To SANDY —

REPORTER'S
NOTE BOOK

LONG LIVE THE
NEWSPAPERS !

July 2022

REPORTER'S NOTE BOOK

*A San Francisco Chronicle Journalist's
Diary of the Shocking Seventies*

BY DUFFY JENNINGS

GRIZZLY PEAK PRESS
350 Berkeley Park Blvd. Kensington, CA 94707

For information contact:
Grizzly Peak Press
350 Berkeley Park Boulevard
Kensington, CA 94707
grizzlypeakpress.com

*Reporter's Note Book: A San Francisco Chronicle Journalist's Diary
of the Shocking Seventies* by Duffy Jennings
is published by Daniel N. David
and is distributed by Grizzly Peak Press.

Design, layout and typesetting by
Sara B. Brownell • sarabbrownell.com

ISBN Number: 978-1-950393-92-3
Library of Congress Number: 2019937959

Printed in the United States of America

"I will never forget Duffy Jennings. I remember going out into the City Hall Rotunda to make the official announcement to the press about the tragic murders of San Francisco Mayor George Moscone and Supervisor Harvey Milk. I saw Duffy, and I don't know why but I kept staring into those blue eyes and that innocent face of his. I couldn't speak for what seemed like a long time. It was like the world stopped. By focusing on Duffy, I was finally able to say those terrible words."

—*United States Senator Dianne Feinstein*

For Bonnie, who inspires and motivates me every day.

For Adam and Danielle, in the hope
you always strive to read, learn, and grow.

For Stacy, my go-to counselor and advocate.

For Dorn, rest in peace, my brother.

Here's to the gallant reporters...
The boys with the pencils and the pads,
Those calm, undisturbable,
Cool, imperturbable,
Nervy, inquisitive lads.

Each time that we pick up a paper
Their valorous deeds we should bless;
The bold, reprehensible,
Brave, indispensable,
Sensible lads of the Press.

—Newman Levy

TABLE OF CONTENTS

Foreword by Bruce Jenkins 1

Preface 4

Prologue 11

CHAPTERS

1. Ten Days in November 1978 16

2. White, Milk and Moscone 19

3. Ambush in the Jungle 23

4. Horror at City Hall 32

5. City in Shock 39

6. The Trail of Dan White 44

7. Crazy-Ass Days 50

8. Leg Man 54

9. We Only Kill Each Other 59

10. Termite 63

11. In Love with a Writer 67

12. Dori and George 71

13. Greenwich Time 75

14. Club Dori 83

15. The Alhambra 89

16. A Letter from Dad 92

17. USMC 97

18. Copy! 103

19. Sudden Death 110

20. Number One Draft Pick 118

21. A Miracle Assignment 124

22. Voice of the West 132

23. Shirt-Sleevers 137

24. I Am Not Avery 140

25. Gas Chamber 143

26. The Note 147

27. No Funeral, Three Weddings 152

28. High Priest 155

29. Fire! Fire! Fire! 161

30. Narc 183

31. A Dark Winter 190

32. On Call with Homicide 197

33. Zodiac and Count Marco 205

34. New Home, Old Threat 208

35. City Hall Beat 212

36. What Really Happened to My Class of '65 216

37. Disco Fever 229

38. Zodiac is Back...Or is He? 234

39. A Detective's Search for Answers 240

40. A Reporter's Search for Adam Goldberg 243

41. Do Something 246

42. The Dan White Trial 250

43. The Verdict 256

44. "I Knew What I Had to Do" 264

45. Don't Talk, Don't Trust, Don't Feel 268

46. Inside Singles Bars 271

47. Softball Question 279

48. The New Yorker 282

49. Giant Changes 284

50. Rookie in the Desert 288

51. Thirty 292

Epilogue 295

Acknowledgements 303

FOREWORD

It was a shocking development when Duffy Jennings left the San Francisco *Chronicle* for the S.F. Giants' front office in the fall of 1980. As sports editor Art Rosenbum put it, "We have lost a slugger." That was true in every sense.

One afternoon at Candlestick Park some years later, in a hardball game arranged by the Bay Area media, Jennings stepped to the plate and belted a home run over the left-field fence. But athletics were a mere sideline for Jennings, who carved out a scintillating reputation as one of the *Chronicle*'s heavy hitters.

I spent most of the 1970s on the *Chronicle* sports desk, right in the heart of Duffy's journalistic prime. Most all of us were envious of the man: blond-haired, blue-eyed, with a background in the Marines and a stylish lifestyle in Marin County. More than anything, though, he had a gift for reporting.

Throughout that tempestuous decade, he crafted a career's worth of Bay Area stories: The Zodiac and Zebra serial killings, the Patricia Hearst kidnaping, the Golden Dragon restaurant massacre. He spent time on the homicide beat and managed to embed himself in a firefighting crew for four adventurous weeks. Most of us felt he was bound for a high-executive job at the *Chronicle*, especially after his superb coverage of the George Moscone-Harvey Milk city hall murders and the ensuing Dan White trial.

As it turned out, we didn't really know everything about Jennings. We didn't realize that he suffered from depression, that he was on the verge of major changes in his personal life, that he had a bitterly contentious relationship with his parents – and that he was deeply affected by his experience with San Francisco's dark side. All of which

1

made it even more remarkable that his work reached the heights of artistic professionalism. Anyone can get the basics down on paper; Duffy let his readers know what it was like to be there.

In many ways, he brought a columnist's touch to his reporting. His most memorable pieces were authentic storytelling, with a beginning and an end. They were concise and clutter-free, with an eye for his subjects' moods and expressions. Beyond the basics, he wanted to know their taste in music, in cocktails, in leisure time, and companionship. Just one example: Confronted with a topic of global relevance — determining exactly how White managed to execute those double murders within the confines of city hall and walk away unseen – he produced a front-page masterpiece of insight and detail.

Those were such different times in the newspaper business. The newsroom was a bustling commotion of activity, rich in conversation and debate, and what a glorious assault on the senses: clacking typewriters, hard copy stuffed into tubes and whoosh! – down a vacuum-delivered path to the back shop. You could smell the place back then: glue from the paste pots, printer's ink, fresh page proofs off the hot-lead press – "an earthy and intoxicating aroma," as Jennings writes in these pages.

Today's newspapers operate mostly in silence, so much of the romance dispatched by technology. And it's a relentless whirl of social media, all about digital innovations, video, and instant online posting. There's never any mystery what anyone else is writing, on any subject, anywhere in the world. It's a matter of public record, instantaneously. In Duffy's time, one had to rely on diligence and instinct. *Chronicle* reporters prayed they wouldn't be "scooped" when they picked up the *Oakland Tribune, San Jose Mercury,* or *San Francisco Examiner*. There was no stopping to put every damned thought on Twitter. Reliable sources were trusted, crazy rumors dismissed. It was world of hard-working journalists looking straight ahead, not down into their cellphones. Write a clear, responsible story and you've set the daily standard. That will forever be Duffy Jennings's legacy.

I was so glad to hear that he decided to share his *Chronicle* recollections with the world. It was a wild, special, important time in San Francisco history, and he understands that as well as anyone. His insecurities and loneliness well behind him, he has found a later-in-life project that will stand the test of time. And he's still a slugger, as readers will discover. He hasn't lost a thing.

—Bruce Jenkins

PREFACE

At some point in my youth growing up in San Francisco, I must have imagined a career in journalism. My father was a reporter, columnist, and author; my mother was a Stanford English grad and publicist; and both of my grandmothers were journalists—extremely rare for women at the turn of the twentieth century. What better gene pool could there be for a reporter? If I did hope to be a journalist, it was only a fantasy. Beyond my afternoon paper route, I never had any plan to make a livelihood in news. But sometimes life makes plans for you.

I became a *San Francisco Chronicle* reporter at the dawn of the 1970s, one of the century's most turbulent decades for crime and social unrest in Northern California. The period was marked by political assassinations, serial killings, kidnappings, a mass suicide, attacks on police, a courthouse shootout, racial murders, gang warfare, and an assortment of counterculture terrorists and whack-job loners with guns and bombs. It was also a time of profound cultural and political upheaval—anti-Vietnam War marches; draft protests; the black power movement; feminism; gay rights; and new excesses in sex, drugs, and rock and roll. In some ways, it was all connected. In just over eleven years, we went from the 1967 Summer of Love to the 1978 winter of hate.

By then I had covered so many major stories that I thought I was at the peak of my career, to the point where I had my eye on the city editor's chair. I loved my work. Newspapers were the kings of news in a pre-digital world. People got most of their news from the daily paper, either delivered to their front door or picked up at a corner news stand.

In stark contrast to recent assaults on the media and journalists, when you were a reporter for the *Chronicle* back then it meant something. You had sway, influence, respect. At least in Northern California. Reporters and editors at the elite East Coast papers frequently ridiculed the *Chronicle* as the "Comical"—soft, lazy, and provincial, lacking in serious attention to significant national stories while favoring off-beat local features. These ranged from such 1960s special reports as Bud Boyd's "Last Man on Earth" wilderness survival adventures and Jonathan Root's exposé about bad coffee in S.F. restaurants ("A Great City's People Forced to Drink Swill") to George Gilbert's "I Was a Hippie" journal. The disdain for the newspaper held by editors in Boston, New York and Washington, D.C. was exemplified in the 1976 film, *All the President's Men*, when actor Jason Robards, as *Washington Post* editor Ben Bradlee, mocked a frivolous proposal for a syndicated feature on yesterday's weather "for people who were drunk and slept all day." "Send that to the *San Francisco Chronicle*, they need it," Bradlee says with a chuckle.

But in my experience, we were serious enough that powerful, high-profile people in politics, government, and business dropped what they were doing to take our calls and answer our questions. Publicists either pitched us for coverage or begged us to kill a story. I regularly received letters, phone calls and anonymous tips about malfeasance, mismanagement, malpractice, and cold cases. People with either a grudge or a sense of civic duty leaked documents to us. At press conferences and media events, all the other reporters knew who the *Chronicle* reporter was. One of my high school classmates said to me years later: "Of all those in our class who became lawyers or doctors or judges or professors, you're the one who ended up with the most power. You're the journalist."

Many of the people and events I personally covered, and other major news that occurred during my years at Northern California's then-largest daily newspaper, are seared into history: George

Moscone, Harvey Milk, Dianne Feinstein, Dan White, Jonestown, Zodiac, Zebra, Patty Hearst, the Symbionese Liberation Army, Juan Corona, the Golden Dragon Restaurant massacre, John Linley Frazier, the Park Station bombing, the Marin County Courthouse shootout, Edmund Kemper, the Chowchilla school bus seizure, the Ingleside Station attack, Herbert Mullin.

In between, I embedded with San Francisco firefighters at the city's busiest firehouse, riding the fire rigs and battling blazes. I spent days on call with homicide detectives, rode along with undercover cops on patrol, worked the police beat graveyard shift, and wrote about the many secret lives of an undercover narc. I covered city hall, local and state government, strikes, elections, storms, earthquakes, floods, a forest fire, and a volcano eruption. There were press conferences, publicity stunts, and "must-go" newspaper promotions. I was up in the darkness for two annual pre-dawn rituals: Easter sunrise services on Mt. Davidson and the 1906 earthquake and fire anniversary ceremonies on Market Street. I wrote obituaries, hot and cold weather stories, and church notices. One day it was a sniper terrorizing Market Street and another it was gunmen taking hostages in a supermarket. In 1970 I described in detail how one man climbed Yosemite's El Capitan and two years later how another daredevil skied off its crest with a parachute.

I waited to interview Smokey Robinson in his hotel room while he sang his latest hit song in the shower. I was there when Bing Crosby sang "White Christmas" at the Laguna Honda seniors' home, when Paul Newman protested waterfront development on the Embarcadero, and when legendary oil rig firefighter Red Adair, immortalized by John Wayne in the 1968 film "Hellfighters," snuffed out a blaze in a Kern County well.

I checked in on and wrote about my baby boomer Lowell High School classmates at age thirty (and again at our fortieth class reunion). Among many surprises, our student body president had shot and killed a sheriff's deputy with his own gun. Another classmate who, as a Lowell lineman in a football game against Galileo High School had once tackled O.J. Simpson, became part of Simson's murder case defense team thirty years later. Still others had dealt with alcoholism, drugs, war, homosexuality, divorce, cancer, drunk driving deaths, and—often worst of all for Lowell grads—failure.

Chronicle editors sent me to cover the disco craze, singles bars, a gay wedding, and war protests. I delved into the ritual of Friday night high school football in Napa, the impact of a sawmill shutdown in the small Mendocino County town of Covelo, and a controversial Vietnam War statue in Auburn. My story about a young Vallejo girl who hand-wrote the same sentence to Barry Manilow ten thousand times to get his attention—"You are my singer and my song"—led to their meeting.

I was just nineteen when I started at the paper as a copyboy in 1967. At twenty-two, I earned a reporter tryout that led to a permanent job despite having few college credits, no formal writing courses, and no experience at another newspaper. I watched, listened to, and learned from the most skilled newspaper journalists and photographers around as we gathered the facts about an especially gory and tumultuous era and reported the news to a half-million readers throughout Northern California every day for the next ten years.

Some of my pieces sang and some missed a few notes. The paper submitted my work for Pulitzer Prize consideration and other honors, but there were also apologetic and embarrassing corrections for my mistakes. Having my name in the paper every week, often on page one, was a very public role that brought me attention and compliments along with pressure and criticism. I was on the front lines for plenty of violence and death and had dozens of front-page articles to show for it. All told, my byline appeared on more than five hundred *Chronicle* articles.

In the background, I struggled with the emotional toll of witnessing and reporting on so much human tragedy while trying to sort out my personal life, often a disaster of its own. My upbringing in a broken, dysfunctional family left me woefully unprepared to form and sustain normal relationships, accept criticism, express my needs, or set personal goals. In middle school and high school, I skated by on sheer wits while acting out for attention. I got plenty, much of it negative. By 1978, my seven-year marriage was on the rocks and my alcoholic mother was in an advanced stage of cirrhosis. I had few tools to cope with either situation. During my twenties and early thirties at the *Chronicle* I got engaged, married, divorced, and engaged again, moved eight times, quit school, smoked and drank too much, stayed out too late too often and grappled with the irresistible pull of drugs.

But before any of that—indeed, at the root of much of it—there was Club Dori.

That was the eponymous gay bar my mother owned and ran in San Francisco's tony Presidio Heights beginning in 1961 when I was thirteen. Think about that. A single mom and gifted Stanford grad with two young boys leaves a secure nine-to-five bank job to run a gay bar in an upscale San Francisco neighborhood in the early Sixties? Who does that? Night after night and all weekend long, she served up cocktails with chasers of motherly comfort to her closeted clientele while defying police harassment and community scorn in a harshly unenlightened era for homosexuals. Scores of men who'd fled from their own parents in the Midwest for fear of being outed and banished found in Dori a nurturing and maternal ear for their insecurities and loneliness.

The more time she spent there, the more it became a popular and discreet refuge for the outcasts of a heterosexual society. Business boomed. Yet, the more successful Club Dori was, the higher the toll it extracted, not only on my mother but on me and my older brother, Dorn. Dori rapidly became more of a consumer than a proprietor, and we became more confused, conflicted, and ambivalent about our adolescence and where in hell life was taking us. Mom thought she was providing for her two teenage sons, but the cost wasn't worth the financial upside.

In the end, Dori got what she wanted out of it—unlimited booze and its inevitable death sentence. It was an outcome she failed to bring about in multiple DUIs, car crashes, and clumsy suicide attempts. My brother got away, far away, from both of us. And never came back. But by then he, too, was an alcoholic. His anger led to drinking and obesity and later to cancer and heart disease, all of which contributed to his early death. What I got was a screwed-up sense of a normal family, a largely absent parent when I most needed one, an unexpected lesson in growing up fast, and total apathy about my future. In spite of that, I found a job I loved and one that brought me the attention I wasn't getting at home. I managed to get through the worst of it with a strong support system of friends and newspaper colleagues that kept me working, mostly sober and out of jail.

These are my best and worst stories from those experiences, at work and at home. I hope they convey a sense of San Francisco history many readers haven't known much about or may not remember.

To be fair, I have forgotten certain people, names, dates, and details from so long ago. I know my memories will be different from others, but I kept a trove of all my clippings, notebooks, letters, photos, family archives and other material that provide the verifiable foundation for the details on these pages. I have changed a name or two where necessary, but this personal journal otherwise reflects my best and most accurate recollection of the people and events that shaped my life before and during my years in journalism.

So, why write this now, decades removed from that job and those events? The easy answer is that I talked about it forever, and now time's running out. I've always worked best on deadline—that term now having a more literal application. At my advanced age, it's a bit like sitting in the newsroom at 4:45 p.m., staring at a blank page in the typewriter, the city editor glowering: "First edition closes in fifteen minutes! Need your copy NOW!"

The more complicated answer is that, despite countless empty predictions about writing a book over the years, I simply wasn't ready until now. To begin with, Ben Bradlee put it in his own memoir, "A Good Life," a memoir goes against the grain for a "newspaperman trained to stay off the stage and keep himself and his feelings out of the story." Plus, it's taken a lifetime to understand who I am—where I come from, who my parents were, what my values are, what I think, why I do and say things, how I relate to others. And to be okay with myself about sharing it. In the words of Salman Rushdie: "Until you know who you are you can't write."

As a San Franciscan I've always been proud of being a native son and of my contributions to a venerable city institution like the *Chronicle*. It's sometimes impossible to describe but I think much of it shows in these pages.

—Duffy Jennings

PROLOGUE

Writing these words now comes with a weighty sense of history. It's been a half-century since tragic and transformative events in 1968 rocked the nation and foretold of a more momentous, more violent decade to come.

A series of shocking, heartbreaking, and establishment-rocking events that year tested the nation and coalesced to a peak of political and cultural change in America that made it among the most turbulent years of the twentieth century. The assassinations of Martin Luther King Jr. and Robert F. Kennedy, North Korea's seizure of the USS *Pueblo*, the escalating war in Vietnam, the black-gloved, raised-fist salutes by two black American athletes at the summer Olympics in Mexico City, deadly riots on city streets and campuses, attacks on police, antiwar protests at the Democratic National Convention in Chicago, the election of President Richard Nixon—it all rolled up into a tsunami of change in America.

Much of this upheaval played out in our own back yard and set the stage for more political and social unrest, more violence and death. The decade from late 1968 to the end of 1978 was as lawless as any in modern Northern California history.

Late one night just before Christmas 1968, a shadowy, thickset man stepped out of the darkness and randomly shot a young couple to death in a popular lovers' lane parking spot in Vallejo, forty miles northeast of San Francisco. No one could have known it was the beginning of a ten-year saga of violence that would shake the Bay Area to its roots as much as any forceful earthquake. Or that the Vallejo slayings were the first in a serial murder case that remains unsolved today, fifty years later: the Zodiac killings. In less than a year, Zodiac

11

murdered five people, ending with cab driver Paul Stine in San Francisco on October 11, 1969, but claimed many more. (A sixth known victim, in Riverside County in 1966, was later tied to Zodiac.) His taunting letters to newspapers, accompanied by cryptic ciphers, set off a decade of public fear and a half-century of police frustration over the hunt for a killer who remains at large. Zodiac's last letter, to the *Chronicle*, arrived in 1978. I was there and reported on it. There's been no verifiable trace of him since.

Then came the shocking, violent, deadly Seventies. Here's a capsule:

January 1, 1970: Just two hours into the new decade, twenty-two-year-old SFPD patrolman Eric Zelms was on foot patrol in the Mission District when he responded to a report of a burglary in progress. Two men surprised him, attacked him, and shot him with his own .357-caliber service revolver. Two other officers soon confronted the fleeing suspects and a gun battle ensued. One of Zelms' attackers was wounded, both were apprehended. They were convicted of the murder and subsequently sentenced to ten years in prison.

Curiously, three months earlier officer Zelms and his partner, Donald Fouke, were on patrol in Presidio Heights the night cab driver Paul Stine was shot, and they may have been the only law enforcement officers ever to have seen Zodiac. They passed by a man walking away from the murder scene who matched the description of the killer, but because he was white, and first reports had said the shooter was black, the officers did not stop him.

Zelms was the first of seven San Francisco police officers to be killed on duty in a two-year period and one of twelve to die between 1967 and 1972. Three of those were killed in attacks on police stations and one died in a police helicopter crash.

On February 16, 1970, a bomb exploded on a window ledge at Park Police Station in San Francisco. The blast mortally wounded Sergeant Brian McDonnell and injured nine other officers. The radical counterculture group Weather Underground was believed responsible for the attack, but no arrests were made.

On June 19, 1970, officer Richard Radetich, twenty-five and a four-year SFPD veteran, was in his patrol car on Waller Street writing a parking citation when he was ambushed by a gunman who shot him three times through his driver's-side window with a .38-caliber revolver. A suspect was arrested, but the case was dismissed due to a lack of evidence.

On August 7, 1970, seventeen-year-old Black Panther Jonathan Jackson attempted to free his brother, George, and two other convicts—the three so-called Soledad Brothers—from San Quentin prison by kidnapping Superior Court Judge Harold Haley and four other hostages from the Marin County Courthouse. As they attempted to drive away in hopes of trading their captives for George Jackson, a parking lot shootout between police and the kidnappers left the judge, Jonathan Jackson and two of his accomplices dead.

On October 19, 1970, bank robbers gunned down San Francisco police sergeant Harold Hamilton when he responded to a bank robbery in progress in the Richmond District. One of the robbers was caught and served seventeen years in prison. Days after the bank shooting, a bomb exploded at the entrance to the church where sergeant Hamilton's funeral was being held, causing several injuries but no fatalities. The Black Liberation Army, a violent offshoot of the Black Panthers that had turned to bank robberies nationwide to finance its activities, was suspected in both incidents.

On July 30, 1971, thirty-seven-year-old officer Arthur D. O'Guinn, a seven-year veteran of the SFPD, was shot and killed while making a traffic stop. Two men were arrested, convicted of second-degree murder, and served seven years.

On August 29, 1971, a trio of gunmen burst into Ingleside Police Station. One of them fired a shotgun through a small opening in the bullet-proof glass separating the lobby from the office area, killing

SFPD sergeant John Young and wounding a civilian employee. Six men, all said to be former BLA members, were arrested in 2017 and charged with the murder of sergeant Young and conspiracy to commit murder for a string of attacks on other officers.

On January 28, 1972, San Francisco police sergeant Code W. Beverly Jr. and his partner, officer James Bailey were walking their beat in the Mission District just after 7 a.m. when they were gunned down by Junious L. Poole, twenty, who said he was striking out against the "system." Beverly died three days later. Poole was convicted and died in prison in 2001.

Between 1971 and 1973, four serial killers—Juan Corona, Edmund Kemper, Herbert Mullin, and John Linley Frazier—murdered a total of fifty-one people in northern California.

On November 6, 1973, two Symbionese Liberation Army (SLA) "soldiers" gunned down Oakland Schools Superintendent Marcus Foster as he left a school board meeting.

Two months later, on February 4, 1974, the SLA kidnapped newspaper heiress Patricia Hearst from her Berkeley apartment. She later joined them, took part in two bank robberies, fled, avoided a nationwide search for sixteen months, and was captured in San Francisco in September 1975.

During the winter of 1973-74, a group of extremist Black Muslims—dubbed the Zebra killers for the "Z" radio channel used in police communications about them—murdered fifteen people in a series of random attacks on the streets of San Francisco. Four men were eventually convicted and sent to prison for life.

That same month in 1975, two assassination attempts on President Gerald Ford occurred within three weeks, both by women, first in Sacramento on September 5 and then in San Francisco on September 22. In the Sacramento incident, Lynette "Squeaky" Fromme pointed a loaded gun at Ford near the state capitol but was intercepted by a Secret Service agent. She received a life sentence, escaped for two days in 1987 and was finally paroled in 2009. In the second attempt, Sara Jane Moore fired a shot at Ford as he emerged from the St. Francis Hotel on Post Street but missed. She managed to get off a second round just as a bystander, Oliver Sipple, deflected her arm. The second shot also missed the president, but a ricochet fragment wounded a taxi driver. Moore was sentenced to life in prison and was paroled in 2007.

On July 15, 1976, three kidnappers seized a school bus in the Madera County town of Chowchilla and took the driver and twenty-six children, aged five to fourteen, to Livermore, where they forced them into a box truck buried in a quarry. The driver and kids managed to escape, and all three kidnappers were sent to prison.

In the early morning hours of September 4, 1977, five members of the Joe Boys Chinese youth gang burst into the Golden Dragon restaurant on Washington Street in San Francisco's Chinatown and opened fire on the patrons, mistakenly believing that members of the rival Wah Ching gang were there. The fusillade killed five innocent diners and wounded eleven others. The shooters were caught, convicted and imprisoned.

Despite all these violent years, nothing had quite prepared San Francisco, or us at the *Chronicle*, for what was to come in 1978.

CHAPTER 1:
Ten Days in November 1978

When November arrived in San Francisco in 1978, balmy fall weather lingered at first, teasing an extended Indian summer even as snow blanketed the High Sierra. It reached seventy-five degrees in San Francisco on election day, November 7. But temperatures dropped rapidly in the days after the polls closed. It wasn't just the weather that changed. Foreboding developments were already in the wind. By the time the month gave way to December, the city would be altered forever.

The month began benignly enough. The *Chronicle* front page on November 1 brought word the Forty-Niners had fired head coach Pete McCulley, who'd lost eight of his first nine games. On November 3, polls showed incumbent California Governor Jerry Brown with a decisive lead over his re-election challenger, California Attorney General Evelle J. Younger, heading into the election. Brown would sail to victory on election day.

That same week, San Mateo Congressman Leo Ryan announced he would visit the Peoples Temple agricultural commune in Guyana, South America, dubbed "Jonestown." He planned the trip to investigate complaints that its leader, the Reverend Jim Jones, was keeping a number of Jonestown's nearly one thousand residents, most of them from the Bay Area, there against their will. "I intend to stay down there as long as it takes to find out what is going on," said Ryan.

A lot had been written about Jones' questionable community leadership and deep paranoia in the months leading up to Ryan's decision. Fearing government interference with his church, Jones moved his followers from San Francisco to the South American outpost to avoid further scrutiny. But Guyana was so far away that the problems there didn't seem all that serious to me.

On election night, reporter Ron Javers, whose desk was next to mine in the city room, covered the defeat of Proposition 6 on the ballot. The measure would have let school boards fire or refuse to hire employees who advocated or encouraged open homosexual behavior. Ron, a slight fellow with dark hair and a trim beard, had been at the paper for a year. A former teacher, he had been a columnist and editorial page editor at the *Philadelphia Daily News*. In 1976, he won a Nieman Fellowship for studies at Harvard University and the Harvard Law School. Following the fellowship, the *Chronicle* hired him as a special projects writer.

I had no specific assignment for election night. I was there on general assignment, standing by for any spontaneous news events to cover. I hadn't had a byline since September when I had covered the final days of the Golden Dragon restaurant massacre shooters trial. I was getting antsy, but election coverage wasn't my thing.

Three days after the election, thirty-two-year-old city supervisor Dan White resigned, ten months into his term, citing financial and personal pressures. White told *Chronicle* reporter Marshall Kilduff that he could not support his wife and four-month-old son on his $9600-a-year supervisor's pay. Adding to the burden, he'd been required to quit his job as a city fireman as a condition of becoming a supervisor. At the same time, White said his wife Mary Ann had to quit her job as a school teacher to raise their child. Hot Potato, a fledgling fast food stand they had opened at the Pier 39 waterfront tourist attraction, was not only losing money but required White to spend up to sixty hours a week there.

Friends had urged him to cut back on his city hall hours, White said, "but I found I wanted to give it a hundred percent and that meant forty hours a week. I didn't have time to be both a good husband and father and supervisor."

Others, Kilduff wrote in an article about the resignation, said White was "frustrated in his first political venture when colleagues voted against him or didn't appear to work as hard," a claim White denied.

Dan White had been elected to the board a year earlier to represent supervisorial District Eight, a conservative, working-class district spanning the Crocker-Amazon, Excelsior and Visitacion Valley neighborhoods in southeast San Francisco. It was the first time in city history that supervisors were elected by district rather than citywide. The same day, voters in the liberal District Five gave a landslide victory to Castro Street camera store owner Harvey Milk, making him the first openly gay elected official in a large U. S. city. Mayor George Moscone had appointed Milk to the Board of Permit Appeals a year earlier, opening the doors of city government to more diverse, underserved groups and paving the way for Milk to pursue political office.

November was only ten days old, but both story lines—the Ryan trip to Jonestown and the White resignation—were on a collision course for an explosive end to the month.

CHAPTER 2:
Moscone, Milk, White, and Jim Jones

In a departure from my general assignment duties and crime reporting, I had spent 1976 and the first half of 1977 as the newspaper's city hall reporter, beginning on the day of George Moscone's inauguration. That entailed covering the day-to-day administration of the mayor, the Board of Supervisors and other city departments. I reported on most anything the mayor did or said, debate and votes by the supervisors' committees and the full board, and newsworthy developments from the chief administrative officer, the registrar of voters, the city clerk, the assessor, the planning department, and other city offices. I often spent time in the late afternoon visiting with Moscone and his press secretary in the mayor's private back parlor or stopping by the various supervisors' offices to check in. I chatted often with board president Dianne Feinstein and had regular interaction with the other supervisors at the time: John Molinari, Terry Francois, Ron Pelosi, John Barbagelata, Dorothy von Beroldingen, Quentin Kopp, Robert Gonzalez, Peter Tamaras, Al Nelder, and Bob Mendelsohn.

By late spring of 1977, however, I'd become weary of the wonky, tedious pace of meetings, the petty politics of city government and spending all day cooped up in one place. I missed the action on the streets, so I asked the city editor if I could come back to general assignment. After that, I occasionally encountered supervisors Dan White and Harvey Milk while filling in on the beat when my replacements there, first Tom Benet and later Marshall Kilduff, took days off or vacation time. I didn't really know Dan or Harvey well, just to say hello or ask a question. I read about White's resignation with only passing interest.

At first, White and Milk got along well despite their oppositional politics. White even invited Milk as one of three other supervisors to attend his newborn child's baptism. Later, when the two men began to take rival positions on matters before the board, their relationship deteriorated. Milk was elated when White resigned. The vacancy meant Mayor Moscone could appoint a new member who would swing the balance of power on the eleven-member board from a six-member conservative majority to a liberal majority.

Mayor Moscone said he was "really very stunned" by White's decision but added that he admired someone "who can push aside the vanity of public service and gauge his life accordingly." Kilduff's article noted that White's resignation was "a clear surprise to city hall observers" and that "the only tip-off of the announcement came when one of his aides was found in tears a few hours before the late afternoon press conference."

On November 15, Dan White declared that he had changed his mind and wanted to return to his Board of Supervisors seat. But a spokesman for the city attorney's office said it would take at least a week to decide whether White was legally allowed to retract his resignation and resume his seat or if Mayor George Moscone had the power to reappoint White.

Moscone, who had already spent several days looking for a loyal ally to replace White, said he would not oppose White's change of heart and returned the letter of resignation. However, chief deputy city attorney Tom Toomey said, "there is a definite problem in revoking resignations" as well as state law and city charter provisions governing the manner of appointing former city officials to new posts.

White told reporters that "all kinds of offers have poured in to me and my wife." He said his family of sixteen brothers and sisters had offered "from about $8000 to $10,000 in interest-free loans" to tide him over, and they also volunteered to work free of charge at the potato stand.

White also indicated he may have underestimated the political forces that had pressured him into reconsidering.

"The 32-year-old supervisor was considered a friendly vote to police and firefighter lobbyists and had also won a following from real estate and downtown interests for his stands against business taxes and a rent rebate issue that failed in last week's election," Marshall Kilduff wrote in his front-page article. "The prospect of a liberal mayor with the power to appoint a like-minded ally to a term with three years remaining had plainly stirred White supporters to action."

White downplayed any conjecture that his quick turnabout made him appear indecisive or fickle. "I think more people are willing to relate to my situation when they see the money problems I was faced with and the way my family came to my side," he said.

White also rejected any suggestion that his relations with the mayor, cool and distant in the best of times, were "now at an all-time low," Kilduff reported. "'The mayor asked me Friday if I'd exhausted every avenue—and I thought I had when I decided to resign,' White said. 'But then I found all this support from hundreds of people who wrote and called.'"

Moscone appeared cheery and friendly at a short session with reporters in which he explained he would allow White to return to office. "As far as l am concerned Dan White is the supervisor from District Eight. A man has a right to change his mind," the mayor said.

As the weekend approached, Ron Javers gathered up his things and left to join the Ryan congressional delegation to Guyana.

Jonestown 'Mass Suicide'

'400 DEAD IN GUYANA'

San Francisco Chronicle
The Largest Daily Circulation in Northern California

114th Year No. 259   ★★★★   MONDAY, NOVEMBER 20, 1978   777-1111   20 CENTS

Reporter's Exclusive Story

I Was in the Airport Ambush

Guyana Says 400 Bodies In Jonestown

By Keith Power
Chronicle Correspondent

Georgetown, Guyana

The Guyana Ministry of Information reported early today that military troops airlifted into Jonestown found "300 to 400 dead bodies" at the jungle settlement, apparently the victims of a mass suicide.

"No living persons were found," said a ministry spokeswoman, who said troops were "going through the bodies seeking to identify the dead."

There was no other immediate confirmation of the report from any other government agency here.

The spokesman said initial reports indicated the dead "appeared to have taken poison," but that this was uncertain, and medical personnel would be sent to the scene today to determine the cause of the deaths.

Guyana police and army troops were sent to the remote People's Temple agricultural mission yesterday after Congressman Leo Ryan and four others were murdered as they attempted to escort fearful and disillusioned settlers out of the jungle.

One report said that eight men and one woman were arrested shortly after the Guyana forces arrived near Jonestown, the compound named after the Rev. Jim Jones, leader of the religious sect.

A government spokesman identified one suspect as Larry John Layton, an American.

The Guyana government expressed official regret over the incident and pledged to make "every possible effort" to arrest the persons who cut down Ryan (Democrat-San Mateo) and five others.

It also said that no Guyanese were involved in the Saturday massacre, which took place at an airfield at Port Kaituma, the nearest landing place to the temple's remote outpost.

Eyewitnesses said the apparently surprise attack came from Americans who were living at the mission.

The vicious assault with pistols, rifles and a shotgun taken from a Guyanese policeman, killed Congressman Ryan and four others, including three newsmen.

The other dead were identified as Gregory Robinson, 27, a photographer for the San Francisco Examiner; NBC news correspondent Don Harris, 41, and NBC cameraman Bob Brown, 36, both of Los Angeles, and Patricia Parks, who was identified as a member of the temple community who was seeking her freedom with Ryan's help.

Ryan and his party — accompanied by several People's Temple followers who wanted to leave

Back Page Col. 1

NBC cameraman Robert Brown got this picture of a man jumping off a trailer and beginning to shoot

NBC newsman Don Harris and S.F. Examiner photographer Greg Robinson were filmed by Brown minutes before all three died

Begin Rejects Egyptian Proposal

Tel Aviv

Israeli Prime Minister Menachem Begin said yesterday that Israel could not accept new Egyptian proposals for a peace agreement because they were not in accordance with agreements reached at the Camp David summit meeting.

Begin told the central committee of his Herut party that he would ask the cabinet to reject the latest Egyptian proposals when it meets again tomorrow to discuss them.

The cabinet, meeting yesterday in Jerusalem on the first anniversary of President Anwar Sadat's historic visit there, spent five hours discussing the new proposals but reached no decision.

After the cabinet meeting, Begin came to Tel Aviv for the meeting of Herut, the nucleus of the Likud alliance which heads the coalition government.

He had been expected to make a lengthy address but spoke only a few minutes.

He said that he could not go into great detail because the cabinet was still considering the new Egyptian proposals and a compromise formula suggested by the United States.

But Begin said that he would ask the cabinet to reject the Egyptian proposals for a timetable for the institution of local autonomy in the Gaza Strip. The strip was under Egyptian administration from 1948, when Egypt captured it, until 1967 when it was occupied by Israel.

Begin said that Israel was ready to sign a peace treaty with Egypt and negotiate the institution of local autonomy for the West Bank and Gaza Strip on three conditions:

• That the Israeli army would remain in the West Bank and Gaza Strip after the Camp David accord.

• That the security of Israel would be maintained.

• That Jewish settlement activity would continue.

The prime minister said he would suggest to the cabinet that Israel accept the draft treaty as contained in the U.S. compromise proposals of November 11.

He also said Israel and Egypt should agree to withdraw two proposals each side had made since then. But he did not elaborate on the nature of the extra proposals made subsequently by the two sides.

Begin and other Herut cabinet ministers were pelted with eggs when they arrived at party headquarters. Demonstrators, many from the ultra-nationalist Gush Emunim ("Faith Bloc") movement that has tried to establish unauthorized settlements in the West Bank, chanted "Begin is a Traitor."

The cabinet debated Egypt's proposals for five hours before postponing decision on the Egyptian proposals.

Reuters

Index

Comics	30
Deaths	31
Entertainment	51
Finance	63
People	30
TV-Radio	50
Weather	31

© Chronicle Publishing Co. 1978

How Rep. Ryan, 4 Others Died

Chronicle reporter Ron Javers was a survivor of the Jonestown attack that killed Congressman Leo J. Ryan and four others. He gave this account from Puerto Rico during a refueling of the U.S. military hospital plane carrying Javers and other wounded to Andrews Air Force Base outside Washington.

By Ron Javers
Chronicle Correspondent
Copyright 1978, Chronicle Publishing Co.

Jonestown is every evil thing that everybody thought — and worse.

We knew that before the shooting started.

All of us who had gone into the People's Temple colony in Jonestown on Friday with Congressman Leo J. Ryan felt lucky to be out of there alive.

Ryan seemed especially lucky. He had been attacked just before we left the jungle settlement and his shirt was stained by his attacker's blood.

Nov. at 4:20 p.m. Saturday we could see two airplanes waiting for us on the nearby airstrip, and the ordeal seemed nearly over.

One plane was the twin-engine craft that had brought us to Port Kaituma, seven miles outside Jonestown, on Friday, and was ready to take us back. A small, single-engine plane for refugees from the colony.

I was standing between Bob Brown and Don Harris, the two NBC men who were to be killed moments later by gunmen charging out of a nearby tractor-and-trailer parked on the edge of the airstrip.

The NBC crew and I became close friends in the course of our stay.

The firing erupted from guns close by. I was hit first. I was knocked to the ground by a slug in the left shoulder, apparently from a 30-30 hunting weapon.

I crawled behind the right wheel of the plane.

Bob Brown stayed on his feet and kept filming what was happening even as the attackers advanced on him with their guns.

He was incredibly tenacious.

While I was trying to decide whether to stay where I was or risk the 100-yard dash across the close-cropped grass field to the jungle, I saw Brown go down.

Then I saw one of the attackers stick a shotgun right into Brown's face — inches away, if that.

Bob's brain was blown out of his head. It spattered the blue NBC minivan.

I'll never forget that sight as long as I live.

I ran, and then I dived head-first into the brush.

I got up and scrambled as far into the swamp as I could. I was about 100 yards from the airstrip and up to my waist in water.

I pushed through the rain forest, walking parallel

Back Page Col. 4

CHAPTER 3:
Ambush in the Jungle

Congressman Ryan and his delegation of twenty arrived in Jonestown on Friday, November 17. The group included his aide Jackie Speier and another staff member, friends and family of Jonestown settlers, Ron Javers, and other journalists. Javers was the *Chronicle*'s third choice for the assignment. Marshall Kilduff, who had written much of the coverage on Jones, would have been the natural reporter to accompany Ryan on the Guyana trip. Kilduff and writer Phil Tracy had co-authored a harshly critical *New West* magazine piece on Jones a year earlier, and there was concern that Kilduff's safety might be at risk. The paper asked reporter Jerry Carroll to go instead, but he begged off with plans to celebrate his tenth wedding anniversary in Big Sur. Javers agreed to go. There was talk of sending a photographer with him, but the perennially frugal paper decided against the added cost. The *Examiner* sent reporter Tim Reiterman and photographer Greg Robinson.

Upon arrival in Georgetown, Guyana, the Ryan delegation, including the media, boarded two small planes for the trip to the Peoples Temple encampment an hour's flight into the jungle. They were greeted warmly by the Rev. Jones, who hosted at a dinner for them. During dinner, one of Jones' followers slipped a note to the NBC news reporter asking for help in escaping from the compound. Others wanted to leave as well. Jones openly agreed to let Ryan take them back, but it was a spurious gesture. He was hatching a sinister plot to stop them and had a yet more evil plan should that fail.

The next day, Saturday, November 18, the Ryan entourage, including some Jonestown residents who asked to leave with Ryan, departed the commune to return home. But as the congressman and the others began to board their two planes at the small Port Kaituma airstrip, several gunmen sent by Jones ambushed the group and opened fire from a flatbed truck. They killed Ryan, NBC News reporter Don Harris and his cameraman, Bob Burns, Greg Robinson, and People's Temple defector Patricia Parks. They also shot Ryan's aide Jackie Speier and several others, including Javers and Reiterman. After the airstrip attack, the paranoid Jones, fearing government investigations and invasions by legions of U.S. troops or law enforcement brigades, ordered some 900 of his followers—men, women, and children—to commit "revolutionary" suicide by drinking a Kool Aid-type drink laced with Valium, chloral hydrate, cyanide, and Phenergan. Those who balked were forced to swallow the poison at gunpoint or were shot to death by Jones's security forces. Jones himself died from a bullet to his brain. Only a few survived by escaping into the jungle.

With limited communications between Jonestown and the outside world, and because it happened on a Saturday, it was hours before reports of the airstrip slaughter began to trickle in to the *Chronicle* and other media. At that time, only a handful of *Chronicle* staffers were in the office, owing to a joint operating agreement between the two newspapers that stipulated the Hearst-owned *Examiner* would produce the news sections of the Sunday paper. As word of the Guyana tragedy began to filter in, key editors started to arrive and called in reporters to work on the story.

Scattered and unreliable reports from the jungle outpost at first created confusion about exactly what had taken place, who was dead and who was wounded. Eventually, as Guyanese authorities reached the scene, reports confirmed the deaths of Ryan and the others. There was no immediate word about Javers, Reiterman, and other journalists.

By the time I came into the office on Sunday for my regularly assigned shift, the *Chronicle* newsroom was buzzing with senior editors, reporters, photographers, copy editors and others, all working to assess the situation, assign and write stories, contact sources for details, and get local reaction from government officials and others.

Like everyone else, I was shocked by the news from Guyana. I wasn't in the office very long before Keith Power, one of the assignment editors, called me over.

"Duffy, we've heard from Javers," Keith said. "He's been wounded but he's okay and he's out of Guyana. He's going to call in shortly to dictate his eyewitness account. I want you to take the call."

Ron had survived the ambush and had hidden in the jungle beside the airstrip overnight. When it seemed safe to come out, he made his way back to the airstrip, where he found Ryan and the others dead, as well as Speier, who'd been shot five times, and the others who were wounded. Eventually, government forces arrived from Georgetown.

Holy shit! I thought. *This is unbelievable. What the hell happened? Reporters don't get shot.*

I sat at my desk to wait. When Javers came on the line I was relieved to hear his voice. "Jesus, Ron," I said. "How are you doing? Where are you?"

"I'm all right," he said. "I'm in Puerto Rico." A U.S. military plane carrying Javers and other Jonestown wounded to Andrews Air Force Base outside Washington had stopped in Puerto Rico to refuel. "I don't have a lot of time. Let's get this done while we have a good connection. You ready?"

I had already rolled a blank sheet of paper into my IBM Selectric typewriter with its spinning metal ball of letters. At the top left corner, I had written the slug, the title that identified the story for editors, "Javers at Jonestown," and below that, centered on the page, the byline style we used for reporters outside the Bay Area: "By Ron Javers, *Chronicle* Correspondent." (Below that, the copy desk later added, "Copyright 1978, *Chronicle* Publishing Co.")

"OK, go," I said. He began, including the punctuation, which was common when dictating from outside the office so the reporter taking the dictation on "rewrite" knew when to include commas or quotes or dashes and when to end a sentence or paragraph. I typed as Ron spoke: "Jonestown is every evil thing that everybody thought, dash, and worse; period, paragraph.

"We knew that before the shooting started; period, paragraph.

"All of us who had gone into the People's Temple colony in Jonestown on Friday with Congressman Leo J. Ryan felt lucky to be out of there alive; period, paragraph."

I was astounded at Javers' composure and clarity under the circumstances. How the hell does a guy who was shot the day before keep it together like this? Could I be this lucid in the same situation? He continued to dictate. This is how it read in the paper:

Ryan seemed especially lucky. He had been attacked just before we left the jungle settlement, and his shirt was stained by his attacker's blood.

Now, at 4:20 p.m. Saturday we could see two airplanes waiting for us on the nearby airstrip, and the ordeal seemed nearly over.

One plane was the twin-engine aircraft that had brought us to Port Kaituma, seven miles outside Jonestown, on Friday, and was ready to take us back. A small, single-engine plane was for refugees from the colony.

I was standing between Bob Brown and Don Harris, the two NBC men who were to be killed moments later by gunmen charging out of a nearby tractor-and-trailer parked on the edge of the airstrip. The NBC crew and I became close friends in the course of our stay.

The firing erupted from guns close by. I was hit first. I was knocked to the ground by a slug in the left shoulder, apparently from a .38-caliber weapon."

As I typed I still couldn't believe what I was hearing. I tried to imagine what it must have been like for him. I'd been near shootouts before, but always far enough away that I wasn't worried about getting hit, let alone being a target. Ron continued:

> I crawled behind the right wheel of the plane. Bob Brown stayed on his feet and kept filming what was happening even as the attackers advanced on him with their guns. He was incredibly tenacious.
>
> While I was trying to decide whether to stay where I was or risk the 100-yard dash across the close-cropped grass field to the jungle, I saw Brown go down.
>
> Then I saw one of the attackers stick a shotgun right into Brown's face—inches away, if that. Bob's brain was blown out of his head. It spattered the blue NBC minicam.
>
> I'll never forget that sight as long as I live.
>
> I ran, and then I dived head-first into the brush. I got up and scrambled as far into the swamp as I could. I was about 150 yards from the airstrip and up to my waist in water.

I was riveted. It was extremely rare for journalists to be attacked, let alone killed on duty back then. Ron continued, saying that when everything quieted down, and it appeared the gunmen were gone, he returned to the airstrip. He found Leo Ryan "on his back in a blue cord suit, lying in the mud in front of the plane's right wheel. His face had been shot off."

Don Harris, Bob Brown, and Greg Robinson all lay dead on the gritty tarmac. Patricia Parks, one of those who had asked to escape from Jonestown with Ryan's party, was also killed. Five others in the group were wounded.

Javers continued with more details of the aftermath and his rescue. I triple-spaced each line to allow for copy editing. He ended his dictation with, "Tim Reiterman, reporter from the *Examiner*—with two bullet wounds in his left arm—and I with my shoulder wound were among the lucky ones."

After each page, I typed the word "more" to indicate there were additional pages to come, and after Ron's last paragraph, I typed "-30-" at the bottom of the final page, a symbol used by journalists to indicate the end of a story. There are various theories about its origin, mostly from its use in the code of telegraphic shorthand to signify the end of a transmission in the Civil War era. "More" and "-30-" are used when writing on deadline and sending pages one at a time to be edited, so the editor knows when a story is still running or finished.

After Ron hung up, I carried the story up to the city desk. On deadline I would have called for a copyboy after each page, but it was early in the afternoon. I was shaken up the rest of the day. All over the newsroom staffers were talking about the tragedy and mourning the loss of Ryan and the others, especially the NBC crew and the *Examiner's* Robinson, just twenty-seven.

"400 DEAD IN GUYANA," read the headline in block type across the top of the front page and above the masthead Monday morning, a number that would more than double in the days ahead. Above that was the kicker, "Jonestown 'Mass Suicide.'" Below the masthead was the headline, "Reporter's Exclusive Story," reversed out in white print on a black background, and below that the headline, "I Was in the Airport Ambush." A subhead read, "How Rep. Ryan, 4 Others Died." The Jonestown stories continued to dominate the *Chronicle* and all the other Bay Area media for the next week.

On Wednesday, November 22, rainy skies dropped a wet blanket over the funeral services for Rep. Ryan at All Souls Catholic Church in South San Francisco. U.S. Senator S.I. Hayakawa, Governor Jerry Brown, Mayor Moscone and fifty-four of Ryan's congressional colleagues were among the fifteen hundred mourners in attendance.

"Everyone in San Francisco feels the way they did after the Kennedy assassination," a grim-faced Mayor Moscone told the Washington Post before the service. "We're sick about it. It's just too much."

* * *

On Friday, two days after the funeral, Moscone told *Chronicle* reporter Maitland "Sandy" Zane that he'd decided to name a replacement for Dan White on Monday, despite the mayor's earlier statement to the contrary and White's claim that his resignation was never actually valid. In his article that appeared Saturday morning, Zane wrote that White had sent a letter to city Attorney George Agnost saying his "purported" resignation on November 10 was not legally effective because he submitted it to the wrong person — Moscone.

"The mayor was the improper authority to whom a resignation should have been submitted, and my lack of intent and appropriate instructions, as well as actual failure, to cause a letter of resignation to the clerk of the Board of Supervisors thereby renders my attempted resignation ineffectual and of no effect," White's letter to Agnost said. "In other words, I am still, and have always been since my election, the Supervisor of District Eight." Moscone dismissed White's letter to Agnost as "an innovative legal approach, but not accurate," wrote Zane.

That Friday was Moscone's forty-ninth birthday. His Sagittarius horoscope for the day warned that an acquaintance "can be quarrelsome for no apparent reason."

It was a quiet holiday weekend. Driving across the Golden Gate Bridge into work on Monday morning, I heard a story on KCBS radio by the station's city hall reporter, Barbara Taylor, who had called White at home Sunday night to ask him about the mayor's decision not to reappoint him. White, she reported, was caught off guard by the news and he grumbled about Moscone "breaking his promise" to give White his job back but gave her no official comment. Then he hung up on her.

I pulled into the alley behind the newspaper building, parked my car, and took the elevator up to the city room.

City Hall Murders

MOSCONE, MILK SLAIN --DAN WHITE IS HELD

San Francisco Chronicle
The Largest Daily Circulation in Northern California

114th Year No. 266 ★★★★ TUESDAY, NOVEMBER 28, 1978 777-1111 20 CENTS

FORMER SUPERVISOR DAN WHITE (LEFT) AND INSPECTOR HOWARD BAILEY
White was hustled into the Hall of Justice for interrogation by detectives

By John Storey/Copyright 1978, Chronicle Publishing Co.

Mayor Was Hit 4 Times

By George Draper

Mayor George Moscone and Supervisor Harvey Milk were murdered in their City Hall offices yesterday morning. Former Supervisor Dan White turned himself in and surrendered his 38 caliber revolver to police about a half hour after the shooting deaths.

White, 32, a tough-on-crime conservative, was questioned briefly by homicide inspectors before being booked into City Prison on two counts of murder.

San Francisco Coroner Boyd Stephens released the preliminary autopsy report last night and found that Moscone was shot four times — twice in the right side of his head and twice in the chest-abdomen area.

The coroner said Milk had been shot five times — two bullet wounds to the back of the head, and three in the chest-stomach area. Milk was also wounded in the right wrist and left arm by bullets that passed through his body.

Stephens said the head wounds caused massive brain damage in both victims and caused "instantaneous death."

The double assassination left San Francisco's liberal political scene without two of its leaders. Moscone, 49, was a specially concerned and liberal Democrat, and Milk, 48, was the city's first avowed homosexual to win elective office.

With the death of Moscone, Dianne Feinstein immediately assumed the post of mayor under a provision of the City Charter that requires the president of the supervisors to serve as mayor until a new chief executive can be selected by the full board.

Apparently, yesterday's violence was politically motivated. It seems to have stemmed from White's futile effort to regain the Eighth District supervisor's seat he had resigned on November 10, explaining at the time that the $9600-a-year salary was

Back Page Col. 1

GEORGE MOSCONE
The slain mayor

HARVEY MILK
S.F. supervisor

Feinstein Becomes the Mayor

By Jerry Burns
Political Correspondent

Dianne Feinstein, president of the Board of Supervisors, became mayor of San Francisco yesterday at the moment Mayor George Moscone was shot to death.

She assumed the tragically vacated job under a section of the City Charter that spells out the process for filling a vacancy in the mayor's office.

Under the law, Feinstein will be mayor until the Board of Supervisors chooses a permanent successor to Moscone.

At the same time, a spokesman for City Attorney George Agnost said yesterday, she will continue to be president of the Board of Supervisors.

Fighting to control her emotions, Feinstein's first official act yesterday was to announce to reporters that Moscone and Supervisor Harvey Milk had both been shot to death.

Two hours later, still near tears, Feinstein presided over a Board of Supervisors meeting that

lasted only long enough for her to urge the public to "go into a state of very deep and meaningful mourning and to express its sorrow with a dignity and an inner examination."

Describing the events as "an unparalleled time" in the history of the city, she said, "We need to be

Back Page Col. 1

Index

Comics 56
Deaths 31
Entertainment 48
Finance 21
People 28
TV-Radio 46
Weather 31

© Chronicle Publishing Co. 1978

CHAPTER 4:
Horror at City Hall

November 27, 1978 - It's 11 a.m. I've been sitting at my desk for more than an hour, drinking coffee, smoking cigarettes, reading the late edition, and waiting anxiously for a story assignment like a fireman pacing near the alarm bell on the stationhouse wall.

This morning's paper carries more follow-up pieces on the Jonestown tragedy, news of a two-alarm fire that gutted the Dance Your Ass Off disco in North Beach, and a report of six people arrested for smoking pot and drinking under the Coliseum bleachers during the Raiders football game.

Man-about-town columnist Herb Caen has an item about Supervisor Feinstein's trip to the Himalayas with Dick Blum and a rumor of their engagement. "Untrue," she told Caen. "I had a wonderful husband and I still miss him terribly. But one can't live in the past and Dick is a great friend. However, no change in our relationship is imminent."

I pour myself a coffee refill and grab the early edition of the afternoon Examiner off a stack of papers on the mailboxes at the front of the room. Walking back to my desk, I hear assignment editor Richard Hemp talking on the phone with Bob Popp, our police beat reporter stationed at the Hall of Justice six blocks away. Even before hanging up, Hemp is beckoning me.

"Duffy, police activity at city hall," Hemp says. "Report of a shooting. Units responding Code Three."

"On the way, Dick," I answer, grabbing my coat and notebook. "What else do we know?"

"Gunfire in the building is all. Bob's trying to get more. Call me from the car."

On the front of Hemp's desk stands an intercom unit with a micro-phone wired directly to an identical unit down the hall in the office of head photographer Gordon Peters. Hemp leans in to the mike, press-es down the button.

"Shots fired at city hall, Gordo. I'm sending Duffy."

"Roger, Dick," Peters responds. "Clem's on deck."

Halfway down the hall toward the elevator, I almost collide with photographer Clem Albers rushing out of the photo lab. At seven-ty-five, he's been around so long he covered stories with my father at the *Call Bulletin* in the 1930s. Clem always seems to be smiling and has a kind face. He looks frumpy in his wool overcoat and fedora, but he's as good as they come with a camera.

We hustle down to his blue Chevy Corvair staff photographer's car parked behind the building and take off up Mission for the short ride to city hall. Rounding the corner at Seventh, I lift the two-way radio microphone from its holder on the dashboard, pull it to my chin and press the talk switch.

"Jennings to desk. Any more details, Gunny?" I ask Hemp. Hemp is not only a Harvard grad but an ex-Marine Corps gunnery sergeant who, at fifty-nine, is still trim, walks with a drill instructor's ram-rod swagger and wears his button-down Oxford dress shirts heavily starched and folded into a military tuck in back.

"Popp says there's been shooting reported in the mayor's office and the supervisors' offices. I'm sending two more teams. Sandy's on the beat today." Sandy is reporter Maitland Zane, who's manning the city hall press room for Marshall Kilduff, the regular beat reporter who took the day off to extend his Thanksgiving weekend. "Call me as soon as you know more."

"Aye, aye, Gunny. Over and out."

Clem guns the accelerator. I feel my adrenaline kicking in. Veteran reporters have a sixth sense about important stories, something in the way people's voices rise and quicken. "Sounds big," I say to Clem.

Clem pulls up to the Polk Street entrance, screeches to a halt diagonally against the curb. Black-and-white units converge from every direction, sirens wailing, tires squealing. People in business attire stream out of the building. Cops are everywhere. This looks like a movie shoot. Did we hear the police radio wrong?

We scramble up the marble front steps of city hall to the gilded doors, flash our press credentials at officers guarding the entry and bound up the inside stairs two at a time to the second floor. A chaotic scene is unfolding outside Room 200, the mayor's office. Plainclothes detectives, officers in uniform and city officials scurry in and out of the mayor's main office door and through two side doors to the inner offices.

Off to my right, the elevator door opens, and out rushes KGO-TV reporter **Peter Cleaveland**. Tall, dark-haired, and TV-handsome, Peter is an imposing figure. Moving with urgency, he almost collides with two fast-moving cops in the corridor, one with his service revolver drawn, another holding a shotgun. "Get down!" one of them barks. Instantly I drop into a crouch against the wall, glancing around for a shooter. *Holy shit, this is no drill.* Cleaveland ignores the warning and tries to enter the mayor's office.

"Not now!" snaps the officer barring the door. Cleaveland retreats.

Two plainclothes officers emerge from a side door of the mayor's offices. "El alcalde ha muerto," one of them says in a hushed tone. I recognize the Spanish words for "mayor" and "dead."

"Is that true, is Moscone dead?" I ask a cop in uniform. "Who shot him? Is Mel Wax here?" I'm hoping that Wax, Moscone's press secretary, will confirm something, anything.

"Wait'll the chief gets here," comes the terse reply. We wait. *This is so unreal, so confusing. Why won't they tell us anything?* I've never seen cops so edgy, so defensive.

A wild rumor spreads among the reporters that Jim Jones had left a Peoples Temple hit squad behind to take out not only Moscone, but other politicians and reporters he viewed as his enemies. Javers had reported from the jungle that Jones and his bodyguards expected to return to the U.S. to "seek out his enemies and kill them one by one." *Are shooters still in the building? Where?* My adrenalin spikes again. Fretful minutes pass without any update from police. More reporters converge on the building, all asking questions of tight-lipped officials.

Near me and Cleaveland, the side door to the mayor's office opens again. This time two coroner's aides wheel out a gurney with a shrouded corpse strapped to it, heading toward the elevator. The small elevator car is so narrow they must stand the gurney upright to fit inside. To my surprise, Cleaveland's cameraman, Al Bullock, squeezes into the elevator with them, dutifully filming the transfer down to the medical examiner's van parked outside.

I dash across the building to the supervisors' suite of offices on the Van Ness Avenue side of the building, where about two dozen reporters and photographers are gathered outside the main door, also guarded by uniformed officers.

Zane, courts reporter Ralph Craib, *Examiner* city hall reporter K. Connie Kang, and another *Chronicle* reporter, George Draper, are there. Zane tells me that an hour before the shootings, he, Craib and Kang met with board president Dianne Feinstein. She was spending the morning preparing to chair the regular Monday afternoon board meeting and to welcome Dan White's expected replacement. It was her first day back at work from a vacation with financial consultant Dick Blum to Nepal, where they visited with the Dalai Lama and had planned to climb Mount Everest. They had reached the 15,000-foot level when Feinstein became ill and had to turn back. She rode halfway down the mountain on the back of a yak to start the trip home. Then the Queen of Nepal's helicopter picked them up and flew them to a nearby airport, where they boarded the flight back to the U.S. Following up the Herb Caen item about Feinstein, the three reporters had gone to her office to ask about her well-being, about rumors she and Blum were planning to marry, and whether she had plans to run for mayor.

Outside the board offices now, we are joined by Barbara Taylor and her colleague Jim Hamblin from KCBS, KYA radio reporter Larry Brownell and news director Greg Jarrett, KPIX-TV newsman Ed Arnow, Dick Leonard from KGO radio, Bob McCormick from KFRC, Cleaveland and a dozen others.

We collect in small knots, compare notes on what's known for sure and what's not. Two men are dead, police have now said, but no names are disclosed. Anxious minutes pass while detectives rush by in all directions, grim-faced and silent. We're buzzing with nervous speculation, fear, disbelief.

I duck back into the *Chronicle* bureau office just across the hall from the supervisors' offices. I call the city desk to check in.

"Word is Moscone and a supervisor, maybe Harvey Milk, are both dead," I blurt to Hemp in short breaths, heart thumping in my chest. "It's not confirmed ... no suspect yet ... the shooter might still be here ... we can't get into the mayor's or supes' offices ... it's total chaos. We're still waiting for some official word."

Just as I hang up, Zane pokes his head in the press room door, shouting:

"Announcement in the hall in five minutes!"

I elbow my way into the crush of news people and others stampeding up the ornate marble stairs beneath the city hall rotunda. The enormity of it all is finally starting to sink in. A double assassination.

At that moment, Feinstein, forty-five years old and in her eighth year on the board, emerges from her office. She is smartly dressed in a royal blue jacket and skirt and a white blouse with a white scarf knotted around her neck. She is flanked closely by San Francisco Police Chief Charles Gain in a business suit on one side and by her aide, Peter Nardoza, on the other. The two men are practically holding her up.

Feinstein stops at the top of the stairwell, ashen-faced, staring straight ahead. I can't remember ever seeing a more horrified expression, on her or anyone else. Looking over the anxious group of reporters in front of her, it seems like Feinstein fixes her gaze directly on me, her eyes drilling into mine as if we're having a private meeting. Months later I will learn that's exactly what she's doing.

She is clearly steeling herself for what she is about to say. The scene falls quiet and the chaos suddenly seems to be in slow motion. In the hush, the only sound is that of shutters clicking. Lights atop TV cameras are ablaze.

"As president of the Board of Supervisors," Feinstein begins, staring straight into my eyes, her voice weak and trembling, "... it's my duty to make this announcement." She pauses, inhales deeply. I try to scribble notes, but my hands are shaking. "Both Mayor Moscone ... and Supervisor Harvey Milk ... have been shot ... and killed."

"JESUS CHRIST!" Zane yells. Even though there'd been speculation about both men being shot, this confirmation was still a shockwave. "OH, MY GOD!" shouts McCormick. A collective gasp goes up, an outburst of audible disbelief and horror I've never heard from veteran news people, hardened as they are to executions, war, riots, plane crashes. All around us, city workers shudder in disbelief, some sobbing.

Feinstein tries to continue. "The ..." But she stops, unable to be heard over the commotion. Shouts of "Quiet!" "Hold it!" and "Shh!" are heard as she waits in silence. After some fifteen seconds, she is able to resume. "The suspect ... is Supervisor Dan White."

Without another word, she turns and walks back inside her office.

Stunned Silence in San Francisco

The Horror That Swept City Hall

By Duffy Jennings

Waves of shock and horror swept through City Hall yesterday at the assassinations of Mayor George Moscone and Supervisor Harvey Milk in their offices.

As news of the tragic shootings spread through the cold marble corridors, scores of stunned public officials, civil servants and other citizens shuddered in disbelief.

Throughout the building, and particularly in the halls outside the cordoned-off second-floor offices of the mayor and supervisors, aides and workers milled about aimlessly, some sobbing uncontrollably.

Board of Supervisors president Dianne Feinstein convened and then recessed indefinitely the regular Monday meeting of the board. She led the supervisors in silent prayer and urged all San Franciscans to "pull together in this unparalleled time."

Earlier, Feinstein had made the first public announcement of the murders of Moscone and Milk.

Hundreds of reporters rushed to City Hall after hearing police radio reports that a shooting had occurred there shortly after 11 a.m., two minutes later Feinstein confirmed what many had heard as a rumor.

Standing in the hall outside the supervisors' offices with Police Chief Charles Gain at her side, Feinstein managed only two sentences:

"As president of the Board of Supervisors," she began, her voice weak and trembling, "it is my duty to inform you that both Mayor Moscone and Supervisor Harvey Milk have been shot and killed."

A collective gasp and cries of disbelief rose from the several dozen people scoot and reverberated from the stone-and-glass corners of the nearby rotunda. Some in the crowd began crying and shouting in horror.

"The suspect," Feinstein continued in tears, "is Supervisor Dan White."

She could speak no more and

A policeman guarded the reception area of the mayor's office as Moscone aide John Monaghan stared in shock

was escorted back from her office by Gain. A short time later, Moscone's press aide, Mel Wax, emerged from his office as the opposite side of the building and repeated the same incredible news.

For the next hour, scores of city officials, police brass, district attorney's staff members and investigators, department heads and other local figures streamed into the building.

Hundreds more gathered along Polk street in front of City Hall, milling about on the sidewalk or in the Civic Center Plaza across the street. Someone placed a bouquet of flowers on the City Hall steps.

Inside the offices of the Board of Supervisors, red-eyed clerks and administrative assistants answered telephones or sat staring amid the chaos as police investigators and news media representatives scurried around them.

By 12:00 p.m. Feinstein had composed herself enough to hold a press conference in the board's committee hearing room on the second floor.

Flanked by several supervisors, and by Chief Gain, City Attorney George Agnost and aides, Feinstein read a brief statement, which began:

"Today San Francisco has experienced a double tragedy of incredible proportions in the loss of our Mayor George R. Moscone and Supervisor Harvey Milk."

"The city and county of San Francisco must and will pull itself together at this time," she said. "We will carry on as best as we possibly can."

Both Feinstein and Gain refused then to answer many specific questions about the episode, but the Supervisor did say she had been to her office three doors from White's when Harvey Milk was killed.

"Yes, I heard shots," she said. "I heard three."

In the corridor after the press conference, Terry Wallace, an aide to Supervisor John L. Molinari was sobbing and screaming about Dan White.

"He's a wild man!" she cried. "He was like crazy."

Peter Nardoza, Feinstein's chief aide, said he saw White enter the board offices and saw him leave the same way, but heard no shots or other noises.

"My office is barely function-

ing," said Chief Administrative Officer Roger Boas, whose offices adjoin Moscone's on the second floor

went off at Barbagelata's home but no one was injured.

In January, 1976, bombs hidden inside candy boxes were mailed to Barbagelata and Supervisor Quentin Kopp, but neither was opened and neither exploded.

But the tightened security didn't prevent a plumber, Walter Jones, 22, from wandering into Mayor Moscone's office with a loaded pistol three weeks after the metal detectors were installed at the entrances to City Hall.

Jones was nabbed by one of the mayor's bodyguards on March 20, and at a subsequent court appearance was sentenced to 90 days in jail.

What the People Are Saying

By Eugene Robinson

A stillness blanketed San Francisco yesterday, the stillness of mourning. Flags, lowered to half-staff, refused to flutter. It was as if the wind had been snatched from the city's sails, leaving it becalmed and bewildered.

Reaction to the murders of Mayor George Moscone and Supervisor Harvey Milk, coming as they did on the heels of the tragedy in Guyana in which hundreds of San Franciscans died, encompassed disbelief, rage, stunned silence.

"Gun control," said financial district cabinetman Katrina Silvers. "That was my first reaction. I've always felt gun control was needed. I just wish people would wake up before something like this happens again."

"You think you've heard the worst of it, with the Guyana thing, and the following week there's this." Silvani said. "My family lives in Europe and they'll all be telling me how violent Americans are."

"It's incredibly shocking," said 35-year-old David Boyd, an advertising executive. "This feels something like a reprise of the Kennedy assassinations. I think it shows a decline in morality."

Boyd said he moved to San Francisco from New York three months ago. "I don't see this as an indictment of San Francisco," he said. "Violence seems to be a pervasive problem — not just in this state or even just this country."

The sadness was tangible throughout the city. In the financial district, normally ebullient lunch-goers gathered in knots and talked quietly of the tragedy. In the predominantly gay Castro street area, Milk's political base, the supporters and friends went from store to store asking local merchants to close their doors for the day, many complied. There was shock too at former Supervisor Dan White's old fire station on Moscone street in the Excelsior district.

Computer salesman Phillip Rows said he had seen White — now booked for investigation of murdering the two officials — on television recently. Rows thought him to be "mature and solid."

"I don't go along with the philosophy that California is the starting point for everything that's weird or kooky," Rows said. "How do you stop something like this? If somebody really wants to kill somebody else, they just do it."

A large, silent crowd gathered on the steps of City Hall and at the edge of Civic Center Plaza across the street. Many were city workers who had known Moscone or Milk. Some were too shaken to comment, and a few were in tears. They watched as police, reporters and city officials came and went.

A white-coated man carrying a transistor radio — the kind of eccentric San Francisco is known for, and of whom the city seemed suddenly weary yesterday — paraded back and forth, reciting the crowd: "What they ought to do," he said of White, "is get a rope and string him up." The crowd looked at him silently. Some shuddered.

"I never thought anything like this would ever happen," said Marge Hall, who now works for the Housing Authority and who once worked in the mayor's office.

"Maybe this will wake people up," she said. "The taking of human life is always a shock."

"They have a metal detector in City Hall," said Susan Johnson. "So how did White get through? They probably just said, 'Oh, this guy used to be a supervisor,' and just let him through. Why have a security system if you're not going to use it on everybody?"

While wax affected yesterday to use the basement City Hall entrance reserved for supervisors and other city officials. There is no metal detector at the basement entrance.)

John Roberts, who works in City Hall, said he feared some people would blame the incident on San Francisco's vaunted "liberalism."

"But this guy White was apparently under a lot of stress," Roberts said. "I really think this could have happened anywhere."

"I guess something like this is hard to prevent."

Someone placed two bouquets of flowers on the City Hall steps under the mayor's window

"I think everyone is still trying to grope for some sense of comprehension," he said. "People all over the building seem to be in a terrible state of shock."

Boas said he was in a meeting downtown when he got word of the shootings.

Boas, whose functions include responsibility for security at City Hall, said all measures would "be tightened, although supervisors have keys and usually enter the building through the basement entrance on Van Ness avenue and Polk street.

"There was recently a suggestion to remove that," Boas said. "Now it will have to be strengthened."

Boas said tighter measures might include 'around-the-clock' security, employee identification tags and other monitoring procedures.

"It's expensive, but we probably have to go that route," he said.

TERRY FRANCOIS, CAROL RUTH SILVER
Ex-supervisor and supervisor after tragedy

By Stephanie Maze

'Leaky As a Sieve'
2 Guards Tell How Security Failed

Security at City Hall is as leaky as a rusty old sieve despite the installation of metal detectors at two entrances nearly two years ago, two policeman guards said yesterday.

Patrolmen Herman Graham and Grant Ellington, who were on security detail screening visitors both denied they saw former supervisor Dan White either enter or leave City Hall after the fatal shootings of Mayor George Moscone and Supervisor Harvey Milk.

"He (White) had keys," said Ellington. "He could go in any door he liked".

Ellington said he was standing on the Polk street sidewalk around 11 a.m. taking a break when he

and another policeman heard gunshots that scattered a flock of pigeons in the Civic Center Plaza.

Ellington and Graham suggested that White may have entered City Hall by way of the unguarded basement entrance at the north, or McAllister street, side. This is the entrance commonly used by supervisors and their aides, who have parking places in the ramp there.

The Grove street entrance at the south end of City Hall has policemen regularly guarding it. This basement entrance is used for deliveries and by top officials who are known by sight to the officers and do not have to open their briefcases for inspection or pass through a metal detector

Patrolman Graham said anyone carrying a gun would have caused the needle on his metal detector on the Van Ness avenue entrance "to go crazy."

"But even if someone was carrying a gun, it would be easy to get in there," the officer admitted.

The metal detectors were installed at the Van Ness avenue entrance and the Polk street entrance to the building in February, 1977, as a result of a wave of violence and threats to city officials. In the winter of 1977, Supervisor Dianne Feinstein's home in Pacific Heights was bombed and shots were fired at former supervisor John Barbagelata's real estate office. The next month, a bomb

CHAPTER 5:
City in Shock

I call Hemp with the confirmation about Moscone and Milk. "Okay," he says. "Draper's writing the lead. Sandy will do the Dan White angle. [City Editor Dave] Perlman wants you to write the city hall scene, the reaction, the mood, what it's like there. Call back when you're ready to dictate." Will do, I say, hanging up. The magnitude of it all still hasn't hit me, but my first thought is a selfish one. *Why Draper? Why aren't I writing the lead?* I knew Moscone better than anyone from my time on the beat. It should be my story. This leads the paper tomorrow. That's my emotional reaction. Professionally, though, I understand it. Draper is one of the top writers on the paper and had been for many years. I sat next to him for a time and learned a lot just listening to him question people on the phone and by reading his copy.

I give George my notes and spend the afternoon talking with people in city hall to capture the atmosphere. As news of the shootings spread through the marble corridors, scores of stunned department heads, civil servants, and citizens shake their heads in disbelief.

Throughout the building, particularly in the halls outside the cordoned-off second-floor offices of the mayor and supervisors, aides and workers mill about aimlessly. Some sob uncontrollably.

Scores of city officials, police brass, district attorney's staff members and investigators, department heads and other local figures flood into the building. Hundreds more gather along Polk street in front of city hall, milling about on the sidewalk or in the Civic Center Plaza across the street. Someone places a bouquet of flowers on the city hall steps.

Inside the offices of the Board of Supervisors, red-eyed clerks and administrative assistants answer telephones or sit staring amid the commotion as police investigators and criminologists work around them.

By 12:30 p.m., Feinstein has composed herself enough to hold a press conference in the board's committee hearing room on the second-floor. Joined by several supervisors, Chief Gain, city attorney George Agnost, and their aides, Feinstein reads a brief statement:

"Today San Francisco has experienced a double tragedy of incredible proportions in the loss of our Mayor George. R. Moscone and Supervisor Harvey Milk. As acting mayor, I order an immediate state of mourning in our city." She extends her condolences to the families of both men, then concludes, "The city and county of San Francisco must and will pull itself together at this time. We will carry on as best as we possibly can."

Both Feinstein and Gain decline to answer specific questions about the episode, but later in the day we learn that Dan White had shot Moscone four times, twice in the chest and shoulder, then twice more in the back of his head at close range after he fell to the floor. He killed Milk in the same coup de grâce fashion, with three bullets to his body and two more into his brain.

Feinstein says she had been in her office three doors from White's when Harvey Milk was killed.

"Yes, I heard shots," she says. "I heard three."

Much later she describes how she was the first to reach the fallen Milk in his office. She bent down to see how badly he was hurt. When she reached out to feel for Harvey's pulse, her finger poked through a bullet hole in his wrist.

In the corridor after the press conference, Terry Wallen, an aide to Supervisor John L. Molinari, is sobbing, and screaming about Dan White.

"He's a wild man!" she cries. "He was like crazy. "

Peter Nardoza says he saw White enter the board offices and saw him leave the same way but heard no shots or other noises. Elsewhere in the building, courts are recessed immediately, and work in most city offices comes to a halt through the noon hour.

With every interview, every note I write down, I remain as astonished and numb as everyone else about the tragedy. Interviewing people at a time like this, people who are grieving at the inexplicable loss of someone close to them, is the hardest, most distasteful part of the job. Other reporters, hard-nosed journalists who'd been around for decades and seen much horror, could be more hardhearted about it.

"My office is barely functioning," Chief Administrative Officer Roger Boas tells me. His offices adjoin Moscone's on the second floor, but he was in a meeting downtown when he got word of the shootings. "I think everyone is still trying to grope for some sense of comprehension," he says. "People all over the building seem to be in a terrible state of shock."

Boas, whose functions include responsibility for security at city hall, says all measures will be tightened, although supervisors have keys and usually enter the building through the basement doors on McAllister or Grove streets. Boas says other measures might include "around-the-clock" security, employee identification tags, and other monitoring procedures.

Feinstein convenes and then recesses indefinitely the regular Monday meeting of the supervisors. She leads the supervisors in silent prayer and urges all San Franciscans to "pull together in this unparalleled time."

White surrendered later that day and confessed to the shootings under questioning by his good friend and former SFPD colleague, homicide inspector Frank Falzon.

My eye-to-eye exchange with now-Senator Feinstein burnished the moment into memory for both of us forever. She still reminds me of it whenever I see her. When she held a press conference on the thirtieth anniversary of the tragic day in 2008, she asked me to be there, then invited me to lunch the next day. The next time I saw Feinstein was nine years later at the *Chronicle*'s retirement celebration for the ninety-eight-year-old Perlman. Other than his two years as city editor in 1977 and 1978, he had been the *Chronicle*'s science writer since 1945. At the Perlman sendoff in 2017, Senator Feinstein was then eighty-four and I had just turned seventy. We connected immediately from across the room as though forty years had whisked by in a flash. She motioned me over, gave me a big hug and kiss and said, "Duffy, it's so good to see you. But it also makes me sad to see you. Seeing you always makes me think of that day, that announcement."

Day of the Shootings

The Trail of Dan White

By Duffy Jennings

Moving with swift precision and the unwitting aid of several trusting city workers, former Supervisor Dan White slipped into and out of City Hall Monday morning in a matter of minutes.

Telling a building engineer he had lost his keys, White climbed in through a basement window and, before anyone even knew two murders had been committed, he had borrowed an aide's car for a hasty exit.

It was during White's brief and unscheduled appearance in the building that Mayor George

Moscone and Supervisor Harvey Milk were fatally gunned down in their offices on opposite sides of City Hall's second floor.

A reconstruction of the events made it apparent that in the scant minutes between the shocking assassinations of Moscone and Milk, the killer methodically reloaded his revolver.

White, 32, was formally charged yesterday with two counts of murder in connection with the killings that stunned the city and left San Francisco without two of its most popular public figures.

From investigators and officials at City Hall

and the Hall of Justice, here is the best available account of White's movements from the time he left his home in the Cayuga Park district of San Francisco shortly after 10 a.m. Monday:

A neighbor who saw White leaving home in mid-morning noticed him getting into a "small red, probably foreign, car driven by a dark-haired woman" who was not White's wife, Mary-Ann.

The woman's identity was not known but it is believed she was White's administrative assistant, Denise Apcar. She could not be reached for comment yesterday.

White was next seen standing outside City Hall on the McAllister street parking ramp that swings down along the basement level of the building. An engineer inside the basement noticed him there.

Parking spaces on the ramp are removed for members of the Board of Supervisors, who each receive two permits from the chief administrative officer.

The heavy double doors at the McAllister street basement-level entrance are locked, but supervisors and their aides carry keys to the door

Page 3 Col. 1

San Francisco Chronicle

The Largest Daily Circulation in Northern California

114th Year No. 267   ★★★★   WEDNESDAY, NOVEMBER 29, 1978   777-1111   20 CENTS

White Is Charged In City Hall Killings

CITY HALL FLAGS AT HALF STAFF
The bodies will lie in state under rotunda
Photo by John O'Hara

Outdoor Tribute At City Hall Today

An outdoor memorial service for Mayor George Moscone and Supervisor Harvey Milk will be held at noon today at the Polk street side of City Hall, Mayor Dianne Feinstein announced yesterday.

The bodies will then lie in state in closed caskets under the City Hall rotunda from 1 p.m. to 6 p.m.

Announcing a weeklong tribute to a mayor and supervisor "who cared very deeply" for the people of San Francisco, Feinstein said she had received two calls of condolence from President Carter.

She said city workers will be given time off to attend today's service, as well as a brief Mass tomorrow at 10 a.m. at St. Mary's Cathedral.

Celebrant at the Mass will be Monsignor Peter Armstrong, and three other priests will take part.

Speakers at the noon service today will include Feinstein, Lieutenant Governor Mervyn Dymally, leading a delegation of Sacramento legislators, Albert Lavin, a close friend of Moscone's, and Ana Kornenberg, aide to Supervisor Milk.

Also today, a memorial service for Moscone, Milk, Leo Ryan and the Guyana victims will be conducted at 12:10 p.m. at Grace Cathedral.

Mel Wax, press aide to the late mayor, announced that a scholarship fund has been established in Moscone's name at the Bank of America office at 315 Montgomery street. The money will help educate Moscone's three younger children, who are still in school.

Death Penalty Possible

By George Draper and Robert Popp

Former Supervisor Dan White was formally charged yesterday with murdering Mayor George Moscone and Supervisor Harvey Milk — "wilfully, unlawfully and with malice aforethought."

He is scheduled to be arraigned at 9 a.m. today before Municipal Court Judge R.J. Reynoso.

If the 32-year-old White is found guilty of first-degree murder by Monday's examination at City Hall, then the jury will have to consider "special circumstances" calling for the death penalty, or for life in prison without the possibility of parole.

Filing of the charges was announced by District Attorney Joseph Freitas. He read the charges at a press conference that refused to comment on the case.

The two-count murder accusation also alleges that White was armed and used a firearm — a .38 caliber revolver — in the killings. These charges could all from one to three years in any sentence he might receive.

According to the complaint, special circumstances could apply in White's case because more than one person was killed and because elected officials were killed.

The killing of Moscone and Milk, according to the complaint, "was personally carried out in retaliation for and to prevent the performance of" their official duties.

This latter special circumstance, the killing of a public official, became law on November 8 following the passage of Proposition 7 at the last general election.

White had been booked on a technical holding charge of investigation of murder following his surrender to police Monday shortly after Moscone and Milk were shot to death.

Attorney James Purcell came to City Prison to confer with White shortly after his arrest. Yesterday, however, attorney Gilbert Eisenberg took over as lead counsel for the defense.

White, according to Sheriff Eugene Brown, has appeared "composed" since his arrest and even chatted with jailers about football.

He was transferred from a cell in City Prison to a special cell in the county jail, where he can be kept under 24-hour guard and also under-

Back Page Col. 4

MAYOR DIANNE FEINSTEIN
'S.F. will not be rudderless'

A Firm Pledge To S.F.

Mayor Dianne Feinstein assured yesterday that the city will remain on an even keel despite the assassinations of Mayor George Moscone and Supervisor Harvey Milk.

"San Francisco is not going to be rudderless," she declared firmly at her first press conference in the mayor's office.

"Government will continue, but this week should be a mourning time, a time of introspection and rededication," she said.

Mayor Feinstein called in reporters after meeting with city department heads and with members of Mayor Moscone's personal staff.

"I think everybody is in a deep state of shock," she said. "I just hoped to wake up and find it was a nightmare, but I know it wasn't."

Feinstein urged the news media to stop emphasizing the "unpleasant and sensational" aspects of San Francisco. Instead, she said, the press should "begin accentuating the positive ... the open, warm, good and stable aspects, as well as all the creativity and cultural

Back Page Col. 5

Dollar Buys Half as Much As in 1967

Washington

A dollar will buy only half as much as it did 11 years ago, the government said yesterday as it released figures showing a new surge in food prices last month.

In its monthly report on inflation, the Labor Department said increases in beef, poultry and pork prices in October helped push consumer prices up 0.8 percent for the second straight month — a rate of 10 percent if averaged over the entire year.

Alfred Kahn, chairman of the Council on Wage and Price Stability, said the October price increases show inflation is now running about 10 percent, nearly 2 percent higher than this July administration official has yet admitted.

"I think the current rate of inflation is about 10 percent."

Back Page Col. 2

Free Speech Program Reported in Peking

Peking

The people of China were told yesterday that a free speech campaign has been launched in Peking with the approval of Vice Premier Teng Hsiao-ping.

Its endorsement brought thousands of people into the streets of the capital for two mass rallies at which they cheered lustily as spoken-demanded democracy and human rights.

One young man told a correspondent: "You are witnessing the greatest thing to happen in China."

The crowds cheered at the mention of Teng, who was quoted in the Chinese press yesterday as saying that the leadership is natural and that Peking's current poster campaign of protest shows the stability of the country.

Newspapers printed direct quotes again by Teng when he spoke to a delegation from Japan's Democratic Socialist party Sunday.

Ordinary Chinese in Peking

told interviewer at the rallies last night that they had long wanted to hear the sentiments directly expressed by Teng.

The vice premier was commenting on the poster campaign in which citizens have expressed complaints about the course China has taken in recent years.

Many posters called for the trial and punishment of prominent figures, accusing them of putting

Back Page Col. 5

Index

Comics	32
Deaths	38
Entertainment	55
Finance	27
Food	21
People	34
TV-Radio	54
Weather	38

© Chronicle Publishing Co. 1978

CHAPTER 6:
The Trail of Dan White

The morning after the shootings, Dick Hemp assigned me to trace Dan White's movements, minute-by-minute, and write a story reconstructing Monday's events from White's vantage point—where he went, how he got into city hall with his gun, how he got out, who he saw, who he spoke to, how he surrendered and what he said.

From talking with officials, aides and investigators by phone and revisiting the scene, I was able to track White's movements throughout the morning. It was some consolation to my ego about Draper writing the lead on Monday that on Wednesday, November 29, my article ran across the top of the front page, above the masthead, with the headline: "The Trail of Dan White."

Moving with swift precision and the unwitting aid of several trusting city workers, former Supervisor Dan White slipped into and out of city hall Monday morning in a matter of minutes.

Telling a building engineer he had lost his keys, White climbed in through a basement window and, before anyone even knew two murders had been committed, he had borrowed an aide's car for a hasty exit.

It was during White's brief and unscheduled appearance in the building that Mayor George Moscone and Supervisor Harvey Milk were fatally gunned down in their offices on opposite sides of city hall's second floor.

A reconstruction of the events made it apparent that in the scant minutes between the shocking assassinations of Moscone and Milk, the killer methodically reloaded his revolver.

White, 32, was formally charged yesterday with two counts of murder in connection with the killings that stunned the city and left San Francisco without two of its most popular figures.

From investigators and officials at city hall and the Hall of Justice, here is the best available account of White's movements from the time he left his home in the Cayuga Park district of San Francisco shortly after 10 a.m. Monday:

A neighbor who saw White leaving home in mid-morning noticed him getting into a "small red, probably foreign, car driven by a dark-haired woman" who was not White's wife, Mary Ann.

The woman's identity was not known but it is believed she was White's administrative assistant, Denise Apcar. She could not be reached for comment yesterday.

White was next seen standing outside city hall on the McAllister Street parking ramp that swings down along the basement level of the building. An engineer inside the basement noticed him there.

Parking spaces on the ramp are reserved for members of the Board of Supervisors, who each receive two permits from the chief administrative officer.

The heavy double doors of the McAllister Street basement-level entrance are locked, but supervisors and their aides carry keys to the door and normally enter the building in this fashion.

White tapped on a window just to the right of the door and told the building engineer on the inside that he had misplaced his keys.

The engineer, identified by police sources as Bill Melia, let White crawl through the window into the Department of Public Works testing laboratory, Room 62 at city hall.

From there, White walked briskly out of the lab into the main basement corridor and headed for the interior of the building.

Investigators assume he walked down the white-tiled hallway, through a set of swinging double doors, past the plumbers' shop and the building superintendent's office to the basement lobby area.

There, he would have entered one of three elevators.

After an eight-second ride to the second floor, White would have gotten out of the elevator at a point within 20 feet of Room 200, the main entrance to the mayor's office.

But White did not enter the main reception lobby, according to aides there.

He most likely slipped through either Room 201 or 202, private, locked doors a few feet to the right of the main entrance. Many city hall insiders enter the mayor's chambers this way, either by knocking or when someone else happens to be coming out.

No one recalls letting White in through either of the doors, nor seeing him enter, but it's possible he entered after someone had gone out because the doors have hydraulic hinges, which cause them to close very slowly.

That would give a person who was leaving time to walk some distance from the door and not see White catch it before if shut and locked. In any event, it would not be unusual for a supervisor to get in this way.

White was then standing in the mayor's red-carpeted inner corridor, between the oak-paneled walls lined with portraits of San Francisco's former mayors.

White walked a few steps down the hall to the office of Moscone's personal secretary, Cyr Copertini, who sits at a desk just inside the door.

As White was asking Copertini if he could see the mayor, Moscone came out of his inner office in shirtsleeves, saw White and cordially beckoned him inside.

Waving away press aide Mel Wax, Moscone met alone with White in the mayor's main office for several minutes, during which the mayor attempted to explain why he was not re-appointing White to the supervisorial seat he had given up earlier in the month.

At some point, according to sources in the mayor's office, the conversation became heated, and Moscone invited White back into a rear sitting room to discuss the matter in a less formal setting.

It was there that Moscone was slain. The mayor apparently had little or no clue that he was about to be shot, one source said, because he had lit a cigaret moments before he was killed, possibly indicating he had been in a relaxed state. The cigaret was found burning beside the body.

Workers in the mayor's office who had heard several loud noises but did not recognize them as gunshots found Moscone dead on the plaid carpet in the sitting room moments later.

But the killer had already left through an unmarked door leading out into the hallway just beside the main entrance to the city attorney's office.

From there, it is about 21 steps to the inlaid marble corridor leading to the supervisors' offices across the building.

Police investigators believe the murderer reloaded his revolver at this juncture, either before leaving the mayor's sitting room or while walking through the south corridor toward the supervisors' offices.

An aide to Supervisor Dianne Feinstein saw White march into Room 237, the anteroom between the board's chambers and the small cubicles that serve as individual work spaces for each board member.

Milk was in his office with a friend when White knocked on the door and asked to see Milk, the friend told police. The two men walked across a narrow hall into the cubicle that had been White's office until his resignation.

It was there that Milk was shot five times, and he died almost instantly, just as Moscone had.

White was seen rushing out of the office area, the first time anyone had noticed him moving faster than a normal walking pace.

The former Army paratrooper went down the hall past the main public entrance to the Supervisors' chambers and into Room 250 on the other side, where administrative assistants to half the board members conduct business.

In what was reportedly a very agitated, excited voice, White demanded that his aide, Denise Apcar, give him the keys to her car, a red foreign compact.

White dashed from the office directly across the hall to a stairwell leading to the main floor behind the rotunda. From there, it was a few steps to the staircase leading to the basement, although it is not known specifically how White left the building.

At some point, White reportedly telephoned his wife at their newly-leased potato stand on Pier 39 and asked her to meet him at O'Farrell and Franklin Streets, but this could not be confirmed.

In any event, White eventually parked Apcar's car near that intersection and met Mary Ann, his wife. The couple then began walking east down O'Farrell toward Van Ness.

They turned the corner south on Van Ness and passed in front of an automobile dealership. One of the salesmen recognized White and said hello. White waved back.

A short time later, White and his wife walked into Northern police station on Ellis street near Van Ness, a block from the auto showroom.

White handed officers there a five-shot .38-caliber revolver, nine expended shell casings and eight live rounds of hollow-point ammunition, an illegal type that expands upon impact.

It was then he was taken to the Hall of Justice.

CHAPTER 7:
Crazy-Ass Days

Not only was the city in shock after the city hall assassinations, so was the *Chronicle*. Carl Nolte, an assistant city editor that day and still a member of the *Chronicle* staff, recalled his reaction to the Moscone-Milk killings when we talked about it years later.

"We didn't know what the hell was going on," he said. "We just had one of our own guys shot down in a South American jungle. Now this. No one really knew much about Dan White. We knew our politicos could be weird, but they didn't just shoot each other. It knocked a hole in what we thought San Francisco was about. It shook the city to its roots. It was a crazy-ass day."

"It was a vivid time that marked us all," another former *Chronicle* colleague, Jerry Carroll, said of the Seventies. Reporters never know what awaits them day to day, but this period was extraordinary. "It was all adrenaline ... very draining." It was as if the newspaper had reverted figuratively to its original name that teenagers Charles and Michael de Young used when they founded it with a $20 gold piece in 1865: *The Daily Dramatic Chronicle*.

I never imagined just how many crazy-ass days there would be during my journalism career when I first started there in March 1967. A week earlier, working for the *Chronicle* was the furthest thing from my mind. I was just back from Marine Corps duty and working as a stock boy in a neighborhood grocery store. I was utterly ambivalent about returning to community college, or any college. Or pursuing a career of any kind, for that matter.

Looking back on it now, I suppose I was destined for the *Chronicle* all along. Not only did I come from a long line of writers on both sides of my family dating back two generations, but both of my parents,

Dean and Doris, had worked together at the *Chronicle*, even after they divorced when I was four. Dean was a columnist; Dori, as she always preferred to be called, was his assistant. I was an infant the first time I came to the *Chronicle*. My mother loved to tell the story about Herb Caen, the paper's legendary three-dot gossip columnist, toting me around the newsroom in my baby basket. As I grew up, she pounded grammar, punctuation, and spelling into me. Often these corrections were delivered with stinging rebuke. There was no room for error. In grade school and junior high school, I excelled at writing essays and book reports. I had no affinity for math or the sciences, but English came naturally. A career in writing seemed inevitable.

Until I was thirteen. That's when my mother went into the bar business.

I didn't know it then, but Mom already had a problem with alcohol before my older brother Dorn and I were even born. Now she had a limitless supply. For the next six years, as he and I went through middle school and high school, she was mostly gone and mostly drunk, and more of a mother to her customers than to us.

The worse she got the more it impacted our teen years in ways we couldn't see. It was like the boiling frog parable. The premise is that if you drop a frog into a pot of boiling water it will jump out immediately, but if you put the frog into lukewarm water and then gradually bring it to a boil, the frog will not perceive the danger and will be slowly cooked to death. Dorn and I were two oblivious frogs in the simmering pot of Mom's progressive disease, confused about what was happening and unaware of the long-term damage her drinking was inflicting on us. We were home alone most nights while she tended bar, though she left money on the kitchen table for bus fare, fast food dinners, school supplies, and clothes.

Worse, Dorn and I both struggled with the humiliation that Mom ran a bar for "homos." We coped by trying to rationalize her as a "businesswoman" and to normalize her clientele as regular guys, even as society perceived their lifestyle as not only repugnant, but in some ways illegal.

Dorn and I never talked about it as kids, not that I remember. I think we just accepted it. What choice did we have? What I do remember clearly is that he and I argued and fought, often and sometimes physically. I don't even recall why, only that we yelled, shoved, wrestled, and punched until one of us got bloodied, or left the room crying. Now I understand we were lashing out, not against one another but at Mom, for choosing the business over us.

There was little we could do to escape this weird, unconventional adolescence until we graduated from high school and turned eighteen. He and I both finally fled by the same means—military service. Five days after Dorn graduated from Lowell High School in 1963 he left for a four-year enlistment in the Air Force, most of it stationed in Okinawa, putting an ocean between him and Mom's "fruit bar," as he termed it.

I graduated two years after him, then squandered a year in junior college. The Vietnam War was escalating, and I had lost my student deferment, so I enlisted in the only service that was still accepting reservists. I left for Marine Corps boot camp in San Diego in July 1966, three days before my nineteenth birthday.

Boot camp was every bit the living hell its reputation has earned over generations. Sure, the physical part was torture, but even worse was the psychological torment. To mold young men for war, their individuality must be erased and replaced with a mental frame of mind that enables them to react instinctively in battle, to follow orders without question, and to put their group objective before their own safety. By mid-1966, the traditional twelve-week boot camp had been condensed to eight to process the increasing number of troops needed in Vietnam. The result was longer days and a higher level of intensity and urgency with every exercise, weapons class, hand-to-hand fighting bout, parade ground drill, and rigid personal appearance instructions. After boot camp, I went to Camp Pendleton for another month of advanced weapons training—rifle range, grenades, rocket launchers, mortars, tear gas—then served the remaining three months as a clerk typist processing deployment orders and stamping out dog tags for Marines headed to Vietnam.

When I returned from active duty in January 1967, I was totally rudderless. By then, many of my Lowell classmates were juniors at Stanford, Cal, Harvard, and Yale. But I was going nowhere. And my combat training wasn't in high demand in San Francisco.

I had no professional work experience, no real direction, and no goals. The *Chronicle*? No chance.

But to truly understand how it came to be, we need to go back a hundred years, to my family origins.

CHAPTER 8:
Leg Man

My father, Dean Southern Jennings, was a writer for nearly fifty years, starting at Lowell High School, then as a reporter and columnist for San Francisco newspapers, then as a freelancer and a prolific celebrity interviewer for national magazines and concurrently as the author of nine books, two that were made into movies. Indeed, he was regarded by his profession as a celebrity in his own right.

At times, my father was also a publicist for government agencies, political campaigns, a world's fair, ad agencies, and other businesses. He had four wives, six children, two yachts, and three heart attacks. He was sixty-four when the last one took his life in Bolinas, California in 1969. I was twenty-two then, and he and I had been estranged on and off for as long as I can remember. But he always seemed larger than life to me, with his books and bylines and boats, the last of which he named Hunter. On our occasional salmon fishing trips, he cut a dashing figure at the tiller in his double-breasted blue blazer and gold-embroidered captain's hat, the bow slapping against the whitecaps as we navigated beneath the Golden Gate Bridge.

Dean began his newspaper career while he was a senior at Lowell in 1923, reporting for the *Daily Journal of Commerce*. In 1924, he worked as a sports writer for the *San Francisco Examiner* and the *San Francisco Herald* and later was a rewrite man for the *San Francisco Call-Bulletin*. He was talented and driven to write, particularly about anything to do with sensational crime and criminals—murders, killers, gangsters, prison life.

Dean freelanced hundreds of articles for crime magazines like *True Detective*, *True Crime*, *Crime Detective*, and others while working as a newspaper reporter. His primary job for the paper was to go out to news scenes and gather information for stories, then call in his notes to a "rewrite" man who would write up the article. In the vernacular of the times, this type of on-scene reporter was called a "leg man," the term he used as the title for his 1940 book about his newspaper career. Among the chapters in "Leg Man," Dean described the first execution he covered for the *Call-Bulletin*. It was the hanging of Charlie Simpson in July 1931 for the murder of Albina Voorhies, a seventy-three-year-old San Francisco grocery store owner who caught him stealing cigars. After he savagely clubbed the old woman, Simpson soaked her in oil and set her afire. Dean's chapter on the hanging, titled "Mother's Boy," included this description of Simpson on the gallows at San Quentin Prison:

"...Charlie went down through the hole sideways, like a sinking ship, and his head thudded against the side of the trap. It made a squish-plop noise, like it does when you bust open a pumpkin, and they started fainting. Charlie jerked like an eel for five minutes, and one of the guards whispered that he must be strangling, that the crooked fall hadn't broken his neck. I thought he must be, too, for I'd heard them say the spine goes off like a shot when the business is handled right."

Afterwards, Dean wrote that he felt "sick and hollow inside" and vowed "no goddam city editor is going to wish any more of these on me."

He covered fourteen more after that.

Dean's first best-seller, *The San Quentin Story*, by Warden Clinton T. Duffy, "as told to Dean Jennings," was published in 1950. (Warden Duffy, you may have guessed, was my namesake.) The book was the basis for a 1954 film, *Duffy of San Quentin*, starring Paul Kelly. In early 1951, Dean was hired to write a daily gossip column, "Inside San Francisco," for the *Call-Bulletin*. That December, when *Chronicle* gossip columnist Herb Caen defected to Hearst's rival *Examiner*, Dean moved over to the *Chronicle* to replace him with a column he called, "It's News to Me." Dean was among several so-called "man-about-town" columnists who filled Herb Caen's regular space in the *Chronicle* during the eight years Caen was gone. Later my father wrote dozens of celebrity profiles for the *Saturday Evening Post*, *Collier's Weekly*, *Reader's Digest*, and *Coronet* magazines. These included John Wayne, Victor Borge, Susan Hayward, George Raft, Red Skelton, Jack Webb, David Niven, Rod Steiger, Sal Mineo, Connie Francis, Edgar Bergen, Kim Novak, Ernest Borgnine, Ann-Margret, and many more. His byline appeared often on the *Saturday Evening Post* cover along with the magazine's trademark Americana artwork by Norman Rockwell.

In addition to his own name, he wrote under several pseudonyms, including Robert Southern, Dorothy Cole, Carlton Russell, John Wesley Noble and Foster Rawls. Using pen names avoided problems with the newspaper, the union and rival magazines.

Dean was born June 30, 1905 in Rochester, New York, to the Reverend Webster Wardell Jennings, an Episcopal minister, and his wife, Mary Southern. Mary once worked for the *Paris Tribune* when her family lived in Germany before World War I. His parents and others in the family always called Dean "Southern," rather than his first name. He was educated in Rochester until he was ten, then in Munich, Germany, while his father served as rector of the American Church of the Ascension there. When the family returned to the U.S. in 1920, Dean went to West High School in Rochester for two years until his father accepted an assignment as rector at the historic and prestigious St. Luke's Episcopal Church in San Francisco, a post he held until 1940.

In San Francisco, the Jennings family, now including Dean's two younger siblings, Roberta and Wardell, moved into a palatial home in swank Pacific Heights. When Dean was eighteen, his parents took in a sixteen-year-old orphaned girl, Rosemarie Thoerner, after her immigrant parents died unexpectedly. Late one late spring night in 1924,

Dean crept upstairs to the girl's fourth-floor bedroom and planted the seeds of scandal. The unexpected pregnancy would surely have brought shame to the socially esteemed minister and his church, so Dean's parents quietly arranged a hasty marriage, sent the girl to Los Angeles to have the baby, and shipped their oldest son off to Paris.

Trunk Killer Ruth Judd Escapes

Dean Jennings Comes to The Chronicle Dec. 9

San Francisco Chronicle
The City's Only Home-Owned Newspaper

FINAL

VOL. CLXXIV, NO. 138 CCCCAAA · FRIDAY, NOVEMBER 30, 1951 · GA 1-1112 DAILY 7c. SUNDAY 15c

FRONT QUIET--BUT BIG RED BUILDUP SIGHTED

DEAN JENNINGS — writer, reporter and man-about-San Francisco, starts as free-lance columnist for The Chronicle on Sunday, December 9. His daily piece, titled *It's None to Us*, will feature entertaining news vignettes, goings-on in the city, flashpoints from celebrities, dignitaries — and characters — around our town.

Jennings has acquired a way with words and a sharp eye for trivia during his long newspaper and writing career. He has written for many national magazines and his best-selling book, *The San Quentin Story*, written with Warden Clinton Duffy, was serialized last year in The Saturday Evening Post.

His new column will present a fast-moving picture of San Francisco personality, he knows "everybody who's here" and he's servicing the beat he knows the best.

His new column will present a fast-moving picture of San Francisco life — with an understanding powerful of daily readings. It's *Keys to Me* will appear every day except Monday. Remember, it starts in this newspaper Sunday, December 9.

ANOTHER CHRONICLE EXCLUSIVE

Remmer Attorney Clashes With Judge at Tax Trial

By FRANK McCULLOCH

The Minor (Bones) Remmer came to trial dragged through the second day in District Court here yesterday. Its first full court session had been a clash between the presiding Judge and one of the four defense attorneys.

Judge Roger T. Foley announced he was not going "to escape the rules of this Court for any San Francisco attorney," and Defense

Which family will enjoy a "pre-paid" Christmas?

The family who've been saving for it — and have a comfortable bank balance to "pre-pay" their Christmas bills.

It could be your family, if you're a member of Wells Fargo's 1951 Christmas Club.

If you're not, why not be "pre-paid" next Christmas? Join our 1952 Christmas Club today.

Get details at either office.

SAVINGS DEPARTMENT

Wells Fargo Bank
& UNION TRUST CO.
SAN FRANCISCO
Market at Montgomery
Market at Grant Ave.
Established 1852

Caudle Tells $5000 Cut in Plane Deal

S. F. Inquiry To End Next Thursday

Purchaser 'Interested' In Tax Case

By CHARLES RAUDEBAUGH

The holdover Federal Grand Jury informed Federal Judge Oliver J. Carter yesterday that it expects to end its six-month-old inquiry into the San Francisco Bureau of Internal Revenue next Thursday.

It gave no indication visitor it will return any indictments.

After a day spent questioning William S. Frank, chief of an outbreak of examiners probing the tax office, the jury asked chief counsel Leslie Gillies of the examiners on Tuesday and Thursday of next week. A five-member chronicle of Review also was authorized to meet today with Internal Revenue agents, and Robert B. Middlemas, chief assistant U. S. attorney, to see also the 1036 pages of testimony taken from 61 witnesses.

The Grand Jury, under U. S. Attorney Chauncey Tramutolo, will end Thursday and the Internal Revenue investigators probably deliver in a document they had been collecting any this summer.

SUBPOENAS SENTENCED

Before convening the hearing could tomorrow when Caudle will resume testimony, Chairman Cecil King (Dem-Calif) issued a state-day-appeal and another last division of Review after the call ordered examination on an "no-book," and "no-book," to the subpoena of the Internal Revenue Service on Wednesday.

The subcommittee also briefly unmasked Charles Oliphant, chief counsel of the Internal Revenue Bureau, who after accusations against Caudle on a piece trip to Florida.

Chinatown Defies Red Ransom

By George de CARVALHO

Chinatown collectively defied the Communists last night and refused to pay any further tribute to the Chinese Red regime's ransom racket.

In an emergency meeting here the Chinese Six Companies, venerable association, overall and most heart of Chinatown's some 30,000 Chinese-Americans.

U. S. Treasury officials hailed the proclamation as "most hopeful and very helpful" in stopping the racket, which has victimized thousands of Chinese-Americans.

Acting Secretary of the Treasury E. D. Foley promptly issued an amended proclamation of the racket, which was revealed by The Chronicle to have the cooperation of the Treasury.

9200 Enemy Trucks Moving to the Front

Van Fleet Stresses Order on 'Lull' Was Misinterpreted; Truce Talks Hit an Impasse

By the Associated Press

TOKYO — Communist trucks rolled in unprecedented numbers last night (Thursday) toward a battle front that was officially stilled.

The Far East Air Forces reported sighting the astonishing total of 9200 trucks rushing supplies and possibly troops under cover of darkness to the front areas on the Korean peninsula.

This is almost double the previous record. The Reds obviously were swinging into a big buildup during the strange lull which paralyzed Wednesday after Allied truce terms agreed on a provisional cease-fire line.

GOP Senate Leader Wherry Dies at 59

WASHINGTON, D. C., Nov. 29 (AP)—Kenneth S. Wherry, leader of the Senate Republicans, died here today of cancer and complications following an earlier operation.

The Senator from Nebraska, one of the most outspoken foes of the Truman Administration strategy elsewhere kept on aggressive to overcome the unexpected.

Truman Says Korea Fighting Will Continue

By the Associated Press

KEY WEST, Fla., Nov. 29 — President Truman announced bluntly today that the fighting will continue in Korea as long as there is a possibility of United Nations forces being "caught off-balance" by the enemy.

Warren to Quit Hospital Today

Governor Earl Warren will leave the hospital here at 3 p.m. today and return to his home at Sacramento.

Reds Expelled 1136 Priests

VATICAN CITY, Nov. 29 (AP)—The Communists have expelled 1136 Catholic priests from their overseas missions in the past year, according to a compilation made public here today.

WINNIE RUTH JUDD
Fourth flight

Ruth Judd, Trunk Killer, Escapes Again

By the United Press

PHOENIX, Nov. 29—For the fourth time, the Arizona trunk murderer of the early 1930s escaped from the Arizona State Hospital last night (Thursday) by dropping down a rope from the window of her room.

Dr. M. W. Conway, who took over as superintendent of the hospital six weeks ago, said the only hope was that she might be found at the residence of some friend.

Sheriff's deputies said there was nothing wrong about the jail because he had "confidence in trust in her residence."

Sheriff's speculate asked by blood-hounds, took up the search.

Mrs. Judd, now 46, served only six years in the state prison after her conviction. She was sentenced to death for the murders of two women friends, whose bodies were found in trunks in Los Angeles. She was judged insane and sent to the hospital.

The disappearance was discovered when attendants making their rounds noticed the screen in the window of her sewing room was out.

Boy Burglar Caught in His Wheelchair

WASHINGTON, Nov. 29 (AP)—A crippled 15-year-old boy was caught in the act of burglarizing a home last night, tried to escape in his wheelchair, and was finally cornered after a chase.

15-Year-Old Cripple Confesses, Brags

First All-Jet Heavy Bomber

WASHINGTON, Nov. 29—The first heavy, long-distance, all-jet bomber—a plane as advanced in secrecy that controlling and war-time drapes will be used to keep its details from public call—will be given the first of several Army tests Monday when it goes aloft from Fort Worth, Tex.

The B-52's will be built, the Air Force said.

21 Shopping Days Till Christmas

Occasional Rain Forecast For Afternoon

Occasional rain is forecast for the Bay Area this afternoon and tomorrow.

Look for the 'CAR WITH THE STAR'

The Index

Bayes Editor 30
Churn 30
Commerce 30
Comics 30
Crosswords 30
Deaths 30
Editorial 30
Finance 30
Leonard Lyons 30
Radio and Television 30
Sports 30
Vital Statistics . 30
Women's World 30

CHAPTER 9:
We Only Kill Each Other

Fluent in French and German from spending much of his childhood abroad, Dean took a Paris apartment one floor above famed American dancer Isadora Duncan, who performed throughout Europe. A few months after Dean moved in, Duncan was riding in a car in Nice when her scarf became entangled in the wheel and axle, strangling and nearly decapitating her. Dean went to work at the English-language *Paris Herald*. On May 21, 1927, Dean, just twenty-one, was the first journalist to reach pioneer aviator Charles Lindbergh's *Spirit of St. Louis* after the aircraft touched down at Le Bourget Field from its historic trans-Atlantic flight. Dean and another Herald reporter, Jack Glenn, had run several hundred yards up the tarmac to get the jump on scores of other reporters and photographers.

"We reached the plane in a dozen jumps, ducked under the wing and peered into the cockpit," Dean wrote in "Leg Man." "'It's empty!' Jack said. 'The door's on the other side.' We rounded the nose of the plane just as the prop wheezed and stopped spinning. We tripped in a chuck hole, sprawled to our knees, swearing, got up—and bumped into a tall, slim, and blond youth who was walking away from the plane with a leather flier's helmet in his right hand.

"'Hey, Lindbergh!' We blurted it out in unison and moved in like bill collectors. But to our utter amazement, he shrank away with frightened eyes, mumbled something between his teeth and took off across the field with great long strides."

When they finally caught up to the man, wrote Dean, "we propelled, dragged and cajoled our hero toward the two-story brick Administration Building... We had Lindbergh between us. There were a hundred reporters at the field this memorable night – and ninety-eight of them were somewhere else."

Finally, the young man spoke for the first time.

"'I beg pardon, sir, but you are making a mistake. I am not Lindbergh! My name's Harry Wheeler. From New York. I was only trying to find Lindbergh. An' all I got was his hat.'"

Rosemarie, meanwhile, delivered Dean's baby in Los Angeles February 9, 1925. The family named him Dean Melvin Jennings and the mother returned to the Bay Area to raise him, with financial support from the Reverend Jennings. From the outset, most of my father's family always treated Mel, as we called him, as if he never existed, hoping to put the shame of this unwanted marriage and pregnancy behind them. The marriage was quickly dissolved, and Dean returned from Paris in 1929. Back home, he took a job as a rewrite man with the *Call-Bulletin*. A year later he married Elsa Virginia Olson in Carmel and over the next eight years they had two sons and a daughter—Dean Southern Jr., Breslau Honeyford, and Suzette Estelle. Naming a second son after himself was an act of hubris consistent with my father's ego, but it had more to do with their denial about Mel as part of the family. My father's second marriage ended shortly after Suzette's birth. Suzette remains my only living sibling.

In 1933, Dean became executive secretary of the Northern California chapter of the American Newspaper Guild and was appointed as the chapter's delegate to the guild convention in St. Paul, Minnesota. The newspaper's management, however, declined his vacation request and fired him for union activities. He appealed to the National Labor Relations Board, which ordered him reinstated. The newspaper appealed, and a complex series of legal arguments ensued, at one point even bringing President Roosevelt into the case over questions of labor relations and press freedom. Roosevelt declined to uphold Jennings's reinstatement and Dean became one of the Guild's first so-called martyrs.

From 1935 to 1936 Dean was regional director of the United States Resettlement Administration in Denver and Indianapolis. The U.S.R.A. was a New Deal federal agency that relocated struggling families to planned communities for that year. For the next two years he was regional director of distribution and promotion for U.S. Government Films in Chicago and Hollywood, then became regional information representative for the U.S. Social Security Board in San Francisco. In 1939, he served as press director for the Golden Gate International Exposition on Treasure Island in San Francisco.

Dean's fascination with Hollywood figures resulted in several books, most of them biographies or autobiographies "as told to" or "with" Dean Jennings, of celebrities that included movie mogul Jack Warner, television star Art Linkletter, hypnotist-to-the-stars Arthur Ellen, and Woolworth heiress Barbara Hutton. Dean's passion for gangster stories culminated in his 1967 book, *We Only Kill Each Other: The Life and Bad Times of Bugsy Siegel*. Some twenty years later, actor-producer Warren Beatty bought the movie rights to the book from Dean's estate and used it as the basis for the acclaimed 1991 film, *Bugsy*, casting himself in the title role. The film garnered ten Academy Award nominations and the Golden Globe for Best Picture. The book title came from my father's conversation with a Vegas mobster. Dean told the guy he'd received death threats while digging into Siegel's unsolved murder. "Aw, don't worry," the thug told him, "we only kill each other."

When my father died in 1969, he was starting work on a book about mobster Mickey Cohen, who had joined forces with Siegel in the 1940s to help open the Flamingo Hotel in Las Vegas. After Siegel was killed in 1947, Cohen was among the early suspects, but was eventually cleared and became "the undisputed boss of Los Angeles gangdom," according to the *Los Angeles Times*. Dean had spent several weeks with the legendary hoodlum while writing the *Post* piece about him that appeared in September 1958. Cohen's wardrobe closets, he wrote, were filled with 300 suits, 25 sport coats, 60 pairs of shoes, 1,500 pairs of socks, $250 silk lounging pajamas and neckties by the hundreds. And he spent forty dollars a week on his favorite cologne.

Cohen was convicted twice of tax evasion, among other crimes. His first conviction in 1951 drew a four-year sentence. Six years after his release in 1955 he was convicted again on tax charges and sentenced to fifteen years in Alcatraz Prison. The prosecution called my father to testify in Cohen's 1961 federal trial. Afterward, Cohen came up to my father and said, "No hard feelings. How about goin' out to dinner with me tonight?" Dean was aware that some of Cohen's previous dinner companions had later died under mysterious circumstances.

Despite one gangster's earlier assurances about their mob victims, Dean declined the invitation.

CHAPTER 10:
Termite

My mother had writing know-how in her veins, too. She was born Netta Lee Conrad on July 13, 1914, in Medford, Oregon, to Halden Conrad, a railroad clerk, and Lucile Rood Conrad, a stenographer and newspaper stringer with three years of college.

I never met any of my maternal grandmother's three husbands and I didn't know her very well beyond the occasional visit to her in Southern California. Lucile spent most of her adult life as a writer and correspondent for major eastern newspapers and was a reporter and editor for several smaller California and Oregon dailies and weeklies—one of few women in the business in her era. She had bylines in the old *San Francisco Call-Bulletin*, the *Portland (OR) Journal*, the *Christian Science Monitor*, and the *New York Herald-Tribune*.

She also worked on the rewrite desk at the San Diego *Evening Tribune* and published one book, *How to Find Leisure Time and Use It Creatively: A Guide for the Busy Woman*. In her later years and until her death, she was a Christian Science Practitioner and a real estate broker who was among the founders of the town of Anza in the high desert east of San Diego.

Dori never seemed to look forward to our visits to see her mother, whom we called "Gromere." That's how my brother and I shortened the French term, "Grand-Mére," that Mom used for grandmother. Dorn and I weren't thrilled about those visits, either. It was a long, hot drive and there was nothing for us to do at her remote little house in the Anza mountains. There seemed to be tension in the air between Mom and Gromere most of the time. Gromere was taciturn and not the least bit nurturing toward us boys. The best part of visiting her was the .22-caliber rifle that she allowed my brother and me

My mother, Doris Jennings, 1937.

to take out into the desert for target practice and pot shots at the occasional jackrabbit that were always off the mark. There was minimal instruction and safety rules and off we went with the rifle and a box of cartridges. That seems negligent for a nine-year-old and eleven-year-old today, but back then it was no big deal.

After Lucile and her husband divorced in August of 1917, she and Doris moved to northern California. Over the next four years, they lived in Berkeley, San Francisco, Oakland and finally Santa Rosa. When Netta was four, her mother married Davis A. Drury, and Netta took the name Doris Drury, though I never learned why. Five years later, Doris's half-sister, Mary Ethel Drury, arrived. Not long after that, Lucile divorced again and soon married her third husband, J.P. Kelley.

A precocious child, Doris was a so-called "Termite," one of some 1500 hundred California children with high intelligence that Stanford psychology professor Lewis Terman studied throughout their lifetimes. Best known as the pioneer of the Stanford-Binet IQ test, professor Terman founded his "Genetic Studies of Genius" in 1921, since renamed the "Terman Study of the Gifted." For the study, Terman selected 856 boys and 672 girls, ages three to nineteen, with IQs above 135. The study subjects were all born between 1900 and 1925, all lived in California, were about 90 percent white, and the majority came from upper- or middle-class families. Doris, at six years old, tested at 142. That figure, Terman noted in her file, applied to fewer than four children in a thousand. More remarkable, Doris' half-sister tested eight points higher when she turned six. Mary grew up to be a writer, too, choosing the pen name Michael Drury to be more marketable than a woman author at the time. She wrote many articles for women's magazines and ten women's advice and self-help books. The best known and biggest seller of them was *Advice to a Young Wife from an Old Mistress*. My aunt Michael was married for many years to Jack Calderwood, but I heard my mother once say her sister had a torrid affair with a well-known Hollywood song-and-dance man.

According to Terman's notes on Doris, she never displayed any interest in dolls of any kind nor did she play with any toys that were kitchen or household items. She did show great interest in sewing and crocheting at ages five and six. She had a great liking for grown up people and preferred to be with them rather than playmates her age. Her home library contained more than 300 books, and she had more interest in dictionaries than the encyclopedia or world atlas, he noted. She accelerated through elementary school, finishing eighth grade at age twelve, and graduated from Analy Union High School in Sebastopol in 1930, four weeks before turning sixteen. Two years later she graduated from Santa Rosa Junior College, where she was her class valedictorian, worked on the Azalea Yearbook and participated in the Thespians, Camp Fire Girls, Spanish Club, Honor Society, Girls League, and Dramatics.

With Professor Terman's endorsement and influence, Doris was accepted as a junior transfer to Stanford University in 1932. She joined the same Class of 1934 with future Silicon Valley icons Bill Hewlett and David Packard. *Stanford Daily* editor Abe Mellinkoff, who would become the legendary city editor for the *San Francisco Chronicle* was also at Stanford with Doris. As a senior, Doris worked to abolish sororities and was elected president of the Roble Club. She graduated with an English degree June 17, 1934, a month shy of her twentieth birthday.

Dori's early jobs after Stanford included social caseworker, publicity assistant with the U. S. Resettlement Administration, secretary in the press office for the San Francisco World's Fair, and society editor and publicist for the Hotel Del Monte in Monterey.

CHAPTER 11:
In Love with a Writer

Dori was a strikingly attractive blue-eyed blonde and Dean Jennings was movie star-handsome with jet-black hair, piercing blue eyes, a cleft chin, and a pencil-thin moustache. When they met in January 1939, he was thirty-three and she was twenty-four. Dean was working as a publicist for George Palmer Putnam, the renowned publisher and author, known also as the husband of missing aviation pioneer Amelia Earhart, who had disappeared over the Pacific Ocean two years earlier while attempting a circumnavigation flight of the globe by airplane. Dori came aboard as Putnam's secretary. Dean had just finished his first book, a novel titled, *The Man Who Killed Hitler*.

From Dori's personal letters to Dean at the time, one can tell she fell hard and fast for the dashing but twice-divorced writer who already had four children. He was romantic and worldly, and she was enthralled by his looks, his family background, and his writing talent. In a questionnaire for Professor Terman later that year, Dori wrote that over the five years since graduating from Stanford she had held various jobs in publicity, editing, and research. And that she was engaged.

She wrote to Terman that she had "a natural interest in things literary—printer's ink in the blood, so to speak (begging your pardon for a cliché). I expect soon to marry a writer, whom I actively assist in research, typing, filing, etc. I prefer this means of expression to trying a 'career' for myself but, if necessary, I would support myself in the publishing field. And I have long felt that my ability lies in execution rather than originality of ideas. It's so natural—and inevitable—that I should be in love with a writer."

In addition to his Putnam job, Dean was also writing freelance magazine articles and his second book, Leg Man. As it neared publication, Doris and Dean traveled to New York, where he met with his publisher, agent, and magazine editors. While there, in October 1940, they got married, then returned to their home in Mill Valley in Marin County, just across the Golden Gate Bridge from San Francisco.

Dori had two miscarriages before my brother was born in May 1945 at what was then Stanford Hospital at Clay and Webster Streets in San Francisco. Naming another son Dean was out of the question. Instead, they cobbled their first names together and came up with "Dorn," and the middle name Webster, an homage to Dean's father. My brother hated his first name his entire life. An unusual name draws unwanted attention, even ridicule, to a child. For an introvert like my brother, it was a living hell. As an adult, Dorn often talked about changing his name to Clay Webster. But he never went to the trouble of applying for a legal change.

I arrived at St. Luke's Hospital in the summer of 1947, three weeks premature and under six pounds. At the time, my father was writing the book with Warden Duffy. The Jennings had become good friends with Clint and his wife, Gladys, and thought Duffy would be a good name for me. Plus, it kept the DJ initials pattern in the family. But my paternal grandfather, the minister, lobbied hard—even demanded—a biblical name. In the end, they named me David Duffy. Dori and Dean liked my middle name so much that they called me by it almost exclusively, except when we visited my grandparents. "Hello, David," the Reverend always greeted me, which caught me off guard. Other than official or legal purposes—government forms, schools, bank accounts, marriage licenses and the like, I have preferred to use and be called Duffy my entire life. Unlike my brother, as an extrovert I liked having an unusual name.

In my life, I can only recall meeting two or three other people with Duffy as a legal first or middle name. It was always a conversation starter. "Is that your real name?" I'm often asked. "You mean like Duffy Waldorf?" or "You must be Irish," or "Duffy's Tavern, Duffy ain't here," after the popular radio show. When I explain I was named after the warden at San Quentin, it always draws curious head tilts and quizzical expressions, even today.

Less than a month after I was born, my father accepted a job as a public information officer with the U.S. Office of War Information in Berlin. That assignment also helped him land a contract with the advertising agency Foote, Cone & Belding to publicize the Swiss watch industry while abroad. We took a cross-country train to the East Coast, where we boarded the RMS *Mauretania* for Europe in September 1947. U.S. civilians weren't yet allowed in post-war Germany, so while Dean worked in Berlin, Mom, Dorn, and I lived in Bern, Switzerland, for the next year. As a frail newborn, I became deathly ill that year. The family story goes that our Swiss au pair began to feed me goat's milk and I eventually recovered. We returned to Marin in 1948, renting a house in San Rafael.

Two years later, Dori confided to Professor Terman that she had her "tubes tied," that she was increasingly depressed and that her ambivalence toward sex was having a chilling effect on her marriage. Also, she told him, she had begun to drink.

"I take a drink occasionally for social reasons," she told Terman in a meeting in his office one afternoon. But in a follow-up memo to her file after the meeting, Terman expressed his concern that she was drinking "...entirely too much. (She said she) begins in the late afternoon when she starts to get dinner and drinks four or five jiggers of hard liquor before the dinner is finished. Then drinks two or three more before going to bed. The fact that she admits to the consumption of a half pint daily could mean that she is probably drinking considerably more than that."

Terman also noted that Dori "looked and talked that afternoon as though she had a hangover, though it may have been only the effects of her emotional upset the night before when she had words with Dean and a long spell of crying. Looks definitely older than she should and less attractive than formerly."

Despite her openness about drinking, Dori did not mention to Terman that she had recently tried to take her own life. Dori took an overdose of sleeping pills, but Dean found her and rushed her to Marin General Hospital. My brother, who was four at the time, said it was one of his first memories. "When she recovered enough to have visitors, Dean brought me to see her," Dorn told me. "Dean pointed to an upstairs window and there was Dori, waving." Dean didn't tell my brother at the time why she was in the hospital, but she acknowledged this when we were grown.

The marriage started to sour soon after we returned from Europe. Between my father's ego and caustic reproaches and my mother's superior intelligence and inchoate drinking problem, there was constant bickering and competition between them. As gifted and prolific as Dean was with a typewriter, it turned out the only parenting gift he had was, well, conceiving. He didn't stick around to raise any of us. My late half-brother, Dean Jr., whom we all called Suddy, short for Southern, said angrily to me one day: "Dean could never keep it in his pants."

Whether it was Dori's drinking and suicidal ideations or Dean's wandering eye, or both, Dean was already moving on. One evening while covering a dance at the Meadow Club in Fairfax for his daily *Chronicle* column, he met Mary Foster, the woman who would become wife number four. Dean's and Dori's divorce was final in April 1952. He tied the knot with Mary in 1954. The ceremony took place in his room at Mt. Zion Hospital in San Francisco, where he was recovering from a heart attack, his first. He was forty-nine.

CHAPTER 12:
Dori and George

Even during their contentious split, Dori continued to work as Dean's assistant at the newspaper. She liked newspaper people and the journalism business so much that it was worth it to her to keep the job. After the breakup, she moved us into a San Francisco flat on North Point Street near the Palace of Fine Arts. Suddenly a single mom with two sons and only intermittent child support payments from Dean, she soon left her low-paying job as his column assistant. She worked as a nightclub hostess, social worker, secretary, restaurant publicist, and eventually as a loan officer for a bank. Never again did she work in anything related to her English degree or journalism.

Mom hired a nanny named Esther, an icy and strict middle-aged woman with stringy gray hair and her own drinking problem. In later years, my brother characterized Esther as "another whisky soak" and "the alky's alky." Esther lived with us in a spare bedroom and imposed her own booze-fueled discipline with frequent spankings. At that age, I don't recall what infractions might have brought them about. Mom swatted my behind once or twice, but she never administered a full-on spanking or any other form of corporal punishment. On the other hand, she occasionally brought home dates who did. One crude, cowboy hat-wearing asshole named Jim walloped both Dorn and me more than a few times over the months he was in the picture. While Mom herself spared us boys from spankings, love and nurturing were in short supply, too. She told us she loved us, but rarely demonstrated it with hugs or kisses.

Our flat was directly across the street from Winfield Scott School, a public elementary school. Every morning I stood at the living room window, longingly watching Dorn walk over to school, and later saw him playing in the schoolyard at recess. I cried because I couldn't wait to start school myself and get away from Esther for the day.

It was about that time when a neighbor woman introduced Dori to George Banda, part owner of the Polk-Vallejo Market, a neighborhood grocery at that intersection. George was a genial Italian man from Wisconsin, the sixth of eight children. He was born with a defect that made his left arm shorter than his right and slightly crooked, but it never impaired him in any way and he rarely talked about it. After his first job shaking hides in a tannery, he became a trucker hauling Coca-Cola and Max Factor cosmetics across Kansas. Then he started his own trucking company with one truck and eventually bought a partnership in the grocery with his brother and brother-in-law. George was divorced with a daughter about Dorn's age. He was masculine, strong and had a warm personality that Dori found engaging. (Ironically, for reasons I never knew, my mother's nickname for my father was George. Many of her letters to him started with, "Dear George...") Dori and George Banda began dating and before long were in a romance that later evolved into a business partnership that would continue for the next twenty years. Despite his blue-collar upbringing and lack of education beyond high school, in contrast to Dori's background, they meshed. She enjoyed teaching him better language skills, etiquette, and social behavior while she reveled in being with a rugged, street-smart man. I always saw George as a father figure and I remained close to him until his death from a stroke in 2002.

In 1955, Dori moved us to a rental flat on Broderick Street. I joined the Cub Scouts and hosted den meetings at our house, but I didn't have a lot of friends. Dorn and I sometimes spent weekends with my father and our stepmother, Mary, who was warmer and more nurturing than any adult woman I had known. From our corner at Broderick and Filbert Streets, I could see all the way across the Bay to the Corinthian Yacht Club building in Tiburon, a few hundred yards down Main Street from where Dean and Mary lived on the water. I enjoyed those weekends with Mary a great deal. Often after returning home on Sunday, I stood on my Cow Hollow corner, staring across the bay, crying, and wishing I was back in Tiburon.

In 1956, Dorn and I spent the entire summer in Connecticut with Mary and Dean, who was there working on a series of articles for the *Saturday Evening Post* about the comic pianist Victor Borge. Borge was a popular performer known as the "Clown Prince of Denmark" and "The Great Dane" who appeared live around the country and on many television variety shows. Dean had rented a house in Danbury, near Borge's ViBo Farms, a 400-acre ranch where Borge raised Rock Cornish game hens for the commercial market. For Dorn and me, it was our first plane trip. After refueling in Kansas City, we arrived in New York, where Dean and Mary spent three days showing us around the city. They took us to our first Major League baseball game, between the Yankees and the Boston Red Sox. This was two years before the Giants moved to San Francisco, and I was awed at the sight of Yankee Stadium and the vast expanse of green grass as I entered the ballpark. The brilliant green and the smell of the fresh mown grass was unforgettable. We ate hot dogs and cotton candy and drank Cokes. I don't recall much about the game itself, but I distinctly remember that Yankees third baseman Andy Carey lined a foul ball into the crowd a few rows in front of us that struck a woman in the head. Ushers carried the woman out on a stretcher right past our seats, bleeding profusely from her scalp.

One day that summer Dean took us for a tour of the Borge estate and the hen factory. We watched as workers electrocuted dozens of the small birds for processing and packaging—both grisly and fascinating for a nine-year-old. Another day at our house there, I was outside walking with my father's German shepherd fifty yards ahead of me when the dog suddenly yelped and bolted back in my direction as fast as she could run. She had disturbed a nest of bees that now pursued her by the thousands. As the dog flew past me, I felt the first stings on the back of my neck and I took off for the house as fast as I could run. Our station wagon was parked in the driveway with all its windows open to ventilate the summer heat. The dog leaped through the right front passenger window and out the driver's window in one bound. When we both got into the house, the dog took cover in a closet. A veterinarian later said she'd been stung more than two hundred times but would eventually be okay. She stayed in the closet for two full days. Meanwhile, I ran crying into the house, where my stepmother comforted me with hugs and a damp towel. Using tweezers, she removed eighteen bee stingers from my neck and shoulders. If you see a bee within five feet of me these days, you'll understand why I can't get away fast enough.

Chapter 13:
Greenwich Time

When Dorn and I arrived back home from Connecticut, Mom picked us up from the airport in our Studebaker—Dorn and I called it the Red Rocket. "I have a surprise for you boys," she said. Once in the city, instead of driving us home, she stopped in front of a pair of Victorian flats on Greenwich Street between Buchanan and Webster Streets. "This is our new house," she said. "We moved while you were back east." Dori had saved enough for a down payment on the flats, which she bought for $17,000. (After our mother died in 1981, Dorn and I sold the property. Today, in the ultra-high-priced neighborhood where it's located, its value is $2.5 million.) Dori, Dorn, and I lived in the lower flat and she rented out the upper unit. For many years, our upstairs tenant was a very pleasant single woman named Barbara Martinelli, a relative of the sparkling apple juice family of that name.

The importance of proper spelling, good writing, and grammar were the backdrop to every dinner conversation, homework assignment and daily communication with our mother. I realized by fourth grade that I could instinctively write much better than I could solve math or science problems. I never kept a journal, wrote any fiction, or took formal writing classes. But my written and verbal communication skills helped get me elected school president both as a sixth-grader at Winfield Scott and three years later at Marina Junior High.

Although she bristled at our grammar and spelling slipups and seemed to always have a book by her bed, Mom did not encourage Dorn and me to read for pleasure. My brother picked that up on his own, but I rarely read books. Nor do I recall ever having a serious

Duffy and Dorn, 1957 Greenwich St.

conversation with Mom about the importance of going to college. Once, when I was seven, Dori and George piled us into the car and drove us down the Peninsula to Palo Alto. As we turned off El Camino Real onto a long road lined with palm trees and headed toward a huge tower in the distance, Dori turned to Dorn and me, pointed her finger at us and said: "This is Stanford University. I went to college here and both of you will go here someday." It was never mentioned again.

George and Dori spent a lot of weekends together at Greenwich Street. He would come to the house after work on Saturday with grocery bags full of Porterhouse steaks from the butcher, fresh mushrooms, baking potatoes, salad greens and sourdough bread. They especially liked sweetbreads, too, and other popular dishes of the day like beef tongue and liver and onions. Dorn and I wouldn't touch them. And always there were fifths of vodka or gin and bottles of chianti. They would have martinis while Dori prepared dinner. During dinner, they drank wine in highball glasses. Both smoked heavily; George liked Parliaments, Dori preferred Salem menthols. Many people smoked then, with no understanding of its dangers. In our generation smoking was not only accepted, it was cool. I took it up myself after high school, intermittently, starting with my mother's menthols. At boot camp, smoke breaks were a welcome reprieve, if only for ten minutes, from the stressful hounding by drill instructors, so I started smoking daily. I smoked all through my newspaper years before quitting on my thirtieth birthday. I relapsed at thirty-two, then quit completely at thirty-six.

Sometimes at Greenwich Street we watched our new little twelve-inch Zenith black-and-white television after dinner. Saturday night favorites included the family comedy "Leave it to Beaver" and the western "Gunsmoke." When it was bedtime, Dori and George disappeared into her bedroom and closed the door. Dorn and I shared the other bedroom, adjacent to Mom's room. It was ten feet by ten feet, with a cork tile floor, our twin beds on opposite walls and a single nightstand between them. We shared the single dresser and the small closet. A window looked over the small concrete yard and the back of two houses on the alley behind us.

We spent months of Saturdays and Sundays refurbishing the house, built two years after the Great San Francisco earthquake and fire in 1906. We recovered the old carpeted hall floors with black-and-white diagonal linoleum squares, remodeled the bathroom, updated the kitchen appliances, rebricked the hearth and fireplace, bought Scandinavian-style fifties living room furniture and painted throughout.

On Sunday mornings, Mom often sent Dorn and me off to the Christian Science Sunday School four blocks away on Lombard Street. Even though her mother was a Christian Science practitioner, sending us to church was more about Dori and George having time alone than it was about exposing us boys to religion. Before long, we stopped going altogether, retaining little of our religious schooling or spirituality.

In the summers, Mom took us on driving vacations to Camp Mather near Yosemite and to the National Parks in California—Kings Canyon, Sequoia, Lassen, and others—or to visit her mother in Southern California. One winter night when I was eleven and Dorn was thirteen, George and Dori packed us into his station wagon with George's daughter, Robin, and told us to go to sleep in the back, that we had a long trip ahead. When they woke us up, we were checking in to a cabin at Squaw Valley near Lake Tahoe. I emerged sleepily from the car to see acres of snow and flakes falling lazily from the dark sky. We spent the weekend sledding, building a snowman, and throwing snow balls. I was very cold and wet, and I couldn't wait to get home. I have felt the same way about snow ever since.

Birthdays and holidays were no big deal at Greenwich Street. Mom wasn't much for decorations and celebrations. We got birthday presents, of course, and sometimes our favorite dinner and a cake. At Christmas, we had a two-foot aluminum tree on the living room coffee table, but little else by way of ornaments, lights, festivities, or seasonal music.

Even as little kids, Dorn and I argued and fought often. I still have a scar on my forehead from a rock he threw at me when I was five. We were so different; he was an introvert who cared about reading, history and keeping to himself; I was an extrovert who liked girls, sports, music, and clothes.

In 1958, when I was eleven, the Giants baseball team moved to San Francisco from New York and we all became instant fans, listening to future Hall of Fame announcers Russ Hodges and Lon Simmons broadcast games on our transistor radios. I'll never forget sitting by the pool at Camp Mather near Yosemite on the afternoon of July 30, 1959, listening to the exploits of Giants' rookie first baseman Willie "Stretch" McCovey on his first day in the majors. He went four-for-four with two triples and two singles off the Phillies' future Hall of Fame pitcher Robin Roberts. Mom became a diehard Stretch fan that day. None of us could have imagined that twenty-seven years later I would be working for the team and would help McCovey write his Hall of Fame acceptance speech.

I wanted to be a first baseman like McCovey, although I'm right-handed. I prodded Mom into buying me a Rawlings "Heart of the Hide," Bill White-model first baseman's glove. It was quite expensive, around forty dollars, and I was surprised she agreed to pay for it. By then, however, she'd been working for a year at Bankers Mortgage Company for its founder, Ray Lapin, who became known as the father of the secondary mortgage market. He would later serve under President Johnson as the creator of the Government National Mortgage Association (Ginnie Mae) and the Federal National Mortgage Association (Fannie Mae). Dori obviously was able to afford the glove, but she never discussed her income or financial situation at home when we were kids. Once I had the mitt, every night I devotedly rubbed the pocket with neat's-foot oil and wrapped a baseball in it. I played "Seals and Oaks" and "Three Flies Up" with my friends at Funston Playground every night until it was too dark to see the ball. I bought a book, "How to Play Winning Baseball," written by Arthur Mann in 1953. I still have it. I taught myself the fundamentals, and a year later I tried out for my junior high school team and made the squad.

Until the ninth grade I had been a decent student, bringing home mostly Bs and Cs, except for As in English and P.E. By then I was nearly thirteen, growing into a six-footer and discovering my interest in girls as well as baseball. When I started eighth grade at Marina Junior High in the fall of 1960, I noticed a new girl in my English class. She was tall, cute, and freckled, with blond hair, blue eyes, a warm smile, and long suntanned legs. We were smitten with one another. At thirteen, I had my first girlfriend.

Becky Van Haitsma had moved to San Francisco over the summer from Holland, Michigan, with her mom and two older sisters. They lived in a third floor flat on Franklin Street near Lombard, five blocks from our house. Becky and I became fast friends and started spending a lot of time together. We hung out between classes and during lunch and would meet at her house after school to study. Like me, her mother worked during the day as a teacher, so we were often on our own in the afternoons.

Becky and I, it turned out, both needed affection and reassurance. Her parents had divorced when she was ten, and, like me at that age, she was often sad and confused about being in a broken home. It seemed like all of our friends had a mom and dad at home. "Being with you was the first time I felt I truly belonged," she told me many years later. When the school year ended, Becky and her sisters went back to Michigan to spend the summer with their father, a dentist. We wrote letters back and forth. In one, she said she had flirted with a boy and felt terrible about it. Another one of her letters had an ugly smudge on it. She later said she had squashed a bug that landed on the stationery while she was writing. We had a big-time case of puppy love and talked about getting married and how we would have two children, a boy, and a girl. When Becky returned to San Francisco and ninth grade began in the fall of 1961, our romance flourished. It seems we spent every spare hour together during the day and all weekend and talked on the telephone into the night.

I was playing baseball for Marina after school during the week and for a Saturday team sponsored by the popular North Beach family-style restaurant New Pisa, and coached by its owner, Dante Benedetti. After games, Dante brought the entire team back to the restaurant and fed us mountains of pasta. Mom never came to any of my games, which disappointed me deeply. She listened when I told her about them afterward, but when I asked her to come, she told me she was just too busy to take an afternoon off.

That fall, with the encouragement of Mrs. Mann, my French teacher, and Mrs. FitzGerald, my English and homeroom teacher, I ran for school president and won. But as the spring came and Mom's absence at home stretched into longer periods, I started to express my anger by being late to school, ditching my homework, ignoring assignments, and fooling around in class.

One day at school I somehow came into possession of a mimeograph sheet that contained a test Mrs. FitzGerald was about to give. Mimeographs were a pre-tech version of today's Xerox machines—a low-cost duplicating machine that worked by printing through a stencil onto paper as it rolled through the ink-fed drum.

I managed to make a printed copy from the mimeo sheet and shared it with several other kids after school at the local ice cream store on Chestnut Street. Cheating was bad enough for any student, but indefensible for a student body president, and I was clearly looking for a way to be liked. After the test, someone ratted me out and I was forced to admit the crime. As punishment, the principal summarily removed me from office for the remainder of the term and suspended me for three days. When I returned to class, I endured untold humiliation throughout the school. When my teachers, my counselor, and my mother all demanded to know why I had done such a thing, I had no answer.

CHAPTER 14:
Club Dori

Around the time I turned twelve, Dori and George went their separate ways, having decided, for reasons I don't know or recall, not to marry. Within a year, Mom met the man who would change all our lives forever. Bart Randle was a wholesale beer salesman for Hamm's, or maybe Pabst Blue Ribbon. He was dark-haired with a moustache and, other than being overweight, was, curiously, the spitting image of my father. He quickly swept Dori off her feet. After they had been dating for a few weeks, he asked her to marry him and she told us she was giving it serious thought. Dorn and I found him cold and aloof and we missed George. Bart told Mom he knew a woman who wanted to sell a small bar and restaurant in Presidio Heights called New Bimbo's, and he persuaded Dori to take out a loan to buy it. She must have thought about owning her own business for some time, but she never talked of it around us. To her, though, this seemed like a dream opportunity. Bart promised to run the place so she could keep her bank job. What Mom didn't know was that the woman selling the bar was Bart's real girlfriend, and they had been plotting to find a sucker to take the money-losing business off her hands. As smart as Dori was, she was blinded by love, or what she thought was love, and the prospect that she would remarry after many years.

New Bimbo's was a small, nondescript place at 427 Presidio Avenue, tucked away in the shadow of the adjacent Jewish Community Center on the corner. Its clientele were mostly lunch customers from the Fireman's Fund building around the corner and other nearby offices, the JCC, and retail stores along Sacramento Street. At night, the bar served locals who dropped in for a drink after work, though a few regulars stayed late into the night.

Within a few months, Bart had purchased new kitchen appliances and spent money on bar equipment, supplies and other improvements. He kept putting off the engagement to concentrate on the business, he told Dori. But one day she arrived at the bar to find that Bart had vanished, taking an untold amount of cash, and leaving Dori with the bar and thousands of dollars in debt. The con had worked, and Dori was devastated.

With bill collectors at the doorstep and only a few months' experience at running the business, Dori turned to the only business owner she knew who could help her. Sheepishly, she called George, explained the situation, and said she would give him half of the business if he helped her bail out from under it all. George said yes. Dori had to quit her job to open the bar in the morning and manage things until George could get there from his grocery store at night. Unfortunately, after a few months it was clear there were never going to be enough regular customers to make up the losses.

One day they were lamenting the situation with their main bartender, a tall, thin fellow named Ted, or as they dubbed him, "Teddy Bear."

"What are we going to do?" asked Dori plaintively.

"How would you feel about going gay?" Ted suggested.

"What?" Dori replied. "How would we do that?"

"Just put a couple of small ads in the gay newspapers and I'll help spread the word," said Ted.

In the early 1960s, much of the city's emerging gay community was spread out along Polk Street and among a handful of South of Market watering holes. Mom never mentioned homosexuals when we were growing up, so I don't know how she felt about them before the bar. She was a capital-D Democrat all the way, and as liberal as they come, so I have to assume she had no qualms about having gays as customers. George knew a number of gay men who were customers at his Polk Street grocery, and I never heard him speak disparagingly about them. He understood that gay men for the most part had no families to support, and plenty of disposable income, and were lonely for companionship.

"OK," said George. "Let's see what happens."

They coined the new name for the bar—Club Dori—hired a new cook, revamped the dinner menu, offered drink specials, and placed some inconspicuous ads in local gay newspapers. The first ad was a simple, one-column, black-bordered ad that listed only four pieces of information about Club Dori: name, address, phone number, and operating hours.

The grand opening under its new name and policy was December 8, 1961. Draft beer was fifty cents, well drinks were sixty-five cents and name-brand liquor was eighty cents a drink. Once the first ads appeared, a few men trickled in for a drink, then word-of-mouth spread quickly. Soon the place was packed with young, good-looking, well-dressed professional men. They knew they were welcome at Club Dori, where they could meet, eat, and drink inconspicuously. They could even dance to the jukebox at a time when it was illegal for men to dance together in public.

Years later, when Monday Night Football began its TV broadcasts, Dori offered free spaghetti dinners on Monday nights, banking on the stereotype that gay men weren't interested in football and had nothing else to do. She was right. They lined up out the front door for free pasta, salad, and French bread—and spent oodles on drinks or wine to go with it. At the same time, word of free food spread to the Haight-Ashbury, where many of the young people who'd converged there during the Summer of Love were struggling to sustain their daily needs. Soon legions of hippies joined the line of regulars at Club Dori on Monday nights, an awkward congregation for both. While they gorged on food, few purchased drinks or wine and were taking up room in the bar. After a few weeks of this, Dori had to impose a drink minimum with dinner, and the hippies quickly faded away.

Club Dori became the "in" place where unassuming gay men could walk in the front door and come out of the closet for a few hours. Scores of men who were revered for their contributions to the mainstream world yet were still society's outcasts for their clandestine personal lives—city officials, legislators, attorneys, bankers, stockbrokers, army officers, doctors, ad execs and TV news anchors—found refuge and respect at Club Dori.

San Francisco cops harassed Club Dori and its customers incessantly. They double-parked their squad cars outside and shined flashlights into the faces of customers as they emerged. They demanded ID and made veiled threats about arrests for lewd behavior. My mother retaliated by going outside with her own flashlight and shining it into the officers' faces. "Leave my customers alone!" she demanded. The woman had balls. Remember, this was fully eight years before the famous Stonewall Inn riots in New York City's Greenwich Village, when gays revolted against a police raid on the bar. A National Monument dedicated to LGBT rights and history now memorializes the Stonewall. Back at Club Dori, the harassment eventually waned, and relationships improved as the cops got to know her and learned that her customers weren't troublemakers or queens who flaunted their lifestyle outside the bar. Before long the cops were coming in to Club Dori on cold nights for a free dinner and a cup of coffee, or I should say, Coffee Royale, made with a shot of brandy.

Eventually the customers were three-deep at the bar most nights. Dori and George made plenty of money, enough to pay off their bills in short order. Eventually she and George bought another place, Jackson's, on Powell Street near Fisherman's Wharf. That also became a trendy gay spot with good food and live entertainment.

In the early 1960s, California's Alcoholic Beverage Control laws prohibited a woman from tending bar unless she owned the business. Dori loved tending bar and she loved her customers. She became what I call the Queen Mother to scores of young gay men who would tell her their most intimate secrets and fears over a few drinks, things they couldn't tell their own mother. In a 1971 *Chronicle* article on the city's gay bars, Dori told reporter Donovan Bess that she had a "marvelous time" with her customers. "Some young men bring their mothers in to meet me," she said. "They may say, 'my son has written to me about you.'"

But in the early years, the more she talked about her regular customers, the harder it was for me to listen. She acted more like a mom in the bar than she did at home. With my own adolescence coming on, I may not have confided in her much, but it would have been nice to feel like I could.

The first time Dorn and I saw the club was one afternoon before it became a gay mecca. We rode over on his Vespa scooter, parked, and went in through the swinging double doors that opened into a small foyer, with a cigarette machine and a coat rack in the corner. Inside it was dark and smelled of cigarettes and beer, with a 25-foot-long bar, a dozen dining tables covered in red-checkered tablecloths, a full kitchen, a jukebox and a storeroom and office in the back. There was one customer at the time and Dori was behind the bar.

"Hi, Mom," I called out. Dori exploded.

"You do NOT call me Mom!" she barked. "You call me Dori. I don't want it known I have children." Maybe she was joking or soused, or both, but my brother and I were stunned. From that moment on I never saw her quite the same way. Dorn and I felt expendable. We both needed to be reassured that she would not abandon us, that whatever happened she would always be there for us. And yet there were incidents and situations that said otherwise.

One afternoon in ninth grade I fell awkwardly over the pommel horse in P.E. class at school and landed on my outstretched arm. I felt and heard a distinctive "snap." The school called Dori, but she said there was no one available to watch the bar for her, so my gym teacher took me to our family doctor on Van Ness Avenue. He diagnosed the fractured left radial and wrapped my forearm in a white plaster cast. Dori never did come. I walked the twelve blocks home, my arm in a sling, with mixed feelings. I was sad to be alone, but proud that I could handle it and not inconvenience her. It took me years to learn, but I rationalized this forced independence, this growing up so fast, as something that made me feel good about myself.

Club Dori's biggest night of the year was Halloween. Long before the Castro District became ground zero as a "gayborhood," with a city-sponsored costume party in the street, Halloween came to the gay community in busloads of drag queens that went from bar to bar to entertain the patrons with flamboyant fashion shows. Club Dori was a mandatory stop on the Halloween bus circuit. Under the disdainful glare of police who stood watch outside the bar, huge Grayline-style tour buses double-parked on Presidio, disgorging chorus lines of exquisitely-dressed men in long sequined gowns, spike heels, elaborate wigs, and impeccable makeup.

They paraded into the bar, sauntered through the appreciative crowd, lingered for a drink or two, teasing the customers with a hair toss or hip bump. Then they sashayed out the door to wild applause, boarded the buses again and headed to the next stop.

Another major showcase for drag queens at Halloween was the annual Beaux Arts Ball, sponsored by the Tavern Guild, an association of gay bar owners. It was at the Beaux Arts Ball that the city's Empress was crowned. George Banda once served as president of the guild.

CHAPTER 15:
The Alhambra

Mom left the house most every morning by eleven o'clock, not returning until three a.m. after closing the bar, cleaning up, and counting the nightly receipts. She was usually sleeping when Dorn and I left for school in the morning, and we were sleeping when she got home. We were on our own for meals, laundry, ironing, transportation, and schoolwork. Every morning, when my brother and I got up for school, there was always cash on the kitchen table for us. The bar was an all-cash business, and wads of bills always stuck out of Mom's purse like small bouquets of green flowers. Sometimes I helped myself to a few extra bucks. She never knew exactly how much she had taken from the till each night. Nor did the IRS, I'm sure. For dinners, Dorn and I regularly walked a few blocks down to Lombard Street. There we split up. One of us went to Bingo's for 19-cent cheeseburgers and French fries while the other went across the street to Miz Brown's restaurant to buy thick chocolate milkshakes and hot slices of cinnamon apple pie. We took it all home and ate by ourselves at our kitchen table.

Eventually, Dori eased up on the "no Mom" rule as her staff and most regular customers knew who we were. Dori made it crystal clear to all her employees and customers that her sons, should they come into the club, were not, under any circumstances, to be touched or bothered. At the same time, however, she told Dorn and me that if anyone ever acted inappropriately in any fashion, we were not to lash out or repel them. For the most part there were no problems, but once in a great while someone new to the place would look one of us up and down salaciously or say something vulgar, which creeped me out.

Still, I followed her rules and just laughed and let it go, but it was hard. Very hard. Dori was my mother, after all, and I was trying to be loyal and help her out. But damn, it was difficult at times. All that open gayness made me uncomfortable, to say the least. I wished that just once Dori asked me how I felt about the whole Club Dori business. She never did.

When I was fifteen, I got a job at the Alhambra Theatre, working as an usher and behind the candy counter. Because of its Polk Street location, the Alhambra was a favorite spot for clandestine meetups between gays, who trolled the restroom and the upper reaches of the second-floor balcony for other men interested in the "coming attractions," as it were.

The theater manager, himself gay, regularly asked me and the other ushers to patrol the mezzanine, balcony, and the men's restroom for lewd activity. We would shine our flashlights down the rows of the loge seats or around the downstairs bathroom, startling men in compromising situations. Embarrassed and grossed out, we'd flee back to the lobby. What I saw in Club Dori and in those in the dark corners of the Alhambra—men grinding together, fondling one another, kissing—made me more and more disgusted and ashamed of my mother and her bar.

Late one night after work, I was walking down the street to my car when I noticed a blond man leaning against a nearby building. He appeared to be in his early twenties and was wearing a plaid shirt, tight jeans, and heavy black boots. As I got closer, he said, "Hey, handsome, want some company?" I'd had it. I snapped. "Fuck you!" I snarled. I belted him once in the stomach and he crumpled to his knees. I took off running down the street, jumped in my car and sped away. But not before the man noted my license plate and called the cops. The next morning my mother confronted me.

"Duff, the police just called. They said you beat up someone last night," she said. "Is that true?"

Imagine the horror! The son of Club Dori's owner punching a gay man? I was busted, and I confessed.

"How could you do such a thing?!" she demanded. I shrugged. She drove me down to the Hall of Justice to meet the detective who had called her. He looked at me with a scowl.

"What you did is battery," he said. "You could go to jail for it."

He got quiet and I started to feel a pit of fear in my stomach as I thought about being locked up. But then he added that the man I hit wasn't badly hurt and did not want to press charges because he was afraid his boss would find out he was a homosexual out cruising for dates late at night, underage ones at that. After a stern lecture, I was let off with a warning. It was awfully quiet in the car ride home. I was so humiliated. I never lashed out at a gay person again, but the shame of my mother's business stayed with me until I matured.

Looking back on it now, I realize that my mother cared a lot for her customers as people and not merely a source of income. In many ways, the bar was a good thing for me. It gave me an understanding, appreciation, and acceptance of gays that I may not have learned otherwise. The basis of prejudice and discrimination, of course, is ignorance and what you learn growing up. Even before the bar, my mother was never critical of gays in any way, so my discomfort and confusion as a kid were based on stereotypes and slurs from other kids, not anything I learned at home. Over time, by getting to know some of Dori's customers and gay employees, and later through my own gay friends, acquaintances and co-workers, I was able to put my misplaced adolescent homophobia behind me.

CHAPTER 16:
A Letter from Dad

Once I arrived at Lowell High School, I detached myself from Becky for reasons I don't recall, but I know it was painful for her. It would become my pattern for ending relationships during my life, not with open, honest conversation but with long periods of silence to avoid the confrontation at all costs. Ghosting, in the parlance of kids today. I worked on the school newspaper and yearbook, played varsity baseball, and produced mediocre grades. I dated three or four girls at Lowell, but none too seriously until my senior year when Linda Morgan arrived. She was the daughter of an Army surgeon who'd been transferred to Letterman Hospital on the Presidio Army Base. Linda and I spent long hours together, many of them in her family's basement after school, supposedly studying.

When my brother left for the Air Force, I got his Vespa, which I rode across town from the Marina through the foggy Sunset District, often arriving at Lowell soaked. Frequently I picked up my junior varsity baseball teammate Steve Somers from his parents' house near Golden Gate Park. Even then Steve talked incessantly about becoming a sportscaster and during baseball season would pretend to broadcast play-by-play of the previous night's Giants game in my ear all the way down Nineteenth Avenue toward school. It got to the point where we gave Steve the nickname Curt, after the renowned broadcaster Curt Gowdy. It wasn't that much of a stretch. While still at Lowell he started doing high school sports reports on KYA radio. After Steve graduated from UC Berkeley in 1970, he had a news talk show on KABL radio and was the announcer for Warriors basketball games before he joined KPIX-TV in San Francisco as a weekend sports anchor and won a San Francisco Press Club Award. Over the next decade and a half,

Steve held TV sports anchor jobs at KOVR in Stockton, WXIA in Atlanta and KNBC in Los Angeles. In 1987, Steve joined New York radio station WFAN at its inception, where he pioneered sports talk radio and became a national sports radio icon. Thirty-two years later, he's still on the air nightly at WFAN, opening with his trademark, "Good evening to you, and how you be? Steve Somers here and you there."

Historically, nearly one hundred percent of Lowell graduates go on to college. Its best-known alumni include titans of business, government, science, medicine, and law, even a Supreme Court Justice, Stephen Bryer. But when my counselor asked me about my college plans, I had none. By then my interest in college or career of any kind had vanished, if they had ever existed in the first place. My grades, already in freefall, dropped further. I was drinking with my buddies every weekend. We made fake IDs and bought cases of beer and pints of vodka and Scotch at mom-and-pop grocery stores in the outer Sunset near school.

I snuck liquor into the senior picnic at the Marin Town & Country Club by hiding small wine bottles in hollowed out loaves of French bread and injecting oranges with vodka using syringes I got from my buddy Bill Berger, whose father was a doctor. Linda got tipsy and had to be pulled from the pool, exposing the hidden hooch caper. The dean of boys suspended me, and the journalism advisor kicked me off the newspaper. The school punished Linda and me by prohibiting both of us from attending our senior prom, which I laughed off since we would have gone together anyway. But the picnic episode marked the beginning of the end of our relationship. Her father was livid, told her to break it off with me, and she started seeing another guy. The principal threatened to banish me from graduation. It was all very embarrassing. I was establishing a pattern of misbehavior like my ninth-grade meltdown. But I didn't care.

After graduation in 1965, I screwed off long enough to miss the registration deadline for City College of San Francisco. One night that summer I heard about a party at an apartment on Monterey Boulevard. I made fast friends with the two guys living there, Dan Parrish and John Crawford. Dan and John were childhood buddies from Woodland, near Sacramento, who had come down to the city to attend CCSF. They had rented a three-bedroom place five blocks from campus and were looking for a third roommate. I told Mom about it and she said I was eighteen and could do what I wanted. I moved in that week.

In August, I made it just under the wire to get into College of San Mateo, mostly to keep my student deferment from military service. The U.S. was sending troops to Vietnam by the thousands and I wanted no part of it. I was neither politically aware enough to be consciously opposed, nor unpatriotic, but my brother was already overseas, and I just had a sense that I needed to stay close to home.

I commuted to San Mateo that fall and worked nights and weekends at the Alhambra. One of the girls working behind the candy counter at the movie, Barbara, said I might like to meet her older sister, a senior at Washington High School. Barbara showed me a photo of a very pretty girl with blond hair and green eyes. "Bring her in," I said. The next Saturday, Barbara brought her sister, Cheryl, to the theatre. I was smitten immediately, and we began dating. I didn't know it then, but I had met the woman I would marry.

My grades at CSM were so-so, but my classes included a journalism course that produced the school newspaper, the Bulldog. Because I had worked on the Lowell paper, the advisor made me sports editor. It was the only class I enjoyed and never missed.

I hadn't been in touch with my father for some time. Dori had sued him a year earlier for back payment of child support and he was furious, so I kept my distance. But I wrote to him, asking for feedback on my nascent journalism skills, thinking he might like the idea that his youngest son was in some small way following in his footsteps. I was naïve. On September 30, 1965, I received a letter back. He wrote:

"Dear Duff: I'm glad you are learning to be a journalist, for this is a fun business, even though the chances of getting rich are nil. But I see you are also learning—or perhaps you were already skilled in it—the art of hyperbole, or, as it is known on the farm, piling up the bullshit. It is fairly obvious that you think I am some kind of a knucklehead, and that may be a natural conclusion. Your mother once told Dorn, long before this junior idiot voted me jerk of the year, that 'you can get anything out of Dad if you just sweeten him up a little.'

"I am amused to note you say my opinions hold a lot of weight with you. Are you kidding? I have not heard from you in one year and four months. You value my opinion? Bologney. Look, Duff, whatever else you feel like saying to me, just don't give me the old soft soap. You have been brainwashed, as has Dorn, and you don't give a living hoot in hell what I think, feel, know, or anything else.

"Now that we've blown the fog away, let's get down to cases. The real reason you wrote to me was to remind me, in a not very subtle way, that you had not received—or your mother had not received—the monthly $100. I can hear her saying to you: Duff, maybe you'd better drop him a note and tell him where you are, and give him the old crap about the newspaper business, etc. He's a sucker for giving out advice in that direction, and he'll be flattered. Then maybe you'll get the hundred. I am your father, and this hundred is labeled child support. What child? My son? LSD, or hallucinations. I have no son. I had two once, named Dorn and Duffy, and I was available when I was needed, for a vacation, or a week-end in Tiburon or a trip to Catalina or Connecticut or Disneyland, or cash in hand, or borrowing a car, or getting new car coats and sneakers or talking to a doctor or giving a speech at the Journalism class or any one of a thousand things."

He added that he didn't have any money because my mother's suit had cost him $8000 and lawyers' fees. There was more to the letter, but no need to go on. He may have been right about Dori indoctrinating us against him, and probably had a good reason to feel estranged from Dorn and me. But at eighteen what did I know about any of that? And who wants to hear that vitriol from his father?

I was stung by this. He had never said anything so hurtful to me. I took it as a thorough rejection of my journalism interest more than the rejection of me personally. By focusing this attack on my writing failures, I subconsciously denied that he was disowning me as his son. My half-sister, Suzette, says that Dean treated both of her brothers the same way, denigrating them to the point that both felt they would never be good enough for him.

Two years went by before I spoke to him again. I called him when I needed a favor and he complied, perhaps out of a sense of guilt. I always hoped that when I became an adult we might someday sit down and talk honestly, one-to-one, about he and my mother, about school, careers, women...so many things. By then, however, he had less than two years to live and neither of us knew it.

CHAPTER 17:
USMC

When the spring semester ended in January, I transferred to CCSF, where my schoolwork continued its downslide. Having fumbled through a year of community college, my grade point average fell below the 2.0 level needed to keep my deferment. The Selective Service wasted no time classifying me 1-A, a guaranteed ticket to Southeast Asia, where the war in Vietnam was escalating. The number of U.S. forces there was approaching 200,000. One night after several beers, my roommate Danny Parrish, a muscular cowboy from the farmlands, announced that he was enlisting in the Marine Corps to fight the Viet Cong.

"Why don't you come with me?" he urged.

"Great idea!" I replied, or some other slurred words to that effect.

"Okay, we'll go down to the recruiting office tomorrow and sign up."

I agreed without giving much consideration to my earlier reluctance to go to war. I was only thinking it would get me out of San Francisco and away from my mother, just as my brother had done.

What also appealed to me about it was the notion that it would make me more of a man somehow. Who's tougher than the Marines? And for sure there wouldn't be any "homos" in the Corps, I reasoned. Not that I ever analyzed it or questioned my masculinity, but having been raised by a single mom and other than Uncle George, there wasn't much of a male influence to shape my manhood. Danny and I went out later that night and celebrated our patriotic decisions in style, ending up at Lyle Tuttle's famous tattoo parlor adjacent to the Greyhound bus station on Seventh Street near Market at one-thirty in the morning. I was both drunk enough and stupid enough to get "USMC" tattooed on my left shoulder in half-inch high block letters.

Me and mom at my graduation from Marine Corps boot camp, San Diego, September 1966.

Parrish, who could hold his alcohol better than anyone I'd ever seen, wised up and declined. He laughed heartily as he watched Tuttle go to work on my arm.

The next day when we got to the recruiting office, I'm the one who came to my senses. Dan signed up for a three-year hitch while I opted for the reserves instead. That meant six months of active duty and then back home for five and half years of monthly weekend duty and two weeks of summer camp training every year. The recruiter, a square-jawed sergeant in Marine dress blues and shoes spit-shined to a patent leather gloss, told me there was no question my reserve unit would be activated for the war eventually, but I figured I'd take my chances. When I arrived at the Marine Corps Recruit Depot in San Diego for boot camp in the middle of July 1966, I took a shit-ton of abuse for that damned tattoo. The first time the drill instructor saw me with my shirt off, he moved in until his nose was an inch from mine. He glowered and screamed:

"WHAT THE FUCK IS THAT ON YOUR ARM, PRIVATE JENNINGS?! You think you're a goddamned Marine? You're no Marine and if I have anything to do with it, you never will be, not in my Corps! You're nothing but a slimy maggot! Drop and give me twenty, you fucking scumbag!"

Just to rub it in, he made the rest of my squad do the pushups with me, which of course endeared me to them for weeks. He had a good point, though. What the fuck *was* I thinking when I got that tattoo? That I would be cool? Tough? Fearless? That it would automatically make me a "mean, lean fighting machine?" Nothing could be further from the truth. Fifty years later, I'm still taken right back there when I watch the opening scenes of Stanley Kubrick's *Full Metal Jacket*. The boot camp scenes and the portrayal of Gunnery Sergeant Hartman by the late actor R. Lee Ermey, a real-life former drill instructor, are as authentic as it gets for me.

After eight weeks of boot camp, I graduated with my company in ceremonies on the MCRD parade ground. My mother and George came down to San Diego for the event. I still have a Polaroid of my mother and me from that day. I am standing at attention in my dress khakis, with a new private first-class chevron on both sleeves and a rifleman's medal above the left shirt pocket. Dori is in a matching skirt and top with a geographic design, flat white sandals and holding her signature, oversized round black-framed eyeglasses. She is smiling into the sun, looking proud of her son in uniform.

I transferred to Camp Pendleton for a month of advanced infantry training, then stayed there for the remaining three months of my active duty requirement. Although I was classified as an infantryman, I was assigned to office work because I knew how to type. I spent my days filling out deployment forms and stamping out dog tags for Marines headed to Vietnam.

At Pendleton, if we didn't screw up somehow during the week, we were given liberty on weekends. Every Friday afternoon at four o'clock I piled into my Volkswagen beetle with three buddies from my reserve unit in the Bay Area—David Middleton, Mike Tognotti and Dennis Jacobson—and we made the eight-hour drive up U.S. 101 to San Francisco. We usually arrived around midnight and regrouped at noon on Sunday for the return trip because we had to be back on the base by 8 p.m.

Jacobson may have avoided combat duty in Vietnam, but he later became a San Francisco cop and was wounded in an ambush. On January 13, 1971, while on patrol with his partner, Robert Martinez, three men opened fire on their squad car at Steiner and Waller Streets without warning. Dennis, who was driving at the time, was wounded in his right leg yet managed to slam down the accelerator and speed away down the block, which likely saved their lives. Martinez was shot in the arm. At the next corner, Jacobson radioed for help and jumped from the vehicle, thinking the gunmen, later identified as Black Liberation Army members, were intent on finishing them off. Both officers survived the attack. I lost track of Dennis after that.

Dan Parrish, meanwhile, was a quintessential Marine. He got through his first tour of duty in Vietnam in one piece and went back for a second. In March 1968, four days after saving many of his patrol members in a fierce firefight, actions that earned him a Silver Star, Corporal Parrish stepped on a land mine. The explosion blew him into the air, and he landed with his other leg on a second mine. He lost both feet. When he finally came home and rehabilitated, he returned to his home town, opened a successful insurance business, and even served as two terms as mayor.

I spent most of those liberty weekends seeing Cheryl. We grew closer by the day. Curiously, Cheryl was my second girlfriend whose father was an Army officer stationed at the Presidio. She was born while her dad was stationed at Fort Benning, in Georgia, and by the time she graduated from Washington High School in San Francisco she had moved from coast to coast and twice to Germany and attended twelve different schools, all while helping her mom take care of her six younger siblings.

When I was discharged from active duty in January 1967, George Banda gave me a job working at his grocery store as a stock boy and delivery driver. I had been working there for three weeks when I came home to Greenwich Street one night and slumped in a kitchen chair. "What's wrong?" my mother asked.

"I hate this job, Mom," I said. "I don't know what I'm supposed to do, but this isn't it. I need to find something else."

"Well, why don't you go down to the *Chronicle* and get a job," she said, as if it were as simple as walking down to the corner news rack and buying a copy of the paper.

"What?" I said. "You don't just go down to the *Chronicle* and get a job. What makes you think I can do that?"

"Because I went to college with Abe Mellinkoff, for one. And your father worked there. And I worked there. We still have friends there. I'll give you Abe's phone number. Call him and ask if there are any jobs."

The next day I called and spoke to Mellinkoff, who, after some pleasantries, said, "Can you come to see me tomorrow afternoon?"

CHAPTER 18:
Copy!

Walking into the *Chronicle* city room to meet Abe Mellinkoff was as much a sensory experience for me as seeing that perfect, green Yankee Stadium grass for the first time. It looked so much like the newsrooms I'd seen in movies—men and women talking on the phone with headsets and typing quickly at the same time, cigarettes dangling from their lips, some wearing green plastic visor-style eye-shades beneath the harsh fluorescent lighting, others reading the newspaper or talking with colleagues. Everyone seemed busy.

Everywhere I looked there were cluttered desktops, scattered news-papers and notes, and cigarette butts on the bare, dark wooden floor. I heard loud shouts of "Copy!" and "Boy!" (no women were yet in this job, hence the term copyboy). I sensed the frenetic movement of people from section to section. Cigarette and pipe smoke rose up from every section and blended with the scents of strong coffee, printer's ink, pencil shavings, gum erasers, gooey mucilage in paste pots and the oily odor of the wood floor, all combining to produce an earthy and intoxicating aroma.

The city room was an expansive open space supported by a strate-gically-placed center row of concrete columns festooned with post-ers and photos. Row upon row of desks, arranged four-across, class-room-style, facing the front of the room, were lined up along one half of the room, overlooking Mission Street. At the front of the room were three desks facing out, for the city editor and his assistants.

On the opposite side was the copy desk, or "slot," a long horse-shoe-shaped desk overseen by the news editor, where a dozen or more copy editors wrote headlines and edited stories for accuracy, consistency, spelling, and grammar. The news editor and others drew up page designs laying out stories and photos. Finished articles were sent out in vacuum tubes to the composing room, where linotype operators converted the copy into hot lead rows of type, or "slugs," and then laid them out in metal page form that were shaped into curves to fit on the presses in the basement of the building. Behind the copy desk were clusters of desks divided for sports, society, fashion, business, entertainment, Sunday's tabloid This World and Datebook, and other specialty news and feature sections.

I did not remember meeting Abe before. He was short in stature, maybe five-five or five-six, with graying hair. He wore a dark blue suit, blue and white-striped button-down shirt, tie, and suspenders. Around his neck on a lanyard hung a monocle that from time to time during the conversation he would insert in his right eye to read something. We talked about what I had been doing and that I was looking for something more satisfying. "Are you going to school?" he asked.

"Yes, I've registered for classes at City College."

After a short time, he went over to talk with Darrell Duncan, the office manager. He returned to his chair, smiling.

"It turns out we have an opening for a copyboy," Abe told me. "It pays sixty-two dollars a week. We can work around your class schedule. If you can you start tomorrow morning, be here at 9 o'clock."

I couldn't believe I'd been hired with so little in my background to justify it. But I had help. Without telling me, Dori called both Abe and Herb Caen in advance to let them know I would be coming in, which no doubt influenced the outcome.

The next morning, Darrell Duncan, who supervised the copyboys, welcomed me, gave me some employee forms to fill out and a stack of papers about company regulations, benefits, and internal phone numbers. He walked me to a large rectangular wooden table in the center of the city room, where I saw a half-dozen young men about my age, all copyboys (today they are called news assistants).

Duffy (standing, left) with other copy boys who were sons of Chronicle employees, 1968.

"Guys, this is Duffy Jennings," Darrell said. "Please show him around and explain what you do."

I circled the table shaking hands, and quickly learned that I wasn't the first beneficiary of nepotism. In fact, several of my fellow copy-boys were sons of *Chronicle* writers, including Bob Bundsen, the son of longtime Herb Caen assistant Jerry Bundsen; David Bess, son of reporter Donovan Bess; Dennis Hogan, son of book review editor Bill Hogan; and Bill Pates, son of managing editor Gordon Pates. Even my brother worked as a copyboy for a time after he was discharged from the Air Force.

The name copyboy derives from a time when reporters, using type-writers, were on such tight deadlines that they couldn't spare the thirty seconds after finishing each page that it took to bring it to the city editor in front of the room, return to their desk and resume writing. To speed up the process, the reporter ripped each page, or "take," from the typewriter carriage and shouted, "Copy!" A copyboy would leap up from his seat at the copyboys' table, rush over, grab the page and take it up to the city editor, even as the reporter was rolling a new piece of paper into the carriage.

Copyboys did every conceivable errand for the newsroom. We delivered materials from the city room to the backroom print shop, took the bus or walked to outlying bureaus to bring back daily stories from correspondents or exposed rolls of film from photographers, picked up the daily shipping report at Aquatic Park, clipped and pasted articles, made up three-copy "books" with alternating sheets of carbon paper and newsprint paper for reporters to type stories, took food orders for takeout runs, and did a variety of other tasks in and out of the building. Among my odder assignments, in 1969 executive editor Scott Newhall dispatched me and other copyboys—including Joel Selvin, who would eventually become the renowned San Francisco rock music critic and author, and managing editor Gordon Pates' son, Bill—to stamp Mexican pesos into Anguillan silver dollars on a coin press in the circulation department garage. As Warren Hinckle told it on the SFGate website in 2009:

"Scott Newhall, The *Chronicle*'s buccaneering, wooden-legged editor—he lost a limb adventuring in Mexico—was gung-ho for the cause of Anguillan independence and put his money where his editorials were: *Chronicle* copyboys were dragooned into service to work an antique coin press outside the newspaper's offices to counter stamp 10,000 foreign coins that Newhall had purchased with the words 'Anguilla Liberty Dollar.' The plan was to sell the coins to collectors to get the foundling republic on a firm financial footing."

Selvin and I still laugh about the nights we spent "minting" Anguillan dollar coins. In another off-the-book errand, Abe Mellinkoff once sent me to deliver a dress to his daughter at the University of the Pacific in Stockton, two hours away. She'd forgotten to pack it.

The city room mesmerized me immediately with its proximity to journalists whose work I had been reading for quite some time, including the *Chronicle*'s distinguished stable of columnists—Herb Caen, Art Hoppe, Charles McCabe, Frances Moffat, Art Rosenbaum, Terrence O'Flaherty, Bill Hogan, Al Frankenstein, Ralph J. Gleason, and Stan Delaplane, among others.

One of the most popular features then was the Question Man, who would pose a question of the day to a half-dozen people on the street and print their answers with a photo. Over its 35-year run from 1959 to 1994, six people—three of them women—wrote the column. Among them was Kristin Conti, the daughter of Pulitzer Prize-winning columnist Stan Delaplane. Her 21-year tenure ended in 1993. (Nearly 25 years later, Kristin—who has reclaimed her Delaplane surname—and I would reconnect to become partners in Our American Stories, a writing and interviewing business that conducts video oral histories for individuals, families, and businesses.)

As a copyboy I worked mostly swing shifts starting at 2 p.m. or 3 p.m. to accommodate my City College class schedule. After the first edition went off the floor at 5:30 and staffers took their dinner breaks, the pace of the day slowed considerably, and we weren't needed as much. I often sat at the copyboy table for long periods doing my homework or reading for a class.

After a few months, when I was feeling comfortable about the job and becoming more interested in being a reporter, I used quiet periods in the office to experiment with writing short pieces of copy, either by rewriting a press release or reworking a story already in the paper.

I stayed after my shift to write and showed my work to the night city editor at the time, Bill Chapin, who became a wonderful mentor. In addition to his *Chronicle* experience, Chapin had been a Dartmouth athlete, a World War II bomber pilot, a prisoner of war, the author of three books, and a professor of journalism at San Francisco State. In fact, after transferring to S.F. State and during my first year as a reporter, I took classes from him and other *Chronicle* and *Examiner* editors who taught there at night. One of them, the *Examiner's* Lynn Ludlow, who was advising the students on the staff of the school newspaper, the *Phoenix*, scolded me for taking the class.

"What are you doing here?" he challenged me in front of the other students on the first night. "You're already working for the *Chronicle*."

"I'm a journalism major," I replied. "I need this class."

"Nonsense," said Ludlow. "Why don't you major in history or literature, something useful?"

Chapin and other assistant city editors from time to time gladly edited my work samples and gave me tips to improve and tighten my writing.

In January 1968, nine months into my *Chronicle* stint, the unions representing production and delivery workers went on strike for higher pay and better benefits.

After a couple of weeks, with the situation growing dimmer amid talk of a long, drawn-out strike, I contacted my father. Despite his awful letter to me two years earlier, I called him. He was in La Jolla, the wealthy San Diego suburb, staying in the home of his friend, Ted Geisel, better known as Dr. Seuss. Geisel was away for a couple of months and Dean had gone to San Diego to research sea lions for a novel about the life of a sea lion, *Valla*, that would be his final published book.

"It looks like it's going to be a long strike," my father said, although I have no way of knowing what made him think so. Of course, he did have some experience with the newspaper guild and strikes, so maybe it was instinctive. "If you move down here I can get you a job as a reporter on the *San Diego Union*," he said. "My good friend Neil Morgan is a very popular and influential columnist. I'll see what I can find out." I'm not sure what prompted this new interest in advancing my journalism career. Perhaps he felt guilty about the nasty things he said to me in that letter, but we never discussed it.

Within a few days my father said it had all been arranged. I withdrew from school, packed my car with everything I owned, moved out of my small Sausalito apartment, and drove to San Diego. When I arrived, my father put me in touch with my contact at the newspaper and said I would start work as a copyboy for the *Tribune*, not the *Union*, with a chance to be promoted to reporter later. I was disappointed, but at least I had a job. I rented a studio apartment on Cherokee Street and worked my *Tribune* shift from 5:30 a.m. to 1 p.m. After work, I often hung out at the beach until it was time to go back for a frozen TV dinner before heading to my night classes at Mesa Junior College. Once a month I made the drive back to San Francisco to attend my Marine reserve meetings.

The newspaper strike lasted two months. San Diego was a great place to be, but I realized early on there would be no reporter's job for me there. Either the paper misled my father, or he misled me, more likely the latter. I can't imagine anyone at the *Tribune* promising to hire a reporter with no experience. Plus, I was homesick. I kept in contact with Darrell Duncan and told him I was returning to San Francisco when the semester ended in June. I said I would very much like to return to the *Chronicle*, if possible. He said the job was still mine whenever I returned. It worked out conveniently for everyone. I gave notice at the *Trib*, and on the day after my last class at Mesa I packed the car and drove back to San Francisco. I stayed with my mother for a short time before I moved into an apartment with an old high school buddy, Steve Watts, who was looking for a roommate.

I went back to my copyboy job at the *Chronicle* in June 1968. New editors and several reporters were helping me with my newswriting technique, giving me tips on how to write with stronger leads, crisper sentences, and tighter lengths. Sometimes the paper would publish a three- or four-paragraph item I wrote. My name wasn't on it, of course, but I was so excited to see my work in the newspaper that I didn't care.

CHAPTER 19:
Sudden Death

On December 22, 1968, the Sunday *Examiner* ran a six-paragraph story about two teenagers, David Faraday, 17, and Betty Lou Jensen, 16, who were shot to death four days earlier in their car parked in a gravel lot near Lake Herman Road in Vallejo. They had driven to the area on their first date.

"Slaying of Teens Still a Mystery," was the headline. The article read, in part:

> Solano County detectives said yesterday they have "nothing concrete" that will lead them to the slayer—or slayers—of a teen-age Vallejo couple Friday night.
>
> "We are still hopeful that residents of the area who may have seen something unusual will give us the lead we need," said Sheriff's Captain H. Malcolm Morris. "There was no indication of a robbery motive or a sexual assault...it was all so needless."

I don't recall the story at the time, and no one at the newspaper could have known that Faraday and Jensen were only the first Bay Area victims of a cryptic serial murderer who would later surface in letters he wrote to local newspapers, calling himself Zodiac.

* * *

One of my original mentors was John Stanley, longtime editor of the Sunday Datebook entertainment section, or what we on the staff called "The Pink," because it was, and still is, printed on pink newsprint. I regularly asked John—pestered was more like it—if there were any freelance articles I could write for him that he didn't have staff to cover. Finally, he said, "I have something I think you can do for me."

He assigned me to write about a communications professor at San Francisco State named Arthur Hough, who was using a powerful new teaching device to engage his students.

I went out to the campus, interviewed Dr. Hough, and then sat in on his class. Afterward I wrote the article and gave it to Stanley. The opening paragraphs read:

> Students fidget with pencils or arrange books under their desks. Latecomers straggle in quietly.
>
> A silence, broken only by whispered murmurs and shuffling papers, presses over the classroom when the professor enters. Setting down his briefcase, he turns to scan the room. His dark eyes, half-covered by thick, black eyebrows, focus on a young lady in the second row and, clearing his throat, he speaks slowly, distinctly:
>
> "Miss Jones..." Her head snaps up quickly in response. "I'm sorry to have to tell you that your father has just been killed in an auto accident."
>
> The girl gasps and stares blankly for a brief moment, seemingly in shock. She begins to sob, quietly at first, then burst into hysteria. She has not even asked for the details.
>
> But there are no details because the tragic news is false. It has been a classroom experiment by Dr. Arthur Hough Jr., an associate professor of communications at San Francisco State College. It is designed to illustrate his point that "true communication is weakened today because people often listen only to words and fail to hear true meanings."
>
> Hough's students are warned well in advance that he is apt to enter the class and pass on false information.

John Stanley ran my article on page fifteen of the Sunday Datebook, January 12, 1969, under the headline, "A Problem for Hough:

Listening Without Hearing." Below that I was both astonished and gratified to see: "By Duffy Jennings." Stanley hadn't discussed a by-line with me in advance, and it was the first time my byline had ever appeared above any of my work for the *Chronicle*. I was twenty-one, and so elated. I clipped and saved several copies.

I continued to produce pieces for Stanley over the rest of the year. Between February and December, he published my Datebook features on local TV personalities: "Anniversary Game" show host Alan Hamel (who would marry Suzanne Somers a few years later), talk show host Owen Spann, and "Point of View" host Gerri Lange, among others.

* * *

On July 6, the Sunday Examiner & *Chronicle* published another brief article about a mysterious shooting of two people parked in a car in Vallejo. The headline this time read: "Woman Slain, Friend is Shot." The opening paragraphs were:

> A young woman was shot to death and her young man companion wounded by a mysterious gunman early yesterday moments after they pulled their car into Blue Rock Springs Park.

> Darlene Elisabeth Ferrin, 22, of 930 Monterey St., was wounded three times. She died en route to the hospital.

> Michael Mageau, 19, also hit at least three times, was reported in satisfactory condition at Kaiser Hospital.

The article, on page nine, noted the shooting was similar to the unsolved murders of Faraday and Jensen in December, adding there were no suspects in the latest case. Ferrin was pronounced dead at the hospital; Mageau survived. Police found seven 9-millimeter shell casings near the car.

The shootings took place just before midnight on July 4. At 12:40 a.m., a man telephoned Vallejo police and claimed responsibility for the attack. He also took credit for the Faraday-Jensen killings. Police eventually traced the call to a phone booth in a nearby gas station, but no clues were found.

Three weeks after the Ferrin-Mageau shootings, the *Vallejo Times-Herald*, the *San Francisco Examiner*, and the *Chronicle* received nearly identical letters from someone claiming to be the killer in both the Lake Herman Road and Blue Rock Springs shootings. Each letter also contained one third of a 408-symbol cryptogram in which the killer said his identity was hidden.

If the newspapers did not print his cipher within a week, the killer warned, he would "go on a kill rampage Fry. night" and throughout the weekend, murdering up to a dozen more victims. The *Chronicle* published a story and its part of the cryptogram on page 4 the next day.

On August 7, the *Examiner* received another letter which began, "This is the Zodiac speaking," the first time he had used the name to identify himself. To prove his authenticity, he included details about the murders which had not been made public.

The newsroom was abuzz over this mystery and the killer's audacity to goad police with such a public confession and a strange puzzle. Paul Avery, a *Chronicle* colleague and veteran police reporter, took on the case and began digging around in earnest to learn as much as he could about the East Bay cases.

Some six weeks later, on Saturday, September 27, two Pacific Union College students, Bryan Hartnell, twenty-two, and Cecelia Shepard, twenty, were picnicking at Lake Berryessa when a stocky man approached them carrying a gun and a large knife. As author Robert Graysmith wrote in his best-selling book, *Zodiac*, the gunman wore "a ceremonial midnight-black hood, square on top, with four corners like a paper sack. He resembled some executioner from the Middle Ages...emblazoned in white on the bib-like front was a three-inch square cross placed over a circle."

The stranger made Cecelia tie Bryan's hands behind his back with a length of clothesline, then he tied her up as well and produced a foot-long knife, sharpened on both sides like a bayonet. "I'm going to have to stab you people," he said. He stabbed Hartnell six times before turning on Cecelia. He plunged the knife into her twenty-four times in all before quietly and slowly walking away.

Shepard and Hartnell were taken to Queen of the Valley Hospital in Napa, where she died from her injuries. Hartnell survived.

A little over an hour after the attack, a man called the Napa Police Department. "I want to report a murder—no, a double murder," the caller said. "I'm the one that did it."

The *Chronicle* story that ran two days later under the headline, "Stabbings Linked to Code Killer," drew parallels with the earlier attacks in Vallejo.

* * *

Four days after the Lake Berryessa attack, on the morning of October 1, 1969, I was at home writing a Datebook piece for John Stanley about local television news anchor Ron Magers when my phone rang.

"Hello?" I answered. My oldest half-brother was on the other end. "Hi, Duffy, it's Dean."

"Mel?" I asked, surprised because I hadn't heard from him in quite a long time.

"I've got some news," he said. "Our father died this morning. He had a heart attack at his house in Bolinas."

Mel said Dean and his wife, Mary, had rented the house for the winter and that Dean planned to write the Mickey Cohen book in the picturesque seaside town. According to Mary, Dean was carrying a box of books up a flight of stairs when he suddenly dropped the box, clutched his chest, and shouted, "I'm having a cardiac!" Mary called the Bolinas Fire Department. They rushed my father to Marin General Hospital, where he was pronounced dead on arrival.

Mel and I talked for another minute or two, and he gave me the details about a memorial service in two days at St. Stephens Church in Belvedere. "OK, thanks," I said, "I'll be there," and I hung up.

I sat quietly for a long time taking it in. I felt an empty sadness, but not because my father was dead. I was sad because I felt no emotion for him at all. None.

I called my mother with the news. Then I went back to work.

* * *

Ten days later, on Saturday night, October 11, a man hailed a Yellow Cab at Geary and Mason Streets and told the driver, Paul Stine, to take him to Presidio Heights. When the taxi stopped at the intersection of Washington and Cherry Streets, the passenger shot Stine once in the head, killing him instantly.

Three teenagers in the upstairs bedroom of a house overlooking the intersection saw the gunman rummaging through the car and the driver's pockets before he took off on foot down the street toward the nearby heavily wooded Presidio Army Base. Police converged on the area, including SFPD homicide detectives Dave Toschi and Bill Armstrong, who were on call, but the killer eluded police. Based on the witnesses' description of the gunman's movements inside the cab and around Stine's clothing, the case was initially treated as a robbery. Until the morning mail arrived at the *Chronicle* the following Tuesday.

It was the copyboys' regular duty to sort the daily bins of *Chronicle* mail into a cabinet of mail slots for departments and individual staff members. Mail addressed to "Letters to the Editor," "Editor," and similar general terms were put in the editorial writers' box and handled by letters editor Carol Fisher.

One letter in a plain white envelope was addressed in blue felt-tip pen to "S.F. *Chronicle*, San Fran, Calif. Please Rush to Editor." The return address was a circle with a cross inside. When Fisher opened the envelope and removed the folded letter inside, a small rectangle of striped cloth stained with blood dropped out onto her desk. Startled, she carefully opened the letter.

"This is the Zodiac speaking," it began. "I am the murderer of the taxi driver over by Washington St. & Maple St. last night, to prove this here is a blood-stained piece of his shirt. I am the same man who did in the people in the north bay area. The S.F. Police could have caught me last night if they had searched the park properly instead of holding road races with their motorcycles seeing who could make the most noise. The car drivers should have just parked their cars & sat there quietly waiting for me to come out of cover."

A Sept. 14 Man's Views on the Draft

By Duffy Jennings

Mike Boland is the kind of person who likes to put things off until the last minute.

Now he may have to change his habits because, if for no clear reason, he was born on Sept. 14, 1950, the first date drawn in last night's draft lottery.

"I hadn't given it much thought before," he said in his dormitory room at the University of San Francisco shortly after the announcement. "But since I heard I've been doing some pretty fast thinking about what I'm going to do now."

A history major in his sophomore year, Boland said his younger brother telephoned to tell him he knows.

PRESSURE

"I wasn't too concerned," he said. "I've been strolling along with a D-5 (student) deferment but now the pressure is really on now. I guess I'll look into the reserve possibility — I don't really know, I think my mother's taking it pretty hard.

"I always put things off. Like a paper I have to do, I'll wait until the last day. Now I'll have to make much definite plans."

Boland was born on that once-in-important date at Children Hospital in San Francisco and is registered at number 427-50-4578 with Local Board 57 in San Mateo where it parents, Mr. and Mrs. Thomas F. Boland, reside.

Mrs. Thomas F. Boland, resides.

RESIGNED

A tall, slim youth with collar-length brown hair and brown eyes, Boland apparently has resigned himself to the fact that his chances of being called are stronger than ever.

"At least Mike knows for sure," said his roommate, Skelton Bass, 20, Fla. In the middle and still don't have one way or the other." Bass's birthday is November 15, the 33rd date drawn.

Meanwhile, four thousand above Boland's room, a crowd of students gathered around a posted list of the numbers. Occasionally a yelp of "Hey, I'm way down at the bottom!" could be heard above the chatter.

Another — "whcih student who drew, blond hair found his birthdate to be No. 76. How did he feel about it? "I am sure could use a beer, but, am sure could use a beer," he said somewhat dejectedly.

MIKE BOLAND
His number is up

John Shaveis, a 21-year-old history major whose birthday is June 28, No. 360 on the list, was noticeably relieved. "I'm a senior in I probably won't be called," he said. "It's a great feeling!"

HOPE

A common belief among most of the students in Phelan Hall, the only men's dorm on campus, is that by the time their student deferments are invalid — in six cases, two years from now — the war will be over.

"I figure the war will be over anyway by the time they get to me," said Laurie Federn, an 18-year-old English major, "so I really wouldn't mind going. But it be nice to know for sure I wasn't going to Vietnam."

A hand-printed sign on a piece of binder paper along-side the lottery results read: "To defray the cost of the Canadian flight, please stick a dime under it door."

"We raised $3.56," said Kim Canfield, 22, a senior. "But I don't care. I'm got the married next month and my birthday is June 14, number 306."

Eisenhower Date With The Draft

Washington

David Eisenhower, President Nixon's son-in-law, may be rope for the draft after his college deferment expires next June.

His birth date, Mareldt, was the 30th drawn in last night's draft lottery.

Those that hot in statof-try are generally regarded as virtually certain to be called for induction.

Young Eisenhower, grandson of General Dwight D. Eisenhower, will be 22 on March 31. He is married to Julie Nixon, the President's youngest daughter.

Eisenhower told reporters at the White House last week he had not decided whether to take his chances with the draft or to enlist in the Navy. Also father-in-law's World War II service.

Young Eisenhower will be exempt until next year, but if his local draft board has exhausted induction for the first 30 birth dates after he graduates from Amherst College, he then would be at the top of the list of draft eligibles.

United Press

House War Critics Lose

Washington

House doves lost yesterday in their effort to open up to amendment a Viet nam resolution which they fear could be construed as supporting escalation of the war.

The resolution, co-sponsored by 333 members, affirms support of the President "in his efforts to negotiate a just peace."

It was whisked through the Foreign Affairs Committee without hearings and sent to the House floor under a procedure that bars amendments.

They wanted to offer amendments clarifying the meaning of the resolution and to make other changes such as supporting rapid troop withdrawals. But they lost, 225 to 133, with the leadership of both parties supporting the so-amendment rule. The resolution is expected to be approved by a big majority today.

Representative Peter Wright (Dem-Tex.) said it has been traditional to send such for-bam, and, because Congress sign policy resolutions to the House under a closed rule. He said it was preferable in this case because there is little time left in the session to get into an all-out war de-

San Francisco Chronicle 11
11th Tues., Dec 2, 1969

should state in in uncertain terms that it supports the President in seeking peace.

Representative Andrew Jacobs (Dem-Ind.) raised the fear that it could prove to be another Gulf of Tonkin resolution — a 1968 resolution thought to be a limited state-ment supporting action to protect American warships but later used as justification for enlarging the war.

Trans-Free Service

Old Fillmore Dance Hall Days Over

The old Fillmore Auditorium at 1800 Geary boulevard, once a mecca for dancing and the San Francisco "sound" will not be a dance hall again, so long as the city's Board of Permit Appeals has anything to say about it.

The board yesterday voted 5 to 0 against the Fillmore's current impresario, Alfred N. Kramer, who wanted to hold dance floor.

Kramer, who has been holding concerts in the building for some months, sought a dance permit for the old hall. He told the board a majority of his audiences always wanted to dance and the permit would help him in his business.

Testifying before the board on Kramer's behalf was the Fillmore's owner, Harry Schiff.

But Police Department witnesses said a new dance permit for the old Fillmore would create "a police problem" and the appeals board agreed.

Kramer will be allowed to continue his concerts, leasing the hall from Schiff.

CHAPTER 20:
Number One Draft Pick

Six weeks after my father's funeral, Abe Mellinkoff called me up to his desk.

"How long is your Christmas break from school?" he asked.

"I get three weeks."

"OK," he said. "We have an opening for a holiday vacation relief reporter for the next three weeks, so I'm going to give you a try-out. But it's on two conditions. When it's over you must go back to copyboy because no matter how you do, I don't have any full-time openings and I don't know when I will. The other is that I can't really promote you without any reporting experience at a smaller paper. Not that it's never happened, but it's rare. But let's see how you do first."

That was the best early Christmas present I remember. I went to see my mother that night. I was excited and wanted her to know, but she was blotto as usual, and little I said was getting through. By then, eight years after starting Club Dori, she was drunk nearly every day, and often could not make it to the place to take care of ordering food and liquor, let alone tend bar.

I was very nervous about my first day, Monday, December 1, 1969. After completing some administrative forms related to my new status, assistant city editor Dick Hemp called me up to the city desk.

"I'm very happy about this," he said. "I agree with Abe that you're ready. I have an assignment I think will be just right for you. Today is the first day of the Vietnam draft lottery, I'm sure you know. They will be drawing the birthday numbers in Washington, D.C. I want you to find a local kid whose birthday is the first number drawn and go talk to him. Ask how he feels about being number one and what he's going to do."

The lottery drawing—the first since 1942—was held at Selective Service National Headquarters in Washington, D.C. to determine the order of call for induction during calendar year 1970. It applied to registrants born between January 1, 1944, and December 31, 1950.

For the actual drawing, three hundred sixty-six blue plastic capsules containing birth dates were placed in a large glass container and drawn by hand. With heavy media coverage, the first date drawn was September 14. That meant any males born on that date and aged eighteen to twenty-six were first in line for conscription.

To find a local man with that birth date, I first went to the newspaper library and asked the librarian for a clipping of the birth announcements for September 14, 1950. Back then, the paper published and saved the birth announcements from local hospitals every day. In a few minutes, the librarian returned with an article that contained the names of a dozen boys born in the Bay Area on September 14, 1950. The brief report included their parents' names and hometowns.

I pulled out a reverse phone directory and began checking the last names and cities against the clipping. I called three numbers and got no response or no one who knew the family in question. Finally, I reached the home of Mike Boland in San Mateo.

"Hello," I said. "This is Duffy Jennings, a reporter for the *Chronicle*," trying to contain my excitement at saying it aloud for the first time. "We're doing an article today about the new draft lottery and I see that your son's birthday was the first number picked. Is Michael at home? May I speak to him?"

"Mike's a student at USF now," his mother told me, and she gave me the name of his dorm. I told Hemp, who said photographer

Jerry Telfer would go with me, and off we went to find Boland. Quite a scene greeted us at his dorm. Dozens of young men were gathered in a large day room, watching the draft lottery reports on television. They had hung a big poster board on one wall, where they wrote down each number as it was pulled from the drum. Every new number was greeted with an equal number of groans and cheers from the boys.

I found Boland in his dorm room and we sat down to talk. Being close in age and having faced the same decision about joining up or waiting out the draft, I felt some empathy for him. (As it happened, my birthdate came up as number 227, which would have freed me from service since the highest number called between 1970 and 1976 was 215.) Plus, Boland was a procrastinator, like me, so I could relate. Turned out Boland was savvy and articulate about his situation, which made for good quotes. I also talked to some of his dorm mates to add more texture to the story.

I returned to the paper, wrote it up, turned it in to the city desk, and went home.

The next morning at home, I retrieved the paper from my front porch and found my article displayed across three columns on page eleven, with a photo of Boland.

I was shocked to see my byline at the top. Even though I had bylines on my freelance articles for Datebook, it was unheard of for a cityside reporter on day one. Some veteran reporters had waited months for their first byline. I heard later through the grapevine that some of them were angry about this, but no one ever said anything to me directly.

Here's my story that ran in the paper December 2, 1969:

* * *

Mike Boland is the kind of person who likes to put things off until the last minute.

Now he may have to change his habits because, if for no other reason, he was born on Sept. 14, 1950, the first date drawn in last night's draft lottery.

"I hadn't given it much thought before," he said in his dormitory room at the University of San Francisco shortly after the announcement. "But since I heard I've been doing some pretty fast thinking about what I'm going to do now."

A history major in his sophomore year, Boland said his younger brother telephoned to tell him the news.

"I wasn't too concerned," he said. "I've been strolling along with a H-S (student) deferment but now the pressure is really on me. I guess I'll look into the reserve possibility — I don't really know. I think my mother's taking it pretty hard.

"I always put things off, like a paper I have to do, I'll wait until the last day. Now I'll have to make more definite plans."

Boland was born on that now-so-important date at Children's Hospital in San Francisco and is registered as number 4-57-50-1578 with Local Board 57 in San Mateo, where his parents, Mr. and Mrs. Thomas F. Boland, reside.

A tall, slim youth with collar-length brown hair and brown eyes, Boland apparently has resigned himself to the fact that his chances of being called are stronger than most.

"At least Mike knows for sure," said his roommate, Shelton Bunn, 20. I'm in the middle and still don't know one way or the other." Bunn's birthday is November 15, the 131st date drawn.

Meanwhile, four floors above Boland's room, a crowd of students gathered around a posted list of the numbers. Occasionally a yelp of "Hey, I'm way down at the bottom!" could be heard above the chatter.

Another youthful student with short, blond hair found his birthdate to be No. 75. How did he feel about it? "I sure could use a beer," he said somewhat dejectedly.

John Shovein, a 21-year-old history major whose birthday is June 20, No. 380 on the list, was noticeably relieved. "I'm a senior so I probably won't be called," he said. "It's a great feeling!"

A common belief among most of the students in Phelan Hall, the only men's dorm on campus, is that by the time their student deferments are invalid — in most cases, two years from now — the war will be over. "I figure the war will be over anyway by the time they get to me," said Laurie Fedora, an 18-year-old English major, "so I really wouldn't mind going. But it'd be nice to know for sure I wasn't going to Vietnam!"

A hand-printed sign on a piece of binder paper alongside the lottery results read: "To defray the cost of the Canadian flight, please stick a dime under the door."

"We raised $2.34," said Ken Canfield, 21, a senior. "But I don't care, I'm getting married next month, and my birthday is June 14, number 356."

* * *

Hemp and other assistant city editors gave me more plum assignments over the course of my tryout, and I earned two more bylines. At the end of the three weeks, Abe called me up, asked me to sit down and stared at me with a serious expression on his face.

"Well, it's been an interesting three weeks," he began. "Honestly, I never expected you to do so well. You have quite a gift for someone so young. Your work is better than some reporters who've been here awhile. So, now I have a dilemma. I'd rather keep you on and not send you back. If I had an opening, I would hire you today. But I don't, so you'll have to go back to copyboy for a while. But the first open reporter job that comes up is yours."

I couldn't believe what I was hearing. I must have been smiling from ear to ear.

"Oh, and one more thing: you have to promise me you'll finish school and get your degree."

"I promise, Abe, of course," I said. "This is great news. Thank you so much."

I did keep my promise to Abe. Thirty-nine years later.

CHAPTER 21:
A Miracle Assignment

I settled back into my old job and returned to my classes. But now that I had produced actual bylined articles as a probationary reporter, I was anxious to do more freelance work while I waited for a full-time opening. In early March, I wrote one more piece for Datebook on a married couple, Geoff and Suzanne Edwards, hosts of the TV show, "The His and Her of It."

A couple of weeks later, I noticed that the popular R&B singing group, Smokey Robinson and the Miracles, was performing in town at a club called Mr. D's on Broadway in North Beach. I was a huge fan of Motown music and I asked John Stanley if I could try to get an interview with Robinson for the Datebook. He agreed, and music critic John Wasserman helped me contact the Miracles' publicist.

The PR guy invited me to come to the show that night and arranged for the interview the next day. Cheryl and I arrived at Mr. D's and were escorted to a front row table. In the middle of the show, Smokey paused the act and introduced me in the audience. "There's a young man here tonight I want you all to meet," he said. "Duffy, where are you? Stand up. Duffy is a reporter for the *Chronicle* who's going to interview me tomorrow. We're glad to have you here, man."

I was embarrassed by the attention. I was afraid someone might know that I wasn't officially a reporter yet.

The next afternoon I went to Smokey's room at the Miyako Hotel in Japantown. Smokey answered the door in a white terry bathrobe, invited me in, offered me a soda, and asked if I minded waiting while he excused himself for a quick shower. "Sure," I said, trying to act nonplussed while I'm pinching myself that I'm in Smokey Robinson's hotel room. Soon I hear the water running and a few moments later

Signed photo from singer Smokey Robinson after our 1970 interview.

his unmistakable falsetto voice carries from the bathroom. Above the running water I heard him singing:

I did you wrong, My heart went out to play,
But in the game I lost you, What a price to pay
I'm cryin'
Ooo baby baby

I was flummoxed just to be in the room with one of the most popular pop singers of the day, but I never imagined he'd be singing one of his top hits in the shower. I wanted to call somebody and tell them, but who? And I would have had to use the room phone, which seemed inappropriate. It was like making a hole-in-one playing golf alone, with no one around to attest to it.

When he was dressed and came out to talk, Smokey was polite, sincere, and genuinely engaged in our conversation.

Back at the *Chronicle*, I wrote the following article, without mentioning the shower serenade. It ran on April 1, 1970.

* * *

"Hey Man, do you wanna be loved?" says Smokey Robinson to a ringside customer at Mr. D's. "Every now and then," the young man replies.

"Every now and then?" Smokey laughs in mock disbelief. "Oh, man, I wanna be loved ALL the time!"

Does he really want to be loved ALL the time? "Sure, man, everybody does. Don't you?" No argument there.

"You know what I really dig?" he asks later in his room at the Miyako Hotel, as he slips a T-shirt over his short, Afro-style hair. "I dig people. I'm all for humanity."

Robinson, at 30, has been digging people ever since he can

remember – and music. Lead singer with the Miracles, now at Mr. D's through Saturday, he is also vice president of the Motown Record Corporation – the main outlet for Rhythm and Blues music in America. He is a composer, arranger, and an extremely gifted lyricist. A dynamo. Bob Dylan calls him today's greatest living American poet.

People say I'm the life of the party 'cause I tell a joke or two
Although I might be laughing loud and hearty, deep inside
  I'm blue
So take a good look at my face
You'll see my smile looks out of place
If you look closer it's easy to trace
The tracks of my tears

But despite all that, Robinson possesses no small degree of modesty. Beneath the glitter of his performing get-up – a gold satin Tom Jones-style shirt with purple ruffled front, a sleeveless purple jacket with gold lame trim, high-waisted bell-bottom pants and black patent leather shoes – is a warm and unaffected person.

"Man, for me life is a whole gob of experiences. Every day you go through so many experiences. They say it's the best teacher. I can dig that, but I don't have to experience everything myself to know what it's like.

"I can just feel it. When I write a sad song it isn't consciously because of some personal experience. I've never consciously written a song from personal experience." He has written hundreds.

"There's just so much sadness in the world today. It's really an abundant thing when you think about it. And I can feel it."

Although he and the Miracles (Pete Moore, Bobby Rogers and Ronnie White) have been making hits for 16 years, Smokey admits that his success long ago surpassed his wildest dreams.

"I used to go to class with a transistor radio plugged into my ear. We were recording when we were in high school and I'd listen for our record."

When he dropped out of junior college in his home town of Detroit to pursue his desire to sing, his father, a city truck driver, was disappointed. "He told me if it didn't work out, to go back to school." He never went back.

The Miracles performance is virtually unchanged after 16 years, except that Smokey's wife of ten years, Claudette, no longer travels with them. She still records with the group in Detroit, however.

"I made her stop, man. It was killing her. I'll tell you how hard it was on her. She had six miscarriages."

The Robinsons now have a son, 19 months old, with a name that reads like the acknowledgements section of a book – Berry (after Berry Gordy, Motown president and Smokey's dearest friend), Borope (a combination of the first two letters of the first names of the Miracles) Robinson.

Smokey's feeling for all people is the reason behind his decision to use the stage as an outlet for a personal crusade for the rights of black people.

"Look here, I don't have to get up on stage and tell the people I'm black. Man, they can SEE that!" Smokey stops, stands up and walks over to the closet. "Don't get me wrong now," he says, buttoning up a knitted leather and wool latticework cardigan, "this is a beautiful history period for black people. They're becoming aware of their blackness and they're digging it!

"But there's a time and place for everything, I think. I'm proud of my black heritage, sure, but I don't think the stage is a place to lecture about it. The people come to be entertained. They want to hear "Ooo baby baby" or "Goin' to A Go Go" or "Tracks of My Tears," not a lecture. Young people get lectures every day.

"Like I said, I'm for humanity first. I don't care if a guy's black, blue, white or orange." He smiles. "Anybody who's not a bigot is cool with me."

Smokey's lyrical talents have won him two gold records and the top composer's award from Broadcast Music Incorporated. "I haven't changed my style much. I try to avoid the new fads, like the psychedelic trend, for instance. I want to write songs that will mean something to people 20 years from now.

"I've got no plans for slowing down yet. Motown still has growing pains and I'm going to keep writing songs for a long time."

Write on, Smokey, write on.

* * *

OK, that closing line was contrived, but in 1970 it played on a common black power expression of the day and Smokey loved it. A short time later I sent him a note asking about visiting Motown and doing an article on the backstory of the record company.

"I really would like you to have a tour of Motown," he wrote back, "but at this time we are undergoing some renovations which makes it very difficult to conduct a tour of the company. Maybe we can get together another time."

Meanwhile, Jann Wenner, who had launched his *Rolling Stone* magazine in San Francisco in 1967, called to ask if I would rewrite the piece for him. I cleared it with the *Chronicle* and my slightly revised version ran in *Rolling Stone* May 28, 1970.

A few months later, Wenner sent me a note asking, "Will you give me a call, make an appointment, so we can talk about you doing some more work for us?"

I wrote back and suggested an "inside Motown" piece once the renovations were done. He replied that he was "very interested...but we would be unable to pay your expenses there or commit to anything in advance without seeing some of the material and an outline of the story after you got back from Detroit."

I certainly couldn't afford to front those travel costs on my $62-a-week copyboy pay, and that was my last contact with Wenner.

Smokey and I exchanged a couple of other letters later that year. He ended one with "Stay cool and 'write on.'" He also sent me a photo of the Miracles. "Hope we can keep in touch," he wrote on it. "To me you're a great reporter. Your Brother, Smokey."

I had no further contact with him for forty-six years. More than once when he appeared in the Bay Area over those decades I tried to reach him through various public relations contacts without success. I had read at some point that he was an avid golfer who played in almost every city where he performed. I sent a query to a couple of golf magazines suggesting a piece about playing a round of golf with Smokey Robinson. Both accepted the idea, but I was never able to get a response from Robinson about it.

In 2016, I saw he was performing at Rodney Strong Vineyards in Healdsburg. I got the name of a new PR contact for him through my old friend Joel Selvin. I arranged to meet Smokey, then seventy-six years old, before the show. I gathered from the PR representative's emails that I might have five or ten minutes to chat with him. I brought my old clipping, along with a copy of a new memoir by a former *Chronicle* colleague, sports columnist Bruce Jenkins, "Shop Around: Growing up with Motown in a Sinatra Household." Bruce's father was conductor and arranger Gordon Jenkins, who worked with Frank Sinatra and other singers of his day. When I arrived at the winery July 23, I found out that I wasn't having a private meeting with Smokey at all. I was just one of two dozen people who had been granted a "meet-and-greet" with Robinson, which was no more than a thirty-second, shake-hands-and-smile-for-the-photo quickie. When it was my turn, I showed him my old clipping and asked if he remembered it.

"No, I don't," he said.

"Smile!" said the photographer. He snapped a couple of shots and called out, "Next!"

I handed the article and Bruce's book to Smokey and left.

Chapter 22:
Voice of the West

The other miracle assignment I waited months for finally arrived in June 1970. There was an opening among the reporters and Abe put me on the staff as a full-time general assignment reporter in a thirteen-week probationary capacity.

I received an official letter from Fred Fletcher, executive secretary of the San Francisco-Oakland Newspaper Guild, dated June 18. "We have been informed by the San Francisco *Chronicle* that you have accepted a temporary replacement promotion to Reporter, less than 1 year's experience," he wrote. After thirteen weeks, he added, the union contract provided that I would be considered "a regular employee in the Reporter classification."

At the time, the *Chronicle* was San Francisco's only morning paper and the ninth largest daily in the country. I was one of about four dozen reporters who covered shifts from 6 a.m. to around midnight six days a week, not counting the one reporter who manned the graveyard shift on the police beat.

Some of the most memorable reporters and editors I worked with were stalwarts of the trade—George Murphy, Kevin Wallace, Charles Raudebaugh, George Draper, Charlie Howe, Michael Harris, Carolyn Anspacher, Don Wegars, Paul Avery, Tim Findley, Julie Smith, Maitland Zane, Keith Power, Kevin Leary, George Williamson, Dale Champion, Birney Jarvis, Bob Popp, David Perlman, J. Campbell Bruce, Larry Liebert, Earl Behrens, Michael Grieg, Peter Kuehl, Jerry Burns, Ralph Craib, Monte Waite, Jim Brewer, Rick Carroll, Tom Benet, Bob Bartlett, Dick Hemp, Rob Haeseler, Steve Rubenstein, Mike Taylor, Bill Chapin, Chapin Day, Steve Gavin, Katy Butler, and many more.

Jerry Carroll, one reporter whose writing style awed me by its grace and erudition, had been one of two dozen journalists chosen from around the nation to be Ford Foundation fellows at Stanford University. The *Chronicle* at that time, he points out, preferred Ivy League graduates but "would settle for someone with a Stanford connection."

The paper also favored reporters with more stylish writing. As Carroll put it, "There had once been many newspapers, the *Call*, the *Bulletin* and later the *News-Call Bulletin*. The *Examiner* was dull and dreary but conscientious. They almost always beat us on the hard news. Ours was the elegant writing, which was cheaper because fewer people were needed to put it out. The hard-boiled Ex types had contempt for our effeminate wiles."

Carroll landed a job on a staff he describes (tongue-in-cheek, I think) as "one of the strangest collection of braggarts, loafers, liars, and oddballs ever assembled."

They ranged from the former publicity agent for Shirley Temple (Raudebaugh), the son of a high society interior designer who was Eleanor Roosevelt's cousin and married to FDR's personal physician (Draper) and two former Marine gunnery sergeants (Hemp and Howe), to an ex-Hell's Angel (Jarvis) who once bit off a man's ear in a fight to settle a point of honor between rival schools of karate. It was Jarvis who introduced Hunter Thompson to the Hells Angels, which led to Thompson's acclaimed book about the legendary motorcycle gang.

In 1969, Hollywood made a TV series based on Birney Jarvis, *Then Came Bronson*, about a disillusioned reporter who takes to the road on his motorcycle to help people in trouble. The Jim Bronson character, portrayed by Michael Parks, was created by a former *Chronicle* reporter-turned-screenwriter, Denne Petitclerc. Birney was larger than life. One night at a party at his house, I stood astounded with the other guests as Birney entertained us by looping a noose around his neck and hanging himself from his backyard pergola. It was a clever illusion, created by a hidden harness under his shirt, but for a few moments there Birney had us all fooled, if his realistic-looking body spasms and the collective gasps were any indication.

As the "investigative reporter" concept flourished in the wake of the Watergate story that led to President Nixon's resignation, the *Chronicle* gave its top talent a lot of leeway to follow leads on corruption and misdeeds by public officials. Some reporters took it a bit far. Charlie Howe, for instance, once marched up to the city desk and announced something to the effect of "...it's about a judge and a truck full of dynamite," then strolled out of the office. He wasn't heard from for days.

My colleagues also included a neophyte in his first newspaper job, a young University of Michigan graduate named Eugene Robinson, who would go on to become the Pulitzer Prize-winning syndicated columnist for the *Washington Post*. Eugene and I shared some dual bylines on stories. African-Americans were in short supply in the newsroom of the 1970s. There were four other black reporters during my time: George Snyder, a former *Sacramento Union* reporter and local TV news producer before starting his twenty-five-year career at the *Chronicle*, much of it as the North Bay correspondent; Karen Howze, who studied journalism at USC; Mike Mills, who later became the longtime publicist for AC Transit; and Huel Washington, who came over from the local *Sun Reporter*, a black community newspaper led by editor-publisher Dr. Carlton B. Goodlett.

Other memorable co-workers included reporter Mel Ziegler and his wife, Patricia Gwilliam, a *Chronicle* artist, who left the paper together in 1978 to start a small boutique in Mill Valley they called the "Banana Republic Travel & Safari Clothing Company." As we know by now, Banana Republic grew into a behemoth, at one point with some six hundred stores around the globe.

Nor can I forget Joseph Torchia, a twitchy, hot-shot feature writer who showed up to work at the *Examiner* in late 1976. He quickly raised eyebrows with his colorful pieces on such disparate topics as a date he had with actress Carol Channing, his work in a porn shop, and the different reactions he got in various neighborhoods when he pretended to faint in public.

Torchia, who was my age, was so good that the *Chronicle* lured him away after just three months in town. On his very first day at the *Chronicle* he sat down at a desk near mine precisely at 9:30 a.m. as scheduled and started frenetically banging away on the typewriter. Office manager Darrell Duncan walked over to him.

"Hi, Joe," said Duncan. "Welcome to the *Chronicle*. Here are some employee information forms and other documents you need to fill out."

"Can't talk now!" Torchia blurted out so fast it sounded like one word. Without looking up or pausing his lightning-fast keystrokes, he snapped, "I'M ON DEADLINE!" Over the next two years, Joe turned in some fine work and then he was gone. He moved to Napa and ran a photo studio until he died of liver cancer in 1996.

Among the photographers I covered stories with, in addition to Clem Albers, were such skilled and veteran shooters as Bob Campbell, Art Frisch, Bill Young, Peter Breinig, Jerry Telfer, Gary Fong, Vince Maggiora, John O'Hara, Chris Stewart, Dave Randolph, Stephanie Maze, Susan Ehmer, and Barney Peterson.

And then there was Joe Rosenthal, the renowned former Associated Press photographer whose iconic shot of the Marine flag-raising on Iwo Jima in 1945 inspired a nation, won a Pulitzer Prize, and served as the model for the Marine Corps memorial statue at Arlington, Virginia. To *Chronicle* reporters, the diminutive Rosenthal was simply known as Joe, or by his nickname, "Mighty Mouse." Joe was already fifty-six when I arrived at the paper, and he retired in 1981 after thirty-five years there. He died in 2006 at ninety-four. Being able to say I worked with him has always been a great privilege.

General assignment reporters don't have a regular "beat" like those who cover just one area, like the state or federal courts, city or state government, education, labor, science. General assignment meant I showed up at work and waited until the assignment editor/assistant city editor dispatched me to cover something. It could be a press conference, a fire, a bank robbery, a feature story, or any other scheduled or breaking event that may have occurred during my seven-and-a-half-hour shift. I always wore a coat, slacks, dress shirt, and necktie to work.

CHAPTER 23:
Shirt-Sleevers

In those days, drinking at lunch was customary throughout the business world, and the so-called "three-martini lunch" was a common practice. Even President Gerald Ford, in a 1978 speech to the American Restaurant Association, said the three-martini lunch "is the epitome of American efficiency. Where else can you get an earful, a bellyful and a snootful at the same time?"

Each city newspaper had its own saloon, and for the *Chronicle* it was Hanno's in the Alley, conveniently located at Minna and Mary Streets behind the newspaper building. Hanno's was "part social club and part psychologist's office," as Carl Nolte put it in a 2000 obituary on Mel Albert, who co-owned Hanno's with Mel Tate. "It was our place," said the late Ron Fimrite, a magazine writer and author who spent many years as a *Chronicle* sports columnist. "It was a place where reporters could commiserate over the atrocities committed on their prose, laugh and talk and play liar's dice by the hour. A wonderful place."

It always amazed me how much some reporters could drink in the middle of the day and return to their typewriters to churn out impeccable, coherent copy on deadline. Often reporters would sneak out for a few pops in the early afternoon. At the *Chronicle*, this phenomenon had its own nickname.

Reporters would meander toward the restroom at the front of the office, leaving their jackets hanging in the coat room or on their chair to appear as if they'd be right back. Once past the city desk they would duck out to Hanno's for mid-day cocktails in their shirt-sleeves. Newsroom lore has it that reporter Monte Waite coined the term "shirt-sleever" for these surreptitious outings. Early on, Waite recommended carrying a piece of paper or a notebook with you, so it appeared you were working on a story that required looking up something in another part of the building. When day editor Carl Latham couldn't find a certain reporter, he would inevitably call Hanno's— there was a direct line from the city desk—and tell the bartender to send the wayward reporter back to the city room. "I know he's there," Latham would say. "Just tell him to get his butt back upstairs."

Jerry Carroll says reporter George Murphy could often be seen seated on a stool at Hanno's, reading a pulp novel, change from a ten-dollar bill on the bar. When his martini was finished, the bartender, without prompting, delivered a fresh one in a shaker and poured. "George was red-faced and loud after lunch," says Carroll. "He liked jokes and puns and had an inordinate store of them. 'I spill more than he drinks,' was one of his favorite terms of dismissal." When the money was gone, George returned to work. Jerry recalls Murphy being summoned back to the city room from Hanno's after being sent to cover the assassination attempt on President Gerald Ford outside the St. Francis Hotel. "George," editor Dick Hemp asked, "what are you doing there? Someone shot at the president." Murphy had picked up the White House press release and headed to Hanno's for a couple of "silver bullets," but clearly lost track of time, remembers Carroll, who ended up writing the story under Murphy's byline because George's version was unusable.

Eventually reporters dropped the cover story altogether. "Going for a shirt-sleever," they announced simply on the way out the door.

Among my assignments over the summer and fall of 1970, I wrote about parent complaints concerning the administration at Galileo High School, the Post Office debut of Jeeps for mail delivery, a controversial new Vietnam War statue in Auburn titled "WHY," angry Market Street business owners frustrated with the upheaval created by construction underground for the new rapid transit line called BART, and a step-by-step guide on how a demolition company took down an old ten-story building at Third and Mission Streets. On August 5, I had a story on page two about an experimental new hydrofoil ferry boat that would whisk passengers across the bay in nine minutes – except that engine failure aborted its test run.

Two days later, the otherwise summer news doldrums blew up with the wild Marin County Courthouse hostage drama and shootout. The city room buzzed all day with accounts of the tragedy as it was covered by Bob Popp, Carolyn Anspacher, Tim Findley, and others.

In September and again in October I received letters from the Guild extending my probationary status as a reporter.

Cheryl, meanwhile, was taking classes at City College of San Francisco and planning to become a teacher. A girlfriend of hers who worked at the San Francisco Playboy Club told Cheryl she would make a great bunny and encouraged her to apply. Playboy founder Hugh Hefner had opened the San Francisco club in November 1965 at the corner of Montgomery Street and Pacific Avenue and it became very popular, very quickly. On something of a lark, Cheryl went for an interview and was hired. For the girls' protection real names were not allowed, so Cheryl became "Bunny Candy."

Somewhere around this time I proposed to her. We were already living together in a flat on Shrader Street in the upper Haight Ashbury. We had been dating for four years and it seemed we were destined to be a couple for the ages. We set a wedding date for June 13, 1971, followed by a Caribbean honeymoon to Puerto Rico, St. Thomas, and Jamaica, with a stay at the Playboy resort in Ocho Rios.

CHAPTER 24:
I Am Not Avery

Two months after the Marin shootout, on October 28, 1970, Zodiac threatened *Chronicle* reporter Paul Avery directly in a Halloween card, the first time the killer targeted a specific victim.

"From your secret pal," taunted the dancing skeleton on the front of the spooky card that the cryptic murderer addressed personally to Avery, although he misspelled it as "Averly."

On the front of the card was a verse that began:

"I feel it in my bones,
You ache to know my name.
And so I'll clue you in..."

Inside, the poem concluded:

"But then why spoil our game! BOO! Happy Halloween!"

Elsewhere on the inside panel, Zodiac printed neatly in felt-tip marker:

"Peek-a-boo! You are doomed!"

We gathered around Paul for a closer look at this brazen new message, cracking jokes about his life expectancy. In the relative safety of the city room, we scoffed at the threat, not only because it was so rare for journalists to be killed on duty in those days but because threatening a specific person was a radical departure from Zodiac's otherwise random choice of victims.

Seizing on the opportunity for some typical macabre newsroom levity, someone quickly produced campaign-style buttons with black block letters on a white background proclaiming, "I Am Not Avery," and we all wore them on our lapels. Herb Caen mentioned it in a funny item that brought TV news crews scrambling to our newsroom.

Still, I had to wonder. If Zodiac was serious about whacking Avery, no silly buttons would throw him off, and he might just as easily take out one of us at the same time. Whenever I left the building with Paul, I couldn't help being more keenly aware of our surroundings. I looked much more carefully around corners, behind us, in parked cars and into the eyes of passing strangers.

Paul went along with the gag and wore an "I Am Not Avery" button on the front of his own jacket. But inside his coat he started to wear something else—a .38-caliber revolver. A former Vietnam War correspondent and a licensed private eye, Paul was not easily intimidated, so he took out a concealed-weapon permit, approved by Police Chief Al Nelder. "Are you really worried?" I asked Paul. "Nah," he shrugged, shaking his head. "It's just a lot of talk. But I'm not taking any chances."

Paul had come to the *Chronicle* in 1959 and had made a reputation as a tenacious crime reporter. He was fourteen years older than me and as a cub reporter interested in police stories, I looked up to him for his experience and persistence at tracking down leads and tips. I began to work with Avery on the Zodiac case when I wasn't busy on another story. I helped him check out phone tips or we brainstormed about the ciphers over beers on his Sausalito houseboat. We spent days chasing blind leads and following potential suspects, hoping to inveigle handwriting samples from them.

Avery's colleagues regarded him as a journalist of consummate skill, but he was not above a little skulduggery to beat a competitor to an exclusive or usurp someone else's turf. "Unsavory Avery" was the not-so-affectionate sobriquet that reporter Charlie Howe hung on Paul for his surreptitious tactics. When the SLA grabbed Patty Hearst, Tim Findley, a dogged investigative reporter who had spent some time behind bars in Soledad Prison for a series on prison issues, had so many sources inside the radical left and in law enforcement that he was the first to discover the identities of the SLA members, led by ex-convict Donald DeFreeze, who called himself Cinque.

On the day of the Hearst kidnap, Avery was in Palm Springs chasing down tips about Mayor Joseph Alioto's missing wife, Angelina, who hadn't been heard from in two weeks. Mrs. Alioto turned up safe and Avery flew home. He wasted no time inserting himself into the SLA story. On February 14 he wrote about Marcus Foster's alleged killers complaining about their treatment in jail, and on April 16 Paul wrote a sidebar about the getaway car used by the SLA and Hearst in the Hibernia Bank robbery in San Francisco. Two days later he uncovered an SLA target list of fourteen other potential kidnap victims. When Hearst was spotted outside a Los Angeles sporting goods store with two SLA fugitives on May 16, Avery flew to LA and ended up covering the massive gun battle between police and the SLA the next day.

Paul became so immersed in the Hearst case that he left the paper in 1976 to write a book on the Patty Hearst kidnapping, *The Voices of Guns*, with Boston writer Vin McLellan. It always baffled me why Avery didn't write a book on Zodiac, and I never had the chance to ask him. It was another ten years before former *Chronicle* editorial cartoonist Robert Graysmith published his book on the case. Paul moved on to the *Sacramento Bee* for a time and in 1985 he returned to San Francisco and joined the *Examiner*, where he ended his career in 1994. Paul died in December 2000, at age sixty-six, not at Zodiac's hand but his own, succumbing to pulmonary emphysema brought on by decades of smoking.

I am sad that he didn't live to see the feature film *Zodiac*. Paul would have loved the idea that a notorious Hollywood star with the stature and reputation of Robert Downey Jr. portrayed him in a major motion picture. Was it simply a coincidence that both men's roguish lifestyles tended to overshadow their considerable career triumphs? In my view, Downey brought Avery back to life brilliantly, if sometimes a bit too realistically for comfort.

Chapter 25:
Gas Chamber

Sometime around noon on Monday, January 25, 1971, I was just back from walking our dog and starting to get ready for my 2:30 p.m. shift at the paper when the phone rang. It was my mother's bar manager Ed Spece calling.

"Oh, thank God, I was hoping to reach you," he said breathlessly. "Your mother just called to tell me she was going down to the garage to 'end it all.' I got ahold of your brother at the newspaper. He's heading over there now."

Ed didn't suggest calling the police or an ambulance, nor did I. We were all inured to Dori's threats of suicide, which she tossed out frequently when she was drunk. We knew to check things out first, before an unnecessary ambulance rolled into the driveway, its flashing rooftop lights attracting curious stares from the neighbors.

"OK, Ed, thanks, I'll go and check on her," I said and hung up. Moments later I was racing across town to my mother's flat on Greenwich Street, hoping to get there before she could turn her garage into a homemade gas chamber.

Peeling down Stanyan Street, I started writing her obituary in my head, just in case. This may seem like an odd thing to do, but I knew that when the time finally did come, I would be the one to write my mother's obit.

Like all reporters out covering news on deadline, I had learned to work out the first two to four paragraphs in my head on the way back to the office. That way, the first page of copy was practically out of the typewriter the minute I sat down. When minutes counted to make the first edition and there wasn't time to get back to the office, I would find the nearest pay phone, call in and dictate to a reporter on rewrite. Either way, it speeds things up to have the lead in your head. As I drove, I formed a lead in my mind:

Doris Jennings, prominent San Francisco businesswoman and former wife of the late Chronicle columnist and renowned author Dean Jennings, died at her San Francisco home yesterday after a brief illness. She was 56.

Instead of "prominent San Francisco businesswoman," I considered using the clause, "who transformed a Presidio Heights neighborhood tavern into San Francisco's most popular woman-owned gay bar." But then I thought better of it. She wouldn't want that. For that matter, she wouldn't want the obit at all. "Brief illness," of course, is the standard euphemism for "committed suicide," or any other embarrassing cause of death families don't want printed.

Mrs. Jennings, the proprietor of the popular San Francisco bar and restaurant Club Dori, had previously worked as a loan officer, publicist, secretary, and restaurant hostess. She was a graduate of Stanford University. She and Dean Jennings divorced in 1953.

Zigzagging through lanes of traffic on Oak Street, I wondered if this wasn't just another false alarm. *What if she really means it this time? What if we're too late, then what? Who should we call? Police? The coroner?* My mother had said often, in that pragmatic tone of hers, that when she died she wanted to be cremated. And the quieter we all were about it, the better. She was an atheist and dismissive of the notion that there was a hereafter.

I sped down Oak, a one-way street that skirts the south side of the Golden Gate Park Panhandle. I passed the weathered park benches, asphalt basketball courts and patchy expanses of lawn where the Summer of Love first flowered four years earlier.

Mrs. Jennings is survived by her sons, Dorn and Duffy, both Chronicle employees, and a sister, Michael Drury, of Newport, Rhode Island. At her request, Mrs. Jennings will be cremated, and no services are planned.

Making the turn onto Masonic, my fear turned to anger. *Goddammit, Mom! I'm getting married in five months!* Then I thought, aw, hell, maybe today's the day her pain—all our pain—will end once and for all. It occurred to me that if she were dead, at least I wouldn't have to worry about her creating an embarrassing scene at my wedding. Immediately I felt guilty for feeling angry.

Without a car at work, Dorn left the newspaper, walked two blocks over to Third Street and boarded the first No. 30-Stockton Muni bus that came along. It was the regular coach, not even the express. Like me, Dorn's first instinct was that this was just another bluff. Over a decade, these panic calls—from her or someone at the bar—had become more annoying than alarming. She had never really gone through with it. Still, we never knew for sure until we got to her. Dorn chided himself for not taking a taxi as the bus snaked sluggishly through Chinatown, North Beach, and eventually down Chestnut Street.

Across town, idling at an impossibly long red light on Masonic at Geary, I banged my palm on the steering wheel fast and hard. "C'mon, c'mon, C'MON!" I yelled, drawing a curious stare from the driver in the lane next to me. The light finally changed, and I swung onto Presidio Avenue, coincidentally passing by Club Dori, where Ed had called from minutes before. *Fucking bar,* I muttered to myself. I wove down through the tall stands of eucalyptus trees on the Presidio Army base at twice the posted limit, watching for the MPs, then out the Lombard Gate and into the Marina.

Dorn got off the bus in front of Funston Playground and ran the last two blocks, stopping twice to catch his breath, cursing his excess weight. The garage door was closed. He used the key she kept in the mailbox to let himself in. Her car, the lime green Challenger with its "DORI" vanity plate, sat there, nosed into the back wall, convertible top up. That was odd, he thought, she rarely put the top up. In its escape from confinement, an invisible veil of carbon monoxide pushed out to the street, temporarily sealing Dorn's nose and throat like a plastic dry-cleaning bag. Covering his face with his jacket, he moved in, yanked open the driver's door. A minute later, I pulled into the driveway. I saw Dorn leaning into the front seat of the Challenger.

"Is she OK?" I called out.

"I think so," Dorn said. "I just got here. I shut off the engine. She's breathing, at least."

The exhaust was now condensed to a grayish-white haze swirling up past the bay windows of her flat above. A powerful odor of petroleum still lingered in the air around the car. My mother was slouched low in the driver's seat, her neck arched backward on the headrest, eyes half closed, mouth agape. She wore a pastel green-and-blue flowered chiffon housecoat, marred by cigarette burns and splayed open over an off-white satin nightgown, and bedroom slippers. Her hair was a snarled nest of blonde straw. Her coral lipstick was smeared. She wasn't moving.

CHAPTER 26:
The Note

After a few moments, Dori moaned and stirred, mumbling something. Her grogginess was from alcohol, not carbon monoxide. In her vodka-saturated state, she simply botched the job. She was just conscious enough to find her keys and navigate the stairs to the garage, but too plastered to attach a hose to the tail pipe, feed the other end through a window and close everything up the way you're supposed to if you're trying to asphyxiate yourself. Just by running the engine and sitting inside the car, even with the driver's window open, the exhaust would have taken a long time to suffocate her.

Standing there, looking at my mother in her familiar stupor, I realized she wasn't dead after all. I was momentarily disappointed, and then disgusted with myself for thinking it.

"Stay with her," Dorn said. "I'm going to call her doctor."

Gently, I shook her shoulder. "Mom?" Another moan, then a fit of coughing. Upstairs, Dorn found the doctor's number by Dori's bedside and dialed it. He told the receptionist he had an emergency and needed to talk to the doctor right away. A few seconds later, Dr. Lake came on the line.

"Hello, doctor Lake, this is Dorn Jennings, Doris's son. My mother just tried to kill herself. My brother and I found her in her car in the garage with the motor running. She's conscious and breathing. She's pretty drunk, but I think she'll be OK. What should we do?"

"I'll send an ambulance," the doctor replied. "Call me back when they leave with her. I will meet them at S.F. General."

"The city hospital?" Dorn asked, incredulous. "That place is a dump. I don't want her going there. Can't you send one from Mt. Zion?"

"It's a lot more expensive, for one thing," said Dr. Lake. "And she might have to stay for a few days."

"Screw the cost!" Dorn insisted. "I don't want any of this on the police channel or the news." This is standard protective behavior for adult children of alcoholics. No one was to know the truth about Dori's "health problem." Dr. Lake relented and agreed to dispatch a private ambulance.

When the paramedics showed up, they checked Dori's vitals and give her some oxygen before lifting her out of the car and onto a gurney. "Hey, guys, no lights and siren, OK?" Dorn pleaded. "Don't worry," replied the driver, "she's stable. We'll give her a nice quiet ride." Dorn climbed into the front seat of the ambulance for the short trip over the hill to Mt. Zion. I followed in my car. We waited there while she was evaluated and admitted, then we were told she was sleeping and that it might be a couple of hours before we could see her. We decided to go back to the house to wait.

A gloomy darkness greeted us at Dori's. All the shades were drawn, and no windows were open. A rank stench of stagnant cigarette smoke, alcohol, and urine pervaded the flat. Dirty dishes were stacked in the kitchen sink, caked in a greasy film. Dori's bedding was disheveled, the bottom sheet stained in the center. On the nightstand sat a clock radio, an ashtray piled with Salem butts, and an empty highball glass.

We found a plain white envelope on the kitchen table. On the outside, scribbled in pencil in Dori's handwriting, it was addressed to me, my brother, George, and several of her co-workers at the bar:

"D & D & G & Ed & Chuck & Billie and all the people I love who have been so good to me. Les & Richard & Andy & Dennis & Fred & Loid."

Inside were five loose sheets of three-by-five, off-white notepaper. The note was scrawled in uneven lines. Some words trailed off in wobbly downward strokes. Dorn and I read it together silently:

"I just can't make it anymore. Not for myself and certainly not for any of you. Leave garage door open for a while. It will be full of odorless carbon monoxide. Keys are everywhere. Tax info is more or less ready." (That was so Dori. It's okay if her sons find her dead, but she's worried about the vapor and doesn't want to inconvenience the accountant filing her 1040.) Call Dr. Lake. He can make it 'accidental causes' or something else euphemistic. I want to go to Daphne (Funeral Home) & be disposed of as quickly and cheaply as John Olson (a former employee) was. If illegal to put ashes in the water, where I belong, then put them in an urn close to Johnny O. Skip memorial services. A lot of 4-letter word that costs $70.00. I love you all enough to do this. Duff knows how to do the paychex. Can be changed if you want. Tell Mother I fell in the bathroom or something & Cissy (her sister) will understand. -D"

My brother and I stood staring at the note without a word for a few moments.

"Jesus," I finally said to Dorn.

"Yeah, I know," he replied.

Dorn looked up from the note, exasperated. His chin dropped, his eyes closed, and his head began moving slowly from side to side. "Let's look around."

We fanned out to scavenge the flat for hidden booze. Almost every drawer or cabinet in Dori's dresser, closet, nightstand, kitchen, and bathroom had a vodka bottle in it, some fifths, some pints. They were squirreled beneath piles of sweaters or scarves or purses or hidden behind rolls of toilet paper and boxes of cereal. On the floor of the hall closet was a cardboard box that held six half-gallon bottles of rotgut Chablis. Four of them were empty, one partially consumed, one still unopened. "C'mon, we need to get rid of this stuff," said Dorn. We poured every bottle into the kitchen sink and dumped the empties in the alley trashcans.

"You know this is totally pointless," Dorn said while we worked. "She'll just call and order more when she gets home."

"I don't know," I said, "maybe a close call like this will scare her enough that she might finally quit for good." His eye roll told me I was kidding myself.

Dori's unshakeable atheism and her obstinate denial of the grip booze had on her was a powerful combination that rejected Alcoholics Anonymous and its Twelve Step program for years. The detox wards, dry out centers, Antabuse – they were all futile. Even though we knew that dumping her stash may only be a temporary impediment, we both felt like we need to do something. Right then, this was the only thing in our control and it made us feel better.

'To Me She Is a Girl'

A Glittering Gay Wedding

By Duffy Jennings

By Vincent Maggiora

Pat Montelcino and Terry Black left church after ceremony

The couple as they departed in car

From the back of the church, you could not tell that the bride, a figure of beauty swathed in a tower of white chiffon, was a man.

But it didn't really matter. "This is what we want for each other," said Terry Black, the tuxedoed groom, minutes before the ceremony. He lit a cigarette and smiled. "I've never been happier in my life."

Terry is 23. At 17, he married a Pasadena girl. Soon afterward he joined the Marine Corps. He has a 4-year-old daughter.

"It didn't work out. I was too young. I turned to the gay life about a year ago." That was when he met Pat Montelcino, a 30 - year - old female impersonator at the 181 Club, 181 Eddy street.

"I love Pat. It's that simple. I think we can be as happy any straight couple. To me she is a girl. She treats me like a husband."

Their relationship bears little difference from any other couple. Pat plays the role of the wife. She cooks ("Mmm, can she cook! Gourmet foods all the time!"), does the housework and handles the finances.

"Their new checks will read 'Mr. and Mrs. Terry Black.'"

Next year they intend to file a joint income tax return — uncertain how it will be received. Terry works as a bartender.

"I'm going to open my own bar next year," he said. "Then Pat can retire. She wants to open a boutique."

Terry's best man, Mike, arrived to escort the groom to the altar. Mike, like the 14 ushers in the wedding party, is also gay. He does not reveal his last name because he works for the National Aeronautics and Space Administration.

Glide Memorial Church had been rented for the wedding. The ceremony was elaborate. Nineteen bridesmaids — all men—took their places to the left of the altar. All were attired in homemade gowns of yellow, pink and blue.

The bride's sisters, Marie, 16, and Debbie, 8, were flower-girls. They knew the bride was their brother.

The Rev. Howard Wells of the Metropolitan Community Church faced the couple and performed his 30th gay "wedding ceremony."

There is no marriage license. The marriage is not recognized as legal in California. But that is not important to Terry and Pat. For them it is an expression of love for each other. They are unquestionably sincere in their feelings. That, to them, is what is important.

The couple exchanged vows. They placed rings on each other's finger. They turned and faced each other. They kissed.

The bride wept.

Resounding applause filled the church as the newlyweds walked back up the aisle and into the street. They led the congregation to a reception at the 181 Club a block away and greeted all their guests at the door.

A Hawaiian honeymoon is planned but "not for awhile." "The wedding set me back 3000 bucks," said Terry. "I'm just a lousy bartender."

"We're just people," said Bill Kruse, 31, one of the ushers. "We're motivated by the same things everyone else is, whether it be home and hearth or a career in show business."

He slipped his drink and set it down. "You can't live alone," he said. "Basically, we just want to be happy. You can accept it or reject it. It's your choice."

CHAPTER 27:
No Funeral, Three Weddings

Dori recovered, was discharged after a few days, and returned to the club as if nothing was amiss.

She was present and well-behaved when Cheryl and I were married at the rustic, non-denominational Swedenborgian Church in Pacific Heights that June. The bridesmaids wore hot pants outfits, all the fashion rage at the time. Cheryl's parents hosted the reception in their backyard in San Rafael, and we left two days later for the Caribbean. It was a welcome break from Dori.

Barely a week after Cheryl and I returned from our honeymoon, my brother married his girlfriend, Sofia, in a civil ceremony in Oakland. I was happy for him, but I couldn't help feeling like he was trying to keep up with me by getting married. He and Sofia were divorced within a year.

Within a few weeks of my return to work, I was assigned to cover a wedding of a different sort – between two men. It was an eyebrow-raising event for the times and ironic for me as both a newlywed and the son of a gay bar owner. The city editor said: "Two guys are getting married and they want the world to know about it." Photographer Vince Maggiora and I went to the ceremony at Glide Memorial Church on Ellis Street. This is my article from Tuesday, August 17, 1971, headlined "A Glittering Gay Wedding":

* * *

From the back of the church, you could not tell that the bride, a figure of beauty swathed in a tower of white chiffon, was a man.

But it didn't really matter.

"This is what we want for each other," said Terry Black, the tuxedoed groom, minutes before the ceremony. He lit a cigarette and smiled. "I've never been happier in my life."

Terry is 23. At 17, he married a Pasadena girl. Soon afterward he joined the Marine Corps. He has a 4-year-old daughter.

"It didn't work out. I was too young. I turned to the gay life about a year ago." That was when he met Pat Montclaire, a 30-year-old female impersonator at the 181 Club, 181 Eddy street.

"I love Pat, it's that simple. I think we can be as happy as any straight couple. To me she is a girl. She treats me like a husband."

Their relationship bears little difference from any other couple. Pat plays the role of the wife. She cooks ("Man, can she cook! Gourmet foods all the time!"), does the housework and handles the finances.

Their new checks will read "Mr. and Mrs. Terry Black."

"Next year they intend to file a joint income tax return — uncertain how it will be received. Terry works as a bartender.

"I'm going to open my own bar next year," he said. "Then Pat can retire. She wants to open a boutique." Terry's best man, Mike, arrived to escort the groom to the altar. Mike, like the 14 ushers in the wedding party, is also gay. He does not reveal his last name because he works for the National Aeronautics and Space Administration.

Glide Memorial Church had been rented for the wedding.

The ceremony was elaborate. Nineteen bridesmaids —all men—took their places to the left of the altar. All were attired in homemade gowns of yellow, pink, and blue.

The bride's sisters, Marie, 10, and Debbie, 9, were flower girls.

They knew the bride was their brother.

The Rev. Howard Wells of the Metropolitan Community Church faced the couple and performed his 20th gay "wedding ceremony."

There is no marriage license. The marriage is not recognized as legal in California. But that is not important to Terry and Pat. For them it is an expression of love for each other. They are unquestionably sincere in their feelings. That, to them, is what is important.

The couple exchanged vows. They placed rings on each other's finger. They turned and faced each other. They kissed.

The bride wept.

Resounding applause filled the church as the newlyweds walked back up the aisle and into the street. They led the congregation to a reception at the 181 Club a block away and greeted all their guests at the door.

A Hawaiian honeymoon is planned but "not for a while." "The wedding set me back 3500 bucks," said Terry. "I'm just a lousy bartender."

"We're just people," said Bill Kruse, 31, one of the ushers. "We're motivated by the same things everyone else is, whether it be home and hearth or a career in show business."

He sipped his drink and set it down. "You can't live alone," he said. "Basically, we just want to be happy. You can accept it or reject it, it's your choice."

Chapter 28:
High Priest

At the height of the Haight-Ashbury spiritual flower-power phenomenon, drugs were becoming more popular than ever—and resulting in more arrests. I had smoked fewer than five joints in my life until then. I didn't care for the soporific effects of pot, and as a reporter I feared being arrested for possession of even the smallest amount of weed. Also, because of my active reserve status in the Marines, I had to stay "squared away," physically and mentally. Nor could I grow my hair long because of my monthly reserve meetings, although a few of the guys in my company wore cheap crewcut wigs over their shoulder-length hair during the duty weekends at the Naval facility in San Bruno.

The Haight-Ashbury, meanwhile, had become the city's epicenter for marijuana and other psychedelics. One drug dealer and self-proclaimed "high priest" of a commune asked to speak to a reporter in his jail cell. Staff photographer Bill Young and I went to see him at the Hall of Justice. My article ran on page one November 11, 1971.

* * *

"I'm into an esoteric religion. White magic. Positive energy.

"They come to me down. Depressed. Uptight. When they leave, they are high again. I just try to do God's will."

Ricky Joe Niemi, self-proclaimed "high priest of a multi-religious, occultist Haight-Ashbury commune," looked tired.

His pale blue eyes surveyed the City Prison walls around him for a brief moment. The real world.

Duffy Jennings

Inside

Most streetcar service was plagued by mishaps, capped by a 30-minute afternoon tieup of downtown traffic. Page 2.

A **San Jose** policeman who is under indictment for manslaughter was discharged from the force. Page 2.

Six who allegedly attempted to escape from San Quentin last August rejected their court-appointed attorneys. Page 2.

A **lack** of agreement over pension benefits will hold up the start of new bus service to Marin and Sonoma counties. Page 3.

Eleven persons in Oakland were charged with income-tax violations that may have bilked the Government of $730,000. Page 4.

TOP OF THE NEWS

The **Bay Area's** new young voters launched a campaign to depose President Nixon and influence nominations. Page 5.

A **Navy** jet whose pilot was accidentally ejected, soared unmanned across two states before crashing into a field. Page 6.

Officials charged with carrying out school desegregation studies got the House-passed antibusing amendments. Page 6.

China advised the United Nations that its first delegation will arrive in New York on Monday. Page 10.

The **State** Department said the new Senate foreign-aid bill would cripple South Vietnam and Cambodia. Page 10.

India's Prime Minister ruled out the crisis over East Pakistan. Page 11.

Mariner 9 is on schedule to transmit pictures of the planet Mars back to Earth early next week. Page 11.

Twenty-two Cubans who came to the U.S. to attend a sugarcane conference and were ordered deported, left the country. Page 13.

Four African Presidents left Tel Aviv for Cairo on a mission to help settle the Middle East conflict. Page 13.

Fresno's Catholic bishop denied his diocese contributed funds to Cesar Chavez' United Farm Workers Union. Page 14.

The **DDT** that is preventing pelicans from reproducing is coming from a Los Angeles chemical plant, a scientists reports. Page 14.

Pro-Franco, anti-Communist youths destroyed 24 Picasso engravings worth $85,700 on display in Madrid. Page 26.

Spent urea from Western uranium mills that is used to fill in housing developments may cause health problems. Page 40.

Weather

Bay Area: Fair Saturday with little temperature change. Highs in the 60s and 70s; lows in the 30s and 40s. Page 33.

San Francisco Chronicle

★★★★ FINAL

107th Year No. 310 ★★★★ SATURDAY, NOVEMBER 6, 1971 GArfield 1-1111 15 CENTS

'High Priest'

By William S. Young

Ricky Joe Niemi of the Sacred House

Ricky Joe and His White Magic

By Duffy Jennings

"I'm into an esoteric religion. White magic. Positive energy.

"They come to me down. Depressed. Uptight. When they leave, they are high again. I just try to do God's will."

Ricky Joe Niemi, self-proclaimed "high priest of a multi-religious, occultist Haight-Ashbury commune, looked tired.

His pale blue eyes surveyed the City Prime walls around him for a brief moment. The real world.

"Psychedelics are all I ever sell. Grass, peyote, acid, mushrooms . . . tools to open up your consciousness — an untouched warehouse of knowledge."

The law doesn't agree.

Niemi and ten others were arrested Thursday night in a simultaneous raid on two houses of the Cosmic Fetus Commune, 1606 Haight, and

See Back Page

Major Shakeup of U.S. Intelligence

L.A. Times Service

Washington

The White House announced a shakeup of the Government's massive intelligence bureaucracy that has given new major import to enabling the President to have more positive and better control over all security and intelligence matters in the United States.

Richard Helms, director of the Central Intelligence Agency, emerges from the long-planned reorganization as an even stronger figure with responsibility for coordinating all intelligence activities. Some sources said Helms' role could double into that of an intelligence czar.

Henry A. Kissinger, the President's assistant for national security affairs, and the National Security Council staff are also given significant new powers in the shakeup.

The Pentagon's huge Defense Intelligence Agency is downgraded and will be reduced.

See Back Page

Big Sale Of Grain To Soviets

Washington

The Nixon administration announced arrangements yesterday for the commercial sale of nearly $136 million worth of corn and other livestock feed grains to the Soviet Union.

The key to the sale was the waiver by American maritime unions of their longtime demand that at least 50 per cent of grain shipments to the Soviet Union be carried in American ships, according to administration officials.

The maritime union agreement to the waiver was made in response to Mr. Nixon's efforts to revitalize American merchant shipping, administration sources said. The Nixon program includes a ten-year system of subsidies to enable domestic shipping to compete with foreign flagships.

The officials turned the sale by two United States grain companies as "the first step" in the expansion of trade with the Soviet Union, and said that the impetus was generated for more sales in the future. They declined to speculate on whether such sales would extend to China in the near future.

The pending sale to the Soviet Union is the first since the late President Kennedy's authorization for a controversial $100 million wheat sale to Russia for 1964.

The sale will be by the Continental Grain Company and Cargill, Inc. Spokesmen for the companies declined to disclose how much of the total sale each company would handle, for competitive reasons. The sale covers 80 million bushels of corn, 24 million bushels of barley and 6 million bushels of milo.

Government officials said the grain sale resulted from a series of events starting last June, when Mr. Nixon lifted some of the barriers for trade with the Soviet Union and China. These included removal of special license requirements for shipments and of the 50 per cent requirements for American shipping.

N.Y. Times Service

Nursing Home Fire -- One Dies

Toledo, Ohio

Fire broke out at a nursing home yesterday and one patient died, apparently of overexcitement, as 57 others were evacuated, fire officials said.

The victim was identified as Stella Mitchell, 99, the mother of Cecil Mitchell, administrator of the nursing home, who was away on business.

United Press

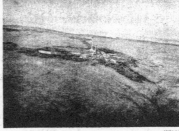

Project Cannikin area was swept by bitter winds as the testing hour approached on bare Amchitka

A Death Is Succeeded By Life

Sheila Smith of Concord gave birth to a baby girl last night at Providence Hospital in Oakland.

In the process, she had another life.

Her husband had died a little more than two hours earlier after the crash scene before ambulance and the Highway Patrol, but Mrs. Nordman III, to the hospital.

She suffered violent labor pains immediately after the accident but was otherwise unhurt.

SAMARITAN

An unknown, passing motorist, who arrived at the crash scene before ambulance and the Highway Patrol, took Mrs. Nordman III, to the hospital.

She suffered violent labor pains immediately after the accident but was otherwise unhurt.

SECOND

It was the second monthly decline in a row. The rate was 6.1 per cent in August and 5.6 per cent in July. It has wavered from 6.2 per cent for a year.

The jobless rate for blue collar workers and Vietnam veterans dropped sharply, but the rate for blacks and other minorities rose to 10.7 per cent, highest since November

See Back Page

U.S. Jobless Rate Drops Slightly

Associated Press

Washington

The Nation's unemployment rate dropped slightly to 5.8 per cent of the work force last month as the total number of working Americans reached a record 79.9 million, the government said yesterday.

The total number of out-of-work job seekers dropped by 200,000, mostly husbands and other adult men, to 4.6 million, the Labor Department's Bureau of Labor Statistics said.

The jobless rate declined by 0.2 per cent from September's 6 per cent. Bureau Commissioner Geoffrey Moore called the drop "marginally significant."

Senator William Proxmire (Dem-Wis.), chairman of the Joint Economic Committee, said it was cause for "marginal encouragement" but showed no breakthrough.

There was no comment from the administration.

Last-Ditch Amchitka Pleas ---High Court Meets Today

5-Megaton Blast Set For 2 p.m.

Washington Post Service

Washington

The seven Justices of the Supreme Court agreed yesterday to sit this morning to hear oral arguments for delaying a five-megaton underground nuclear explosion on Amchitka Island only hours before the weapon is due to be detonated.

In an unusual move, the full Supreme Court agreed to hear the last-minute appeal of eight environmental organizations for a temporary injunction against the test so that they can argue their case that the test violates the National Environmental Policy Act.

The petition to the Supreme Court could have been handled by Chief Justice Warren E. Burger on the basis of written briefs alone, but the seriousness and legal novelty of the case apparently prompted the decision to hold court to hear the oral arguments for and against the test.

The hearing on the test needs-named Cannikin is only the second Saturday session of the Supreme Court since the Rosenbergs were tried for treason in 1953. In late June, the court held a Saturday session on newspaper publication of secret Pentagon papers.

The hearing will start even on the Atomic Energy Commission presses ahead with its plans to detonate the Spartan anti-ballistic missile warhead at 2 p.m. PST in the Aleutians.

FOCUS

Cannikin Waits, 6000 Feet Down

N.Y. Times Service

Amchitka Island

The hole where Cannikin is buried was sealed off with gravel and topped with plastic slugs yesterday but foul weather tormented technicians as they hurried to complete final adjustments for today's hydrogen bomb test. Cannikin is the test's code name.

The men scurrying around toward zero-were perhaps and task gear for protection against the chill wind, fog and continuous driving rain brought in overnight by a typical Aleutian Islands storm. The forecast for today is for some clearing.

Two television cameras are aimed at the site which is on a low hill where the island rolls northward down to the Bering Sea, less than a mile away. The Pacific surf pounds the southern shore, which is less than two miles away.

The source of these two cameras is 2600 feet and the test will not be fired if the weather is such that the camera cannot see ground zero.

See Back Page

Few Are Working-- Fewer Aren't

By Jackson Rannells

California's unemployment rate was 7.0 per cent in October — the first time since July, 1968, that it was below the same month of the previous year, state officials announced with some optimism yesterday.

"This may be an indication that the upward trend in unemployment has been stopped," said Sigurd I. Hansen, director of the state department of Human Resources Development.

The 7.0 seasonally adjusted rate was below both September's 7.1 and last October's 7.2.

Both the number of jobless persons and the total unemployed declined since October, 1970.

This paradox may indicate

See Back Page

Index

Comics	18
Deaths	33
Entertainment	35
Finance	45
People	42
TV-Radio	34
Vital Statistics	33
Weather	33

© Chronicle Publishing Co. 1971.

"Psychedelics are all I ever sell. Grass, peyote, acid, mushrooms, tools to open up your sub-conscious — an untouched warehouse of knowledge."

The law doesn't agree.

Niemi and ten others were arrested Thursday night in a simultaneous raid on two houses, the Cosmic Fetus Commune, 1626 Haight, and Niemi's Sacred House, 290 Frederick Street.

He is charged with conspiracy, possession of an opiate, possession of dangerous drugs and marijuana for sale, and selling narcotics.

"I decided if I was going to survive. I'd have to deal. That's the only way I was going to make it.

"I dealt, made money. But I never got into a money trip. I've seen what that can do to people. I just made enough to pay my rent and my bills. I knew it was illegal but I sell psychedelics for sacraments."

His is an oft-told story. Finished eighth grade. Ran away from his Stockton home at 16. Stock boy, waiter, busboy. The Haight. Then, five years ago, lost within and without, he turned to religion. He will be 23 tomorrow.

His religion was his own, self-taught from Christianity, Judaism, and others. And the occult.

"I belong to an occult order that is the seed of the same order in which Christ was taught everything he knew. The new Messiah is coming. I don't know when, but soon. It really started coming together in the last year. Getting heavy."

He said his mother was a divorcee who had been suffering miserably from alcoholism for 15 years.

"Three years ago. I turned her on. She practices here now." His mother, Constance Azevedo, 40, was arrested with him in the raid.

"Shane," as Niemi is known by his followers, soon became a popular figure in the Haight, a spiritual leader to whom the wayward could go for confession and a cleansing of their sins. And, the police say, for dope.

Three months ago he rented the upper flat of a pale green house at the corner of Frederick and Clayton Streets.

In a short time, he had transformed the flat into Sacred House, with altars, religious symbols, a ritual room, hanging canopies — and a complete nursery.

In one sun-bathed front room, there are begonias, a pot of sedums, peppermint, geraniums and hanging baskets of Boston and maiden hair ferns.

On the opposite wall is an altar with a life-size statue of a black-faced nun cloaked in robes of white and royal blue, flanked by paintings of Jesus Christ and the Virgin Mary.

One of the arresting officers said the house was "eerie, it gave me the creeps." In the light of day, however, the house was more like a church.

"I live life," said Niemi.

"I surround myself with living things. Plants are alive. And I have fish. And a small dog, Spring Garden."

Niemi is a vegetarian, "but in this evolution it's okay to eat plants. Meat deteriorates the body. As a vegetarian, I'm less uptight. I feel healthy.

"Pretty soon, we won't have to eat anything. Man will live on cosmic energy. He'll just have to breathe to survive."

Niemi, wearing a long sleeved, bright yellow undershirt and Navy bellbottom jeans trimmed from the knee down in an Indian fabric, assessed his current situation as he would minister to those who come to him.

"This is not going to change my head about the Spirit. It bums things up a little, though.

"I don't know what's going to happen now ... how long I'll be in here. I'll just put it in God's hands. Whatever happens, it will be His will."

While I was learning the ropes as a new reporter, Cheryl was looking at a new career direction of her own. Being, a bunny was fun, but Cheryl knew it wasn't a long-term career. For an assignment in a women's studies at city College of San Francisco to write about women in broadcasting, she interviewed local TV anchors, including Karna Small and Marcia Brandwynne, who inspired her to pursue a radio and TV career of her own.

To get her foot in the door, Cheryl applied for intern work at twenty Bay Area radio stations. All turned her down except KNBR, and soon she was working fifty hours a week there. She helped on-air hosts Frank Dill and Mike Cleary with traffic reports for five months and later worked as switchboard operator and secretary. After a year and a half, the station made Cheryl its overnight and weekend news reporter. From there she became a reporter and later news director at K101 radio working for the legendary Jim Gabbert.

Married just a few months, I encouraged Cheryl in her broadcast career at first. I wanted to be supportive, but at the same time I was jealous of the attention it took from me as the journalist in the family. I never said as much to her. As I often did when such emotions posed a conflict for me, I let those feelings fester in silence, cultivating a grudge that would eventually explode abnormally out of proportion to the reality of it.

FIRE! FIRE! FIRE!

Photo by Chel Born, San Francisco Fire Department

Answer the bell with the firemen of the busiest Engine Company in San Francisco. Chronicle reporter Duffy Jennings rode the fire rigs and fought fires with the men of Engine 21. Read his exciting story.

Starting Monday

San Francisco Chronicle

CHAPTER 29:
Fire! Fire! Fire!

Late in March 1972, one of my early mentors, *Chronicle* editor Steve Gavin, returned from a trip to the East Coast raving about a new book by New York City firefighter Dennis Smith. "Report from Engine Company 82" was a graphic diary about life in a Bronx fire station that was answering 700 calls a month.

Smith's vivid account of the busiest fire station in the country was the first of its kind to open the firehouse doors to the public, revealing the day-to-day routine and the life-and-death heroics firefighters face every time the alarm sounds.

"We've got to do this story here," Gavin said to me. "You should do it. Go be a fireman. Live with them, work their shifts, fight fires with them, hang out in the firehouse, sleep and eat there, find out what it's like every day."

I had covered a few major fires during my first two years on the job and I always marveled at the efficiency and fearlessness with which firemen went about their work. But I knew nothing about them beyond the fire scene itself. Living among them, getting to see what goes on inside the firehouse and how fire crews live and work together—now that sounded like a great assignment. Besides, what kid didn't want to be a fireman when he grew up?

City editor Abe Mellinkoff wrote to San Francisco's fire chief at the time, Keith Calden, asking about our idea. "We will be very happy to have Mr. Duffy Jennings share the life of a fireman in the San Francisco Fire Department for one month," Calden wrote back on April 4. "We will have him sign a release for insurance purposes while in station quarters and riding on apparatus. Looking forward to an exciting month with Duffy Jennings and the readers of the San Francisco *Chronicle*."

A short time later I took a three-day crash course at the department's Fire College to learn enough of the basics to keep from getting myself hurt or killed. Then I donned my own genuine SFFD uniform with an official silver badge, turnouts (firefighting coveralls) and a distinctive yellow press helmet to help other firemen identify me at fire scenes. I joined the crew at the busiest firehouse in San Francisco, Engine Company 21 on Grove Street between Broderick and Baker Streets, two blocks from the Golden Gate Park Panhandle.

This was the 1972 equivalent of what journalists now call being "embedded." At first the guys at 21 Engine were none too happy to have a reporter in their midst. It was a closed group that relished and guarded their privacy once the firehouse doors closed. Gradually, I was able to earn their trust by keeping up my end at fires and in the kitchen.

After four weeks of working with them 24 hours on, 48 off, I came back to the paper and spent almost as much time writing a series of six articles titled, "Riding with Engine 21."

The newspaper promoted the series with a full-page ad, reading: "FIRE! FIRE! FIRE! Answer the bell with the firemen of the busiest Engine Company in San Francisco. *Chronicle* reporter Duffy Jennings rode the fire rigs and fought fires with the men of Engine 21. Read his exciting story. Starting Monday."

Here is the series:

Part 1 – July 24, 1972 – A Fireman's Life

The bells hit. Onetwothree. Onetwothreefourfive. Onetwothree. Onetwothreefour.

With the last four, a thunderous clatter of wooden chairs and benches. Heavy black boots pound across the linoleum.

The men of Engine Company 21 scramble out of the communications room and slam through the big double doors to the apparatus floor. Paul Arvonen shouts into the firehouse intercom:

"Inside for the engine! Chief goes too! Box 3534, Fillmore and McAllister! Everybody!"

The huge automatic overhead garage door grinds open. Men run down both sides of the pumper, jump on. Seventeen tons of glossy red steel, rubber and hose.

Paul guns life into the big diesel. Biff O'Brien, on the back step, gives the go-ahead. Paul jams down the accelerator. Siren. Red lights.

The rig bolts out onto Grove street, into the night. Mike Keating grips the handrail on the right side with one hand, snaps up his turnout coat with the other.

Paul takes a wide turn at Broderick street. Up the block, tear around the next corner. Down Fulton street jostling through traffic. Two ear-shattering blasts of the air horn drown out the siren.

Inside the cab of San Francisco's busiest fire engine, Joe Medina barks into a radio headset:

"21 Engine responding to Box 3-5-3-4!"

Past Scott street, Pierce, Steiner. Gotta be doing sixty, seventy maybe. Moving van on the right! Swerve! No sweat.

Paul pumps the brakes at Fillmore. Two more rigs tear up Fulton from the opposite direction. 14 Engine and 6 Truck. Sirens everywhere.

Mike points to a decayed hotel up ahead on Fillmore. The Manor Plaza. It is abandoned. (Later, Battalion Chief Bill Favilla says there used to be so many pimps, junkies and whores in the joint, no fireman would go in alone. And never without an ax.)

On the fourth floor, at the rear of the building, an orange glow beats against the window.

Lieutenant Medina is on the radio again: "Box 3-5-3-4, workin' fire." He bends out the cab window and yells, "Drop the hydrant jumper!"

Biff hooks his arm through a loop of "big line," yanks a 50-foot length off the hose bed and heads for the hydrant. The pumper pulls up to the front of the building. The coupled hose snakes out behind it, flops on the pavement.

The Manor Plaza's outer foyer is boarded. Old campaign posters splashed on rotting plywood sheets. Can't make a lead from the street.

Chief Favilla orders 6 Truck to "ladder" the front fire escape – take the line up from the outside. The men haul the hose up, through a splintered window on the fire floor. Down a pinched hallway, thick with soot and smoke.

Mike humps the nozzle to the doorway of the crackling room. The opposite wall is curtained in flame. Another wall is blistered and bubbly, the ceiling scorched.

Mike swears at the lifeless hose flaked out behind him. "Charge the line, dammit!" he yells. Outside in the street, a fellow fire fighter with a wrench opens the valve on the hydrant. The hose ripples up the hall, swollen with water. Sixty gallons a minute.

Mike cracks the nozzle open, floods the room. Choking black steam hisses up the walls and ceiling. Cruddy hot smoke belches out in the hall. The truckmen crouch beneath it, coughing, eyes red and runny.

Mike, wiping a moustache of black snot from his lip, moves in another two feet. He drives the powerful stream against the window on the blazing wall. The glass explodes, showers the empty lot below.

The smoke pours out the window. A smoldering mattress, now a pile of soggy cotton and crusty springs, is visible in the far corner. The fire is out. Mike gives the room a final washdown and shuts down the line.

Two truckmen throw the mattress out the window. Others move in with ceiling hooks and axes to pull the walls, checking for hidden fire.

Cause of this fire – unknown. "Probable discarded smoking materials," the official report will say. Someone had been living in the room. No plumbing, no electricity, no heat. Just a mattress, a shirt, a pair of shoes.

In another room, more clothing, an empty bottle of white port. Fresh human waste in the corner. Still another room, empty wine bottles knee deep along the back wall. Favilla says: "They'll be back when we leave."

He tells 21 to "pick up." Uncouple each length. "Bleed" the water out. Recouple. Feed the hose back onto the engine. Go home.

The box – the bells sounding the alarm – hit at 9:07 p.m. Fourteen minutes later, the fire is out. Engine 21 dropped the most line; they are the last to go home. First there, last back. It is after 10 p.m. when the pumper backs into the firehouse.

Mike and Biff leave their turnout coats and black leather helmets on the rig and walk back to the kitchen. The coffee is hot and fresh.

It is past midnight when Paul climbs the stairs to the second-floor dormitory. He goes to a bank of small open cubicles to get his turnouts – heavy canvas pants "turned out" over clumpy rubber boots.

He carefully sets them on the floor beside his bed, boots pointed toward the glistening brass pole in the center of the dorm.

His body jerks forward as a box hits on the big bell over his bed, but it is for another company.

"You know what they say," he says, turning back the covers. "Only two people get paid in bed – whores and firemen."

Part 2 – Firemen's Life of Bells and Death

Chief's operator George Dwyer glances fitfully at the big chrome bell on the wall above him, curses its muteness and returns to the kitchen.

"Haven't turned a wheel all day," he says. He sits sidesaddle on a long bench, lights a cigarette, stands up, walks around, sits down again. "C'mon, c'mon!" he says. "Due for a big burner."

On slow nights like this, when every box is for another company and even the TV movie is a rerun, the guys at 21 Engine fidget about like so many wiredrawn fathers-to-be and talk stoically about last year's fires. And death.

Thirty-seven persons died in fires here last year. And tonight, the faces around the kitchen table reflect them.

"My first stiff looked like a department store wax mannequin," says John Sweeney. "All his features were gone, like someone just wiped his face right off. All you could make out were his teeth. He was an invalid. His old lady torched him."

The chilling voice of Captain Cronin at the Fire College comes back: "When they're cooked, they smell like meat, like a roast burning in the oven."

"It's always tough to lose somebody," says Mike Keating. "But it doesn't really bother you until it's a kid.

"We were up on Laurel one night, near Geary. It turned into a third. We found the boy in his room. He was about 14. Just sitting there on the floor, Indian style."

In a bedroom crematory — charred corners of pennants and posters ironed to the steaming walls — the boy sits, "Indian-style," sudden death branded across his young face.

The firemen shiver at the sight of crisp bits of roasted flesh pasted to the boy's boiled arms. They force down the vomit rising in their throats and go outside to wait for the coroner.

"There's usually a lot of joking around and grab-ass when we're picking up after a fire," says Keating. "But that night, but you coulda heard a pin drop. You always wonder if you couldn't have done just a little more..."

He is interrupted by the bells. The bells. An explosion of silence rocks the room. Everyone stops to count the bells.

Four, pause. Five more, pause. One, another pause. Then the last three.

"That's good!" Sweeney yells. "Four-five-one-three, Page and Ashbury!' In 20 seconds the pumper is out the door, racing up Baker street. Across Hayes, Fell, Oak. Siren howling.

German shepherd on the corner, snout up, bays with the siren. Owner waves.

Right on Page to Ashbury. Nothing showing. False alarm.

The route back to the firehouse is notched with blackened window frames and boarded up Panhandle flats. Soiled souvenirs of 21's busier, dizzier days.

Cook points out each one like a tour guide. "Had a third there one night ... that joint went to a fourth . . . lost a girl in that one."

Back in the kitchen, Sweeney lights a cigarette, and stares thoughtfully at the glowing match.

The tiny flame dances before his round, freckled face and illuminates the tips of his reddish-blond moustache. He fans out the match with a flick of his wrist.

"Fire's weird," he says. "It just sorta floats around. People don't understand fire. It makes them think they can jump 15 stories and live, like that guy in that hotel in Korea.

"It's crazy. You can't see, you can't breathe. It's claustrophobic."

Sweeney, like many other firemen, is a third generation firefighter. His grandfather died in a fire here in 1900. His father wore the uniform 38 years. Firefighting in this town has always been a family affair.

"Wherever I go," he says, "I look for another way out. The movies, a restaurant, somebody's house for dinner. Everywhere."

Eleven thirty. Half the crew goes up to bed, the other half pores over the TV log. Cavett or Carson?

Twelve forty. Bells. Freeze! Count. Four, two, four, six. Broderick and Haight. Cook, Sweeney and Limberg go for the rig. Dwyer and Favilla hustle out behind them to the chief's buggy.

Days, weeks seem to pass before Keating and Ackenheil spin down the pole in turnouts a minute later. Ackenheil's eyes are closed all the way to the box. It's false. Back home.

Dwyer, a pleasant man with smooth round cheeks and smiling eyes has taken two drags off a fresh cigarette when the bells start in again. He stops to decipher the code.

Firemen count bells wherever they are. They count bells in a department store, on a streetcar, at a gas station. They always count.

But this box is for another engine company. George crushes his cigarette in a tiny metal ashtray and goes upstairs. "F...in' bells," he says, taking a toothbrush from his locker. "Probably be ringin' all night long."

Part 3 – Firemen as the Enemy

The dumpy third-floor flat is foggy with the putrid odor of burned food. The wreckage of dinner hisses in the kitchen sink.

The halls are filled with firemen, checking rooms, opening windows. Small children in pajamas, choking and bawling, paddle out of every room.

On the living room sofa, a middle-aged man is asleep. No, passed out. Dead drunk, embalmed in bad gin.

For ten seconds, he comes to and wonders what all the commotion is about and what are you guys doing here and what the hell's going, on and would you turn off the goddamned light, please.

In a fire, he would be dead.

During the ride back to the firehouse, Paul Davis shakes his head in disgust and shouts above the night wind punishing his face.

"That's what bothers me the most. You see those kids? They haven't got a chance. I mean, what kind of life is that? Hell, in a few years they'll be out on the corner pulling the box."

Back at Engine Company 21, Jimmy Cook bakes Irish soda bread. From scratch. The sweet aroma of raisins and rye floats through the kitchen as he gently draws the steaming loaf from the oven.

Before he can cut the first slice, Box 3521 comes in, and two minutes later Jimmy is inside a cavernous garage beneath a housing project at Webster and Fulton streets, swamping a flaming debris box with the tank line.

"Notice anything odd about this garage?" asks Chief Lane. "Must be 200 parking places in here, but no cars. These kids strip 'em-in a minute."

Cook, O'Brien and Davis are peculiarly silent as they rewind the smooth red hose on the big metal spool. They all remember like it was yesterday.

It happened six blocks from here, on a warm October night three years ago. They had responded with 14 Engine to Eddy and Laguna. Box 3366. It was a false alarm.

"Davis and Samuels were resetting the box," Jimmy says. "We heard this popping. It sounded like a lot of firecrackers.

"Then someone yelled: 'We're being shot at!'

"I sank down in the jump seat, and I heard Brodie say, 'I'm hit!' I jumped off the rig, then Samuels took one in the arm. I felt some chips hit my face from a ricochet."

Biff was in the other jump seat when he caught it. A copper-jacketed .30-06. The slug plowed into a chrome bar near the hose reel and sprayed fragments in Biff's eye and face. The sniper was never caught.

Of the 30 "incidents of harassment" against San Francisco firemen, firehouses and firefighting apparatus here last year, only one was a shooting. Half were reports of rocks or other missiles thrown at firemen and responding apparatus.

Because of this, the department has now put enclosed cabs on all the rigs working in the areas where most of these attacks have occurred. 21 Engine works the Western Addition, the Fillmore and the Haight. It has an enclosed cab.

Jimmy lights a cigarette and drops into a kitchen chair. He leans way back, so only the two rear legs are on the floor, and his rubber boots dangle above the linoleum.

Even in his crusty old turnouts and sweatshirt, he still bears an uncanny resemblance to actor Russ Tamblyn. The gymnast physique, the wavy hair, the tight lips.

"I was gonna quit after the shooting," he says. "Then I told myself, well, if I quit now it's because I'm running scared. And once I do it the first time, it'll be easy as hell the second time."

The fire alarm boxes in the Haight and the Fillmore are much quieter now. Indeed, they are even somewhat predictable.

But back when the streets of the Haight were redolent of incense and patchouli oil, and bouquets of flower children garnished every stoop, 21 Engine was making ten, 15 runs a day across the Panhandle.

"We got up there one night," says Cook, "and this hippie girl is lying under the box with her arm slashed open, bleeding like a sunuvabitch.

"So I'm holding her down, waiting for the ambulance, and she's fighting me like mad. And there I am, holding the pressure point on her arm to stop the bleeding, and she's calling me a mother-----g pig!

"All I had to do was let go and let her bleed to death. But then I thought, what the hell, she doesn't know what she's doing anyway.

"Besides, who the hell else was gonna do it?"

Part 4 – False Alarms and Worse

3:01 p.m.— Box 3622 hits on the bells.

3:05 p.m.— Box 3514.

3:11 p.m.— Box 3523.

Engine Company 34 is having a busy weekday afternoon. As usual.

At Engine Company 21, ten blocks away, Gil Moreno writes in a small notebook used to log fire alarm boxes and the time they are struck.

As the last of the three boxes comes in, he looks at the clock, then, with a throwaway gesture, says:

"School's out."

He is still jotting down the numbers when another box comes in. This one's for 21.

"Inside!" Moreno hollers into the intercom. "Four five-one-three, Page and Ashbury!" Seconds later, the pumper is out the door, rumbling across the Panhandle.

Cars pull over on Baker, block both lanes. Across the double yellow line. Red light. Run it! Black Chevy coming down Oak. Not gonna stop! Siren, air horn. Guy must be deaf! Brakes, hit the brakes! Misses by a foot. Okay, go.

At Page and Ashbury, six youngsters huddle around the fire alarm box, bobbing and weaving at the firemen.

A skinny girl, about 12 years old, roller skates over to Lieutenant Baggetta. She is pale, wearing a crinkled yellow dress.

"My little brother did it," she says. "He pulled it. I saw him do it."

"Really?" says Baggetta. "Where is he?"

"He ran home." she says. "Want me to get him? Will I get the five hundred dollars reward for turning him in?"

Moreno resets the hook inside Box 4513 and replaces the broken glass with a new one from the supply kept inside the small red door. Baggetta picks up the radio:

"Box 4513, a false alarm. Strike Signal 22. 21 Engine in service."

Last year, the San Francisco Fire Department responded to an average of 84 alarms every day. On average, 35 of them were false. Not all of them were pulled by children.

"I pulled a false alarm once," says one of the men, as he leaves his turnout coat and helmet on the rig and walks back to the kitchen.

"I came out of this bar one night about one-thirty with a big heat on, and I said to myself, 'I'm gonna wake those bastards up!'

"So I went to the box on the corner and broke the glass — it was real easy to break — and I pulled the hook. Then I stood there and laughed my ass off when they came down the street. It was my old company.

"Ever since I was a kid I wanted to know how it felt to pull one. So I did it. But I'm not proud of it ... Yeah, well . . . how 'bout a game of ping pong?"

Before he can serve the first volley, Box 4361 hits, and the game is forgotten as the rig tears down Grove to Central.

At the box, a little girl in pigtails tells Baggetta she pulled it by mistake.

"We was just foolin' around," she says. "I'm sorry."

The bells are ringing as the engine backs into the firehouse. Four, one, four, six. Divisadero and Grove.

"That's right down the street," yells Tishma.

At the corner. Baggetta tells Keating to drop the hydrant jumper. The rig grinds down the street to the front of a wheat-colored apartment house.

Tishma leaps down from the sidestep, goes to a side compartment, grabs a shiny aluminum extinguisher. O'Brien plucks an axe from its clamps over the front tire. They race into the building.

Up three flights, three steps at a time. Gotta quit smoking. In an open door. Down a long, curled hall. Smoke, banked down to the baseboard.

In the kitchen. Young man, mid-20s, hair to his collarbone, beard, pouring a bowlful of water on a sweaty sack of garbage. "It's out," he says.

"You live here?" Tishma asks, opening a window.

"Hell, no! Not in this dump. I live across the hall. Smelled the smoke and ran in here, saw this bag of garbage burning. Goddam hippies are gonna burn this place down yet."

O'Brien kicks the soppy heap to one side. He and Tishma kneel with their pocket knives to chisel away the crusty linoleum. Underneath, the wooden floor is badly charred, but not burning. Okay, Baggetta says, it's out, let's go.

"Too bad you had to drop all that line," says George Dwyer back in the firehouse. "But at least somebody had sense enough to pull the box.

"You wouldn't believe how some people stand around watching some joint going really good and wonder where the hell the firemen are.

"All that smoke and flame, everyone just assumes the firemen are coming. They say some woman watched the Pelosi house burn for 15 minutes. Weird. You either get a lot of calls or you don't get any.

"Or sometimes you get this: A woman calls, and she's excited as hell, and she yells into the phone:

"'IT'S A FIRE!

"And the dispatcher says: 'Where?'

"And she says: 'IN THE KITCHEN!' and hangs up!"

Part 5 – A Night of Flames and Screams

Lights. Lights on. Bloody fireballs explode behind the eyelids. Eyes, pinched shut, won't open. Bells. Can't count, groggy. More bells. Louder now.

Head off the pillow. Punchy. A voice, loud, electric. What? Where? Up on one elbow, waking up now. The voice again, like thunder. Clearer this time:

"Fell and Buchanan! Engine! Chief! Fell and Buchanan! Everybody, get out!"

Roll out, stand up. Boots, there. Yeah, the boots. Left foot, right foot. Pull up the pants, clip the waist ring. Go, GO! The pole, go for the pole. Hit it. Down, down... thump. Run, run.

Engine, get on. Awake now. Mouth, dry. Helmet on, heavy. Coat, smells of diesel, fumes, old fires. Fingers still puffy, fumble with the clips. The clock, look at the clock. Five something.

Out, out. Out in 45 seconds. Grove, Scott, Hayes. Past the paper boys and garbage trucks. Faster. Icy wind spanking the face. Shivering, eyes watery. Gloves, that's it, put on the gloves.

Up Buchanan, two blocks away, smoke tumbles out the second-floor windows of a four-story apartment house. A soft, Confederate gray mushroom speckled with tiny orange cinder balls. Working fire.

14 Engine at the corner, dropping big line. They're first due, gotta get water on the fire. Right now. No time to strap on a Scott Air-Pak, the fireman's third lung. Seconds mean lives, get a line to work. Any rescues to be made, the truckmen or the rescue squad will make them.

Flames are blowing out the windows in both rooms and up the outside wall of the tiny apartment. The officer of 14 Engine races out, gulping air on the run.

"We're takin' a helluva beating in there, Chief," he says. "Door was jammed like a bastard. First room's gone already. Tryin' to keep it out of the hall, dunno if we can hold it. We need Scotts."

The chief sends 21 to the floor above the fire to help ventilate the smoke and heat, take the pressure off 14. Going up, the stairs are crowded with barefoot people in nightclothes hop-scotching over hose on the way out.

On the third floor, a sucking liquid heat, camouflaged in bleary smoke, heaves against the ceiling.

Mike Keating kicks in the door to the apartment above the fire. The men pour in, opening windows that will, breaking those that won't.

Behind them, a man from 5 Truck hacks at the hot floor with his ax. Another skewers the walls and ceiling with a long iron hook.

Peppery smoke from the fire floor below bubbles up through the ax holes. Jagged chunks of chalky plaster and wood rain from the ceiling. Powdery dust clings like fresh snow to helmet brims and cheekbones.

Every breath of boiling air sears the throat and lungs. Long rubbery gobs of mucus ooze from the nostrils.

A hoarse, agonized scream slices through the ceiling from the room above, electrifying the men.

In the hall, Pete Ackenheil instantly drops the coiled bundle of hose he is carrying and races upstairs.

Blinded by smoke, he relies on his ears to lead him through a narrow doorway and into a small room where a screeching woman lies on her bed. Her wheelchair is nearby.

She is a bony black woman in her 40s or 50s. She is lying on her back in a long, creamy nightgown, paralyzed with terror, screaming wildly.

Pete squats firmly beside the bed, slides a weight-lifter's arm beneath her knees, another behind her back. He lifts her gently and carries her out and down the stairs.

As he passes the third-floor landing, the sweat is popping out of Pete's forehead, and his face is glowing red, as though his whole head is lighted from the inside.

He takes each step slowly, carefully side-stepping the bulging hose. In the lobby, Pete sets the woman in a lumpy armchair, beside a wilting rubber tree plant.

"You're OK now," he says. "Just take it easy. Do you want a drink of water? You'll be all right, now, just sit here and try to calm down. OK?"

One of the other tenants comes back inside the lobby to comfort the woman and Pete returns to the fire.

The fire is out now, except for a few stubborn window sashes that continue to flare up again as the truckmen shovel charred debris into heavy canvas tarpaulins.

Outside, an ice-blue sky.

The engine sparkles like a teacher's apple in the early sunlight. The men shed their turnout coats and helmets and pass around cigarettes while they pick up.

They work quickly because they will all be off duty when the engine rolls home.

George Dwyer straddles a leaky hose coupling to sip the wet spray. He stands up slowly and looks at his watch.

"Six-thirty," he says. "Not bad. I sure hope my old lady's up when I get home. I look forward to her after a good fire."

Part 6 – The Talk in the Firehouse

Eight-thirty on a crisp, flawless San Francisco Saturday morning. Gonna be hot, they figure.

Fireman Jim Thompson sets his coffee on the kitchen table beside the latest issue of Gourmet, "the magazine of good living."

"It's a pleasure to come to work," he says. His face is suntanned and fresh, his teeth white, hair yellow. Picture of health.

"There's no politics or competition here like there is in the business world. We all get along great.

"No matter how intense a man is, firemen keep everything at a basic level. And that makes this a smooth-running operation."

In the communications room at Engine Company 21, Bill Jasey cradles the house telephone and scribbles an illegible message on a small green blackboard. He shouts into the intercom:

"Still alarm for the Engine! Fell and Baker, auto on fire!"

A minute later, the pumper swerves into the Department of Motor Vehicles parking lot. A new turquoise Lincoln is smothered in smoke and flame.

Pete Ackenheil spins the tank line off the hose reel. They pry the crumpled, molten hood with an ax. Pete gives the engine block a quick washdown. Duck soup. Back to quarters.

"It's like being on a football team," says Les Terry. "It doesn't seem like work. Every time we go out, it's to help somebody. Every time a cop does his job, he offends somebody. We have great rapport with people.

"But take something like a stupid mattress fire. You're the guy goin' in there, and you're starving for oxygen, and the roaches and everyone else is takin' a hike. That's what wears a guy's heart out."

"Remember that time we were making a lead into that place over on Diviz?" Jimmy Cook asks. "This room is dusty as hell, and I'm at the door waiting for 'em to charge the line.

"Then I see Davis coming out with this baby in his arms. I didn't even know he was in there.

"He comes out coughin' like hell, and he's got this baby, and he's thinking hero all the way down the stairs. Class A medal for sure.

"A few minutes later I see him tryin' to sneak the kid back in. When he got outside with it, he found out he'd made this great rescue of a kid's doll."

"Yeah," Dwyer says amid the laughter, "firemen do crazy things sometimes. If you climbed Mt. Everest, you'd probably find a fireman at the top."

Tony Simi returns from the market and begins to prepare lunch. Spareribs with pineapple sauce, French fries, garlic bread.

Cook pokes around in the groceries and spies a plump standing rib roast.

"Hey, you guys," he says, "guess what, we're havin' for dinner? Elephant's foot. Terrific, Tony boy, terrific. We had that last watch."

"Don't worry, Jimmy," says Sonny Armada. "I'm cooking next watch. My special recipe."

"That right, Sonny?" Ackenheil asks, "Well don't forget we've got an extra man here. You'd better get a bigger dog this time."

Twelve forty-five. Young couple driving up Masonic. At Golden Gate, smoke under the hood. Man jumps out, runs to the small red box on the corner, breaks the glass, pulls the hook.

Ackenheil is halfway through his second helping of spareribs when the bells ricochet off the kitchen walls 15 seconds later. Four . . . four . . . six . . . two. Golden Gate and Masonic.

The men hustle out to the rig. John Sweeney skips out from the john, zipping up his pants.

"Chrissakes!" he hollers, running for the backstep. "A guy takes one lousy dump all day ..."

Another auto fire. Dwyer says sometimes a guy calls to say his car is on fire — but forgets to say it's in his garage. Next thing you know, third alarm.

So when a box comes in, the old-timers move just as fast as the rookies. They never know.

"One night," Thompson says, "Keating got halfway to a box before he noticed he'd forgotten his turnouts. He was standing on the backstep in his skivvies! But that's not as embarrassing as getting left behind."

"When I first came in the department four years ago," says Sonny, "other firemen told me, 'Never tell people what you do for a living, and if they find out, never tell them how much you make.'

"You see, if your neighbor sees you home mowing your lawn for two or three days during the week, he wonders what the hell kinda job you've got.

"Then he finds out you're a fireman, and that you work 24 hours and get 48 off. And he finds out you make eleven hundred a month for it.

"So when the next election comes along with something on the ballot for firemen, he says to himself:

"'Geez, that guy next door is a fireman, and he's home all the time. I ain't gonna vote for that. He makes too much dough as it is.'

"That doesn't really happen so much anymore, though. I tell people I'm a fireman. I'm proud of it. And they're really interested, you know.

"Most people only see us on the rig, passing them on the street. They don't know where we came from or where we're going.

"That's why this is a mystery job. When the rig comes home, and that big door rolls down, nobody really knows what goes on inside."

* * *

Some firefighters complained to the newspaper about certain aspects of the series, as might be expected. Surprisingly the biggest complaint wasn't about the firefighter who admitted pulling a false alarm late one night, but about this phrase describing my first ride to a fire: "Gotta be doing sixty, seventy maybe."

I knew, of course, that fire engines rarely exceed 35-40 miles per hour, but I wanted to convey what it felt like riding on the side step of the apparatus with the wind slapping my face. Several firemen from the chief on down feared people would think they were really flying across town at dangerously high speeds.

The comments and feedback were otherwise all positive. Several months later, in April 1973, I received a letter from Howard Mc-

Clennan, president of the International Association of Fire Fighters, based in Washington, D.C.

"The International Officers and the Public Relations Committee of the International Association of Fire Fighters, AFL-CIO, offer their congratulations to you for having been designated a second-prize winner in the 1973 International Awards Program," McClennan wrote. "Approximately 300 entries were received in the major categories, so the task of the judges was far from an easy one." The award cited the series "for outstanding achievement and distinguished reporting in bringing to public attention the efforts of professional firefighters to safeguard their community from fire and disaster."

A few weeks later Chief Calden and Jim Ferguson, president of the Fire Fighters Local 798, held a ceremony at Engine Co. 21 to make a formal presentation of the award and a check for $250, a portion of which I gave back to the guys in the firehouse toward a dinner.

Three weeks after that, Congressman Robert H. Steele of Connecticut made note of the award and entered my opening article of the series into the Congressional Record. "The quality of the winning entry is very high, and in my estimation deserving of the widest readership, including the attention of my colleagues," Rep. Steele said on the floor of the House.

The Dozen Dangerous Lives of Pat Wolfe

By Duffy Jennings

A man who had been a different man sat in the small restaurant booth.

He was a long-haired freak strung out on heroin, a slick cocaine dealer from Miami, a wild biker in leathers and boots, a shrewd marijuana smuggler from Ohio.

He was Bill Borders and William Richardson, Pat Gordon, and a man named Jesler. He was Bill Yost too, and The Wollman. All of them.

You couldn't really see them, but they were there. All the private ghosts of Patrick Wolfe, banding him in a very private sort of way.

ALONE

Wolfe sat alone in the booth, looking oddly uneasy in his gray knit suit, blue and white shirt, navy blue tie. He is 33.

"When I became a policeman," he said, "my whole life changed."

Three years ago, Wolfe — a rookie cop who'd never even seen marijuana — slipped quietly into San Francisco's enemy underworld as an undercover narcotics officer.

He grew his hair long, and grew a beard. He changed his name. He studied the language of the street. He bought a motorcycle.

WET

He fell effortlessly into the role. He became a none of a thousand faces with identifiers and never stories to match. He was tough, and versatile, and possessed a keen wit that kept him alive — barely.

He worked on hundreds of cases, made some 1300 narcotics "buys," and figured in so many arrests he can only say they're "in the thousands."

He is an assistant inspector now, with a fresh haircut and shave, and back in the office.

"I'm glad it's over," he said, a bit unconvincingly. "You get down in the dumps because of the way you look. That was the worst part.

"Even when I wasn't working, I couldn't put on some decent clothes and go downtown for dinner. I had to being dirty and grubby.

"I would never have long hair now. Or a beard. Maybe a mustache. But I wasn't brought up that way. I'm very conservative. I always have been."

The simple fact that Wolfe stayed in undercover work for so long attests to his effectiveness in the role.

"People used to talk to me about me," he said. "I sat in a restaurant one day with a guy who spent an hour warning me about Pat Wolfe. He even gave me a perfect description of myself.

"I thought he was trying to tell me he knew who I was, and I was getting pretty nervous. But when he left, he sold me two balloons of heroin.

"I used to say, 'Just call me The Wollman.' Or sometimes I liked to say my name was Jesler, and even when I busted 'em, I'd say I was turning 'em in for silver."

Sergeant John O'Rea, Wolfe's immediate supervisor, spoke of his uncanny ability to fool some of the people all of the time.

"You wanna know how good he was?" says O'Rea. "He would make the connection, make a few buys, arrest the suspect, and testify against him in court. And when he got out of jail, the man would sell Pat more narcotics."

Wolfe often got busted along with his prey. He was taken to jail, booked, mugged, fingerprinted and locked up. In court his real identity, one man was mistaken...

'People just thought I was another bad guy on the street with a gun'

Patrick Wolfe in disguise

Patrick Wolfe's real appearance

There were times, too, when his arrest was not contrived.

"I was walking along upper Grant avenue one night with this dealer. A radio car pulled up, and the officer threw us both in the back seat.

"He gave me this long lecture about why didn't I get a haircut and look for a job in...

stead of hanging around with guys like this. Later, I went over to Central station and left him a note: 'Thanks for the lecture,' and signed it 'Officer Wolfe.'"

Although Wolfe said less than 5 per cent of his cases involved marijuana, it was one grass bust that gave him the most satisfaction.

"I rented a truck for this

guy and he delivered 384 kilos to me at a San Francisco motel. I convinced him I had $58,000 to pay for it, but I didn't have a cent.

"He was no hot from loading all this stuff, he went in the room at the motel and took a shower. When he come out in a towel, I busted him. That case took three months."

Wolfe's secret identity gradually began to overcome him.

ROUTE

He began taking a long, roundabout route home in Daly City.

He would confer often with his superiors, sometimes on a secret phone installed in his home on which dealers would call him to set up meetings. His wife and young son were instructed never to answer it.

His neighbors began to shun him, either for his looks or because they knew what he was doing.

He endured three years of insults and degradation from close friends as well as strangers, and was often told to leave a bar or restaurant because of his shaggy appearance.

'GAME'

"It's just like playing a part," he said. "For each case I'd be somebody different, whatever seemed to fit. It was almost like a game — except I had the advantage.

"But it was hard for me to adjust to a 30-cent vocabulary and mingle with people that I had nothing in common with.

"I never married a badge or handcuffs. I always had a gun, but not a police gun. A .45, whatever. People just thought I was another bad guy on the street with a gun.

"There's so much violence connected with narcotics. People have no idea how much violence there is. Right people I knew during the past three years have been murdered. That's the worst part of it, the violence."

Violence, though, is no stranger to Wolfe. He was born and reared in a Spring-field, Ohio neighborhood where "fighting was a way of life."

After high school, he joined the Navy, but failed to make regular promotions because of his short temper and quick fists. He spent a year in Vietnam as a frogman.

He was in the Navy for ten years. His last duty station was on Treasure Island, and after his discharge he joined the San Francisco Police Department.

"I figured I was going to be a policeman for 10 years," he said. "I wanted to do something interesting."

His undercover work hastened him even further against narcotics, particularly when he saw 16-year-old shooting heroin.

He bought a Four Le Mans, a Pontiac was pushed discontinued in 1938, at a pawn shop and wore it constantly. "It's a blue Max," he said. "My good luck charm. I still wear it.

"I'm just trying to adjust back to normal now. It's still

hard for me to carry on a normal conversation.

"It was a dangerous job, sure. But I suppose I'd do it again if they wanted me to."

Wolfe glanced casually over his shoulder, a reflex he may have to live with for a very long time. He knows there are those who would like to kill Bill Borders, or Jesler, or The Wollman.

"It was very lonely," he said, as he and the dozen other men who live inside him walked quietly outside into the pouring rain.

Methadone Center Security Blasted

By Charles Petit

A city official said yesterday he "wandered around unchallenged" in three San Francisco methadone clinics and "could have walked out with all I wanted."

Dr. Nicholas Cummings, a member of the city's Mental Health Advisory Board, told the board members, "I would be loath to recommend expansion of the program" until security measures are tightened.

Cummings was made chairman last month of a committee to evaluate the program, which treats about 500 heroin addicts with daily doses of Methadone.

REPORT

A full report won't be ready until next spring, he said. However, just to get it started, he said he walked into three clinics unannounced during the past several weeks.

"I was very disturbed by what I found," he said.

He told the board he was "not bothered" by staff members at any of the clinics, even when he walked into where the methadone was stored. I could have walked out with all I wanted."

He said he was also disturbed "to find addict counselors still on drugs," and these off-hands still on have methadone "after three years."

STREET

Methadone in city containers is found "in large amounts" on the street, said Cummings, giving as his

sources persons in the sheriff's department.

When asked whether his position might have given him greater access than the public might have, Cummings said, "They didn't know who I was. I didn't introduce myself until I got ready to leave."

The clinics he visited, he said, were at 239 Hyde street, 19th and Howard streets, and 1167 Van Ness avenue — the program's headquarters.

When asked yesterday afternoon how methadone is safeguarded in the six clinics in the city, a spokesman for the Methadone Maintenance Program of the Department of Public Health said, "It's always in a safe, or under direct observation of staff members."

The spokesman, Tony Sanchez, the program's public information director, said he "doubted very much" that Cummings could have walked out with any methadone, or that he did indeed wander unmolested in any of the clinics.

San Francisco Chronicle

Published by
The Chronicle Publishing Co.
901 Mission Street
San Francisco, California
94119

Second-Class Postage Paid
at San Francisco and at
additional Mailing Offices.

Monthly by Carrier
Daily & Sunday $4.75
Daily only $3.25
Sunday only $1.70

CHAPTER 30:
Narc

It was hard to go back to my regular general assignment duties after those exciting weeks with the SFFD. One day in November 1972, the city editor said, "There's a cop named Patrick Wolfe who's been an undercover narc for the past three years and now wants tell his story. Go talk to him."

I was drawn to stories about cops and police work, and I frequently imagined what it would be like to be a police officer. If I hadn't found the newspaper, I might have joined the SFPD. Wearing that uniform and all its accessories appealed to me. I loved uniforms, from the moment I buttoned up my first little league jersey and heard my spikes clicking on the pavement to my Marine fatigues, starched and ironed and tucked into spit-shined boots. In a uniform I felt like I belonged to something, that others had my back, a need I traced back to growing up and feeling alone.

But after two years covering cops and crime, I'd seen up close how their daily duties differed widely from the glamorized version we saw on our TV and movie screens. Two months before this assignment, the new weekly TV crime drama, *The Streets of San Francisco*, starring Karl Malden and Michael Douglas, made its debut. It was a hit that ran for five years, and it showcased the city in nearly every scene, but the script and action were, of course, all Hollywood.

Real police work could be tedious, frustrating, depressing, and dangerous. Police were under attack by radical groups nationwide, and six San Francisco officers had died in the line of duty over the previous two years. I may have dodged a bullet by choosing another line of work, but I remained fascinated by the motivations of those who chose it. I was not disappointed by Patrick Wolfe.

I met Wolfe in a restaurant on Ocean Avenue. He was a square-jawed, clean-cut man in his 30s, with thick black hair nicely trimmed, his face clean-shaven and he wore a suit and tie.

My story ran in the paper November 15, 1972.

* * *

A man who had been a dozen different men sat in the small restaurant booth.

He was a long-haired freak strung out on heroin, a slick cocaine dealer from Miami, a wild biker in leathers and boots, a shrewd marijuana smuggler from Ohio.

He was Bill Borders and William Richardson. Pat Gorders, and a man named Judas. He was Bill Fent too, and The Wolfman. All of them.

You couldn't really see them, but they were there. All the private ghosts of Patrick Wolfe, haunting him in a very private sort of way.

Wolfe sat alone in the booth, looking oddly uneasy in his gray knit suit, blue and white shirt, navy blue tie. He is 33.

"When I became a policeman," he said, "my whole life changed."

Three years ago, Wolfe — a rookie cop who'd never even seen marijuana – slipped quietly into San Francisco's seamy underworld as an undercover narcotics officer.

He grew his hair long and grew a beard. He changed his name. He studied the language of the street. He bought a motorcycle.

He fell effortlessly into the role. He became a man of a thousand faces with identities and cover stories to match. He was tough, and versatile, and possessed a keen wit that kept him alive — barely.

He worked on hundreds of cases, made some 1500 narcotics "buys," and figured in so many arrests he can only say they're "in the thousands."

He is an assistant inspector now, with a fresh haircut and shave, and back in the office.

"I'm glad it's over," he said, a bit unconvincingly. "You get down in the dumps because of the way you look. That was the worst part.

"Even when I wasn't working, I couldn't put on some decent clothes and go downtown for dinner. I hated being dirty and grubby.

"I would never have long hair now. Or a beard. Maybe a mustache. But I wasn't brought up that way. I'm very conservative. I always have been."

The simple fact that Wolfe stayed in undercover work for so long attests to his effectiveness in the role.

"People used to talk to me about me," he said. "I sat in a restaurant one day with a guy who spent an hour warning me about Pat Wolfe. He even gave me a perfect description of myself.

"I thought he was trying to tell me he knew who I was, and I was getting pretty nervous. But when he left, he sold me two balloons of heroin.

"I used to say, 'Just call me The Wolfman.' Or sometimes I liked to say my name was Judas, and when I busted 'em, I'd say I was turning 'em in for silver."

Sergeant John O'Shea, Wolfe's immediate supervisor, spoke of his uncanny ability to fool some of the people all of the time.

"You wanna know how good he was?" says O'Shea. "He would make the connection, make a few buys, arrest the suspect, and testify against him in court. And when he got out of jail, the man would sell Pat more narcotics."

Wolfe often got busted along with his prey. He was taken to jail, booked, mugged, fingerprinted, and locked up. In court the next morning, one man was missing.

There were times, too, when his arrest was not contrived.

"I was walking along upper Grant avenue one night with this dealer. A radio car pulled up, and the officer threw us both in the back seat.

"He gave me this long lecture about why didn't I get a haircut and look for a job instead of hanging around with guys like this. Later, I went over to Central station and left him a note: 'Thanks for the lecture,' and signed it Officer Wolfe."

Although Wolfe said fewer than 3 per cent of his cases involved marijuana, it was one grass bust that gave him the most satisfaction.

"I rented a truck for this guy and he delivered 204 kilos to me at a San Francisco motel. I convinced him I had $38,000 to pay for it, but I didn't have a cent.

"He was so hot from loading all this stuff, he went in the room at the motel and took a shower. When he came out in a towel, I busted him. That case took three months."

Wolfe's secret identity gradually began to overcome him.

He began taking a long, roundabout route home in Daly City. He would confer often with his superiors, sometimes on a secret phone installed in his home on which dealers would call him to set up meetings. His wife and young son were instructed never to answer it.

His neighbors began to shun him, either for his looks or because they knew what he was doing.

He endured three years of insults and degradation from close friends as well as strangers, and was often told to leave a bar or restaurant because of his shaggy appearance.

"It's just like playing a part," he said. "For each case I'd be somebody different, whatever seemed to fit. It was almost like a game — except I had the advantage.

"But it was hard for me to adjust to a 50-word vocabulary and mingle with people that I had nothing in common with.

"I never carried a badge or handcuffs. I always had a gun, but not a police gun. A .45, .38, whatever. People just thought I was another bad guy on the street with a gun.

"There's so much violence connected with narcotics. People have no idea how much violence there is. Eight people I knew during the past three years have been murdered. That's the worst part of it, the violence."

Violence, though, is no stranger to Wolfe. He was born and reared in a Springfield, Ohio neighborhood where "fighting was a way of life."

After high school, he joined the Navy, but failed to make regular promotions because of his short temper and quick fists. He spent a year in Vietnam as a frogman.

He was in the Navy for ten years. His last duty station was on Treasure Island, and after his discharge he joined the San Francisco Police Department.

"I figured I was going to be a policeman for 20 years," he said. "I wanted to do something interesting."

His undercover work hardened him even further against narcotics, particularly when he saw 10-year-olds shooting heroin.

He bought a Pour Le Merite, a Prussian war medal discontinued in 1918, at a pawn shop and wore it constantly. "It's a Blue Max," he said. "My good luck charm. I still wear it.

"I'm just trying to adjust back to normal now. It's still hard for me to carry on a normal conversation.

"It was a dangerous job, sure. But I suppose I'd do it again if they wanted me to."

Wolfe glanced casually over his shoulder, a reflex he may have to live with for a very long time. He knows there are those who would like to kill Bill Borders, or Judas, or The Wolfman.

"It was very lonely," he said, as he and the dozen other men who live inside him walked quietly outside into the pouring rain.

Inside

S.F. police terrorized occupants of a Grove street apartment house in their Zebra search, two residents charged. Page 2.

Police have about a Zebra-type cult of murderers seven months ago, an intended murder victim disclosed. Page 3.

One conversation after another in the transcripts returned to the idea of phasing the rap for Watergate on John Mitchell. Page 6.

A House Judiciary subcommittee approved rules permitting Mr. Nixon's lawyer to participate. Page 7.

The edited transcripts reveal the close relationship that built up between Mr. Nixon and the

TOP OF THE NEWS

first Watergate prosecutor. Page 9.

The Northrop Corp. and its chairman pleaded guilty to illegally contributing $150,000 to President Nixon's re-election campaign. Page 10.

Three meetings in Mr. Nixon's office on April 16 provided some of the most striking conversations in the edited transcripts. Page 12.

The U.S. Senate passed a bill establishing no - fault insurance systems in every state. Page 12.

The king of Jordan laid down his terms for agreement of forces with Israel. Page 13.

The Senate defeated an effort to give Mr. Nixon power once more to control wages and prices. Page 13.

Anwar Sadat said he is confident that Henry Kissinger will achieve an Israeli-Syrian disengagement. Page 13.

A report released yesterday implied that the coastal protection commissions have leaned toward the developers. Page 18.

Twenty-two women, who had waited all night outside the Carpenters Union Hall, applied for cabinetmaking apprenticeships yesterday. Page 19.

Misty-eyed fans reliving the '50s are flocking to see singer Johnny Mathis who's back on the road again. Page 20.

Hardsell ads on TV for children are softening, due to law suits and profit motives. Page 22.

The United Nations adopted a third world economic aid plan in preference to one offered by the U.S. Page 24.

The stock market enjoyed a rally on the end of wage and price controls and hopes for lower interest rates. Page 52.

Weather

Bay Area: Fair Thursday. Lows, in the mid 40s to low 50s; highs in the 70s. Page 26.

A 'Victim' Tells His Story

See Page 3

San Francisco Chronicle

**** FINAL

The Largest Daily Circulation in Northern California

110th Year No. 122   ****   THURSDAY, MAY 2, 1974   GArfield 1-1111   15 CENTS

House Committee Vote

Probers Say Nixon Failed to Comply

Dramatic Raid at Dawn — See Page 2

7 Blacks Arrested In Zebra Killings

Suspects in S.F. Seized For Murder, Conspiracy-- A 'Death Angels' Cult

By Duffy Jennings

Squads of heavily armed police arrested seven black men in San Francisco yesterday as suspects in the series of Zebra street shootings.

Mayor Joseph L. Alioto said the suspects were members of a "vicious ring of murderers called 'Death Angels,'" a group "dedicated to the murder and mutilation of whites and disident blacks."

Oakland Attorney Clinton White, retained to defend the seven suspects, denied they belonged to a group called Death Angels and said he understood that they were hard-working Black Muslim members or Temple 26 of the Nation of Islam.

"I can say this: none of these men are involved in Zebra killers. I've talked to all of them," White said.

Chief of Police Donald M. Scott said officers carried out simultaneous pre-dawn raids on "more than one location," but refused to say where or how many. The Chronicle learned that two men were arrested at a Grove street apartment.

An eighth suspect, according to Alioto, was already being held. He is believed to be Larose Doctor, who was convicted last December of assaulting a Pacific Gas and Electric Co. employee the month before and sentenced to prison.

Another man, Jessie Lee Cooks, 30, is serving a life sentence at San Quentin prison for the murder of Frances R. Rose, 28, of San Francisco. She was named by Alioto as a victim of the "Death Angels."

Miss Saari, a physical therapist was shot while in her car near the University of California Extension at 35 Laguna street last October 30.

Cooks pleaded guilty to first-degree murder and was sent to prison on December 14.

None of the seven arrested yesterday offered any resistance, according to Chief Scott.

He identified those arrested as:

J. C. Simon, 29; Larry C. Green, 22; Manuel Moore, 29; Tom Manney, 25; Dwight Stallings, 25; Edgar Douglas Barton, 28; and Clarence Jamerson, 27.

Scott refused to give details or occupations say they were present, saying:

"There is still a hunk of a

Back Page Col. 1

Alioto Says Slayings Are Nationwide

By Jerry Carroll

The seven suspected Zebra killers arrested yesterday belong to what is believed to be a well-heeled nationwide cult of fanatics "dedicated to the murder and mutilation of whites and dissident blacks," Mayor Joseph L. Alioto said yesterday.

He said a concerted drive by local, state and federal law enforcement agencies is "desperately needed" to crack the shadowy organization but it reveals new members to replace those arrested.

Alioto's call for the crackdown met with a chilly reception a short time later from state Attorney General Evelle Younger and Charles Paton, special FBI agent in charge for San Francisco.

Younger said, "We have no evidence of a statewide conspiracy. Regarding Mayor Alioto's comments, I have no comment on that. Whether it is true or untrue is for him to determine."

For his part, Paton said he has no information that any federal law has been broken. "If they get a warrant for unlawful flight to avoid prosecution we could come in," he said.

But U.S. Attorney James Browning—who has met with Younger but not Paton —said, if requested, the FBI could enter the case

Back Page Col. 2

When Nixon Knew Of Aides' Roles

By Bob Woodward and Carl Bernstein
Washington Post

Washington

The edited transcripts of President Nixon's recorded White House conversations indicate that Mr. Nixon was aware of the possible involvement of his top aides well before March 21, 1973, the date he has maintained he first learned of the Watergate coverup.

The tapes show that on Sept. 15, 1972, and Feb. 28, March 13 and March 20, 1973, Mr. Nixon, a lawyer, made statements, asked questions and received indications that indicated he knew there was far more to the Watergate story than government investigators said they had been told by that time.

For example, on March 13, 1973, according to the transcripts, White House Counsel John W. Dean III specifically told Mr. Nixon that White House aide Gordon Strachan was aware of the illegal Watergate bugging operation during the period in still more telephones at Democratic National Headquarters were tapped.

"I will be damned," the President responded, then referring to his White House chief of staff, H.R. Haldeman. Mr. Nixon added: "Well that is the problem in Bob's case." Strachan worked directly for Haldeman in the White House.

Advised by Dean that investigators "would

Back Page Col. 6

White House Bid To Kill Subpoena

Washington

President Nixon's lawyers moved to quash a prosecution subpoena yesterday and hinted strongly they are moving toward a Supreme Court showdown over whether the White House must give any more tapes and documents to Watergate investigators.

In a motion filed to U.S. District Court, the President's attorneys asked Judge John Sirica to quash a subpoena seeking tapes and records of 64 White House conversations for use by the Watergate special prosecutor in the coverup trial of seven defendants.

A spokesman for the office of Special Prosecutor Leon Jaworski said the White House motion would be resisted. A hearing was set for this morning in Sirica's courtroom.

"Yes, we will resist," the prosecutor's office said. "This is material we need. We will do everything we have to to secure it."

While White House chief Watergate lawyer James St. Clair at a news conference earlier in the day had avoid-

ed a direct answer to questions about a Supreme Court fight, the motion filed later indicated he is preparing to take the battle to the high court.

At his news conference, St. Clair said the transcripts turned over to the House Judiciary Committee Tuesday contained all that the committee and the prosecutor need.

In the petition asking that Jaworski's subpoena be quashed, St. Clair maintained that the material sought covered "confidential communications of the President" and that it should be up to the President "rather than for a court," to decide when the public interest requires that he exercise his constitutional privilege "to refuse to produce 'information.'"

The motion was accompanied by a statement to the court signed by Mr. Nixon saying portions of the conversations sought had already been made public but that the rest are confidential and that it would be against the public interest for him to turn them over.

Associated Press

Pay Negotiations Set

Brief Dock Walkout Ends

About 12,000 dock workers who shut down Pacific Coast ports yesterday will be back to work today as union leaders and officials of the Pacific Maritime Association meet to hammer out worker demands for higher pay.

The announcement that workers would return to their jobs came early last night, following lengthy meetings. Union officials said their men were expected to report to their regular assigned jobs this morning.

The sudden shutdown of West Coast ports was called by the International Longshoremen and Warehousemen's Union to dramatize demands for pay increases now that government wage controls have expired.

Talks will begin today on that issue between the union

and the association, both sides announced.

Union leaders said they refused the right to reopen the wage terms of their contract two years ago, after the Pay Board cut 14 cents an hour from settlement terms of the longshoremen's 130-day strike.

Yesterday's walkout—conducted without picketing in many places — tied up 10 major ports — tied up cargo ships in the Bay Area and more than 30 others at ports from San Diego and Seattle.

Union spokesmen reiterated to the action as a "demonstration" rather than a strike.

Union leader Harry Bridges and Edmond J. Flynn, president of the 130-member Pacific Maritime

Association, met to discuss the dispute yesterday afternoon.

The union had presented its demands in two earlier meetings with the management association in recent weeks.

PMA spokesmen said yesterday's walkout was called without the normal 84 - hour notice. They also disputed the union's contention that the contract still has a wage opener.

A new two-year contract was signed last summer.

"The agreement contains a no-strike clause, and we fully expect the union to live up to its commitment," a spokesman said.

Union officials said resentment has been smoldering

Back Page Col. 6

Germans Place The Spy Blame

Bonn

West Germany's counter-intelligence service yesterday blamed the chancellery for giving a "top-secret" security rating to Guenter Guillaume, the personal aide of chancellor Willy Brandt arrested as suspicion of espionage.

The service took the unusual step of issuing a statement to news agencies here following reports that counter-intelligence chief Guenter Nollau had offered his resignation in connection with the spy scandal.

Reuters

ONE OF THE ZEBRA SUSPECTS AT THE HALL OF JUSTICE
Police put jacket over his head to hide his identity

By Clem Albers

Index

Comics	54
Deaths	26
Entertainment	42
Finance	52
People	20
TV-Radio	40
Vital Statistics	27
Weather	26

— Chronicle Publishing Co. 1974.

189

CHAPTER 31:
A Dark Winter

By comparison with 1972, most of 1973 was uneventful for me. I wrote articles about a shortage of roses for Valentine's Day, a teachers' strike, the so-called "Fillmore Arsonist" who set twenty-eight fires in a short span, a U.S. Customs dog that found forty-four pounds of heroin at San Francisco International airport, the city's critical shortage of firemen, the deaths of two Oakland police officers in the fiery crash of their department helicopter, and an interview with state questioned-documents expert Sherwood Morrill about his knowledge of the Zodiac's handwriting. Until December, my biggest story was a front-page piece in May about the grand opening of the forty-million-dollar, twenty-story Hyatt Regency San Francisco (now the Embarcadero Hyatt), with its innovative atrium lobby and revolving rooftop restaurant.

The last quarter of 1973 and early months of 1974, however, brought another violent new chapter to the Bay Area.

Beginning in October 1973, a group of extremist Black Muslims carried out a six-month series of random attacks of mostly white men and women on the streets of San Francisco. They killed at least fifteen people, wounded several others and, some authorities believed, may have slain more than seventy people in all. By year's end, nine were already dead and four others had survived, including future San Francisco Mayor Art Agnos, who was shot twice in the chest and stomach outside a community meeting in Potrero Hill December 13.

In an unrelated attack the night of November 6, Oakland Schools Superintendent Marcus Foster was shot to death and his assistant superintendent, Robert Blackburn, was wounded in the parking lot behind the administration building as they left a school board meeting. Three men confronted Foster and shot him eight times with hollow-point, cyanide-tipped bullets. Two days after the shootings, in a letter to the *Chronicle*, a group calling itself the Symbionese Liberation Army claimed responsibility, blaming Foster for what they misconstrued was his support of a program requiring ID cards for all high school students. My colleague Tim Findley, writing about the letter, reported the group had issued a "shoot on sight order" that would remain in effect for other school officials "until such time as all political police are removed from our schools and all photo and other forms of identification are stopped."

In a letter received by the *Oakland Tribune* November 15, the SLA, now calling itself the Western Regional Youth Unit of the Symbionese Liberation Army, had rescinded its "death warrants" because Oakland school officials were obeying its demands. I was assigned to write the *Chronicle* article about the latest letter. "The fascist Board of Education has made an attempt to heed and respect the rights and wishes of the people by stating that they will not continue to take part in crimes committed against the children and the life of the people," I quoted the letter as saying. It was certainly not the last we would hear from the SLA.

Meanwhile, the random street murders in San Francisco continued. On December 22, I wrote that Police Chief Donald Scott announced investigators had linked five of the shootings to the "same person or group," and that a special task force had been formed to work on the case. Chief Scott assigned the "Z" police radio frequency exclusively to the task force. Since Zebra is the common phonetic word for the letter Z in police, military, and other government agencies, the attacks became known as the Zebra murders. Rather than arrests, the new year brought an escalation to the violence. On January 29, 1974, five more victims were shot in separate random attacks; only one survived.

Somewhere in the Bay Area that same night, Zodiac was writing a new letter to the *Chronicle*, his first in nearly three years. It contained the killer's familiar misspellings and abbreviations. "I saw & think 'The Exorcist' was the best saterical comidy that I have ever seen," he said in the brief note, referring to the new horror film gaining wide popularity across the country. "Signed, yours truley." Beneath that he added lyrics from a song in Gilbert and Sullivan's 19th century comic operetta, The Mikado: "He plunged himself into the billowy wave and an echo arose from the sucides grave. tit willo tit willo tit willow." The lyrics come from a second act aria sung by Ko-Ko, the Lord High Executioner. Zodiac had referenced The Mikado in a 1970 letter, quoting the lyrics, in part, "I've got a little list. I've got a little list, of society offenders who might well be underground who would never be missed who would never be missed." In this new note, Zodiac added: "p.s. if I do not see this note in your paper, I will do something nasty, which you know I'm capable of doing. Me – 37 SFPD – 0."

There was no evidence, however, that he had killed anyone other than his five Bay Area victims and Cheri Jo Bates in Riverside. Paul Avery mentioned that case in his Page One article about this latest letter. "Zodiac eventually acknowledged that he indeed had been responsible for the Riverside slaying in a letter mailed on March 15, 1971 from Pleasanton in Alameda County," the article noted. "That was the last communication from the killer—until yesterday."

Just one week after the newest Zodiac letter, the Symbionese Liberation Army struck again in spectacular fashion.

On February 4, the leftist urban guerrilla group violently kidnapped Patricia Campbell Hearst, the granddaughter of publishing tycoon William Randolph Hearst, from her Berkeley apartment. She soon joined forces with her captors, took part in a San Francisco bank robbery with them, which set off a 19-month, nationwide police search for her and the SLA.

The shocking crime sent the *Chronicle* into an all-hands-on-deck coverage mode as the case moved from Berkeley to San Francisco to Los Angeles. Reporters Charles Raudebaugh and Tim Findley took the lead for us, but they were soon joined by, or, depending upon whom you asked, shoved aside by, Paul Avery. The Zodiac case had gone mostly quiet and Avery couldn't resist nudging his way into a good police action story.

One of the early ransom demands made by Patty Hearst's kidnappers – with her own vocal support by audio tape over the telephone – was the distribution of millions of dollars in free food to the poor. The city desk asked me to cover the food giveaway, dubbed the "People in Need" program by the SLA, in late February. I wrote two page one stories, one about preparations to feed as many as 20,000 families, and a second one two days later after violence flared at the distribution center in Oakland. Sixteen people, including two reporters, were injured at the Oakland site, but I wasn't among them.

I also became part of a rotating team of *Chronicle* reporters that was stationed daily outside the Hillsborough home of Randy Hearst in the event of any developments or impromptu FBI updates. The vigil continued at all hours, with reporters and cameras positioned outside the Hearsts' front door and spread out across their front lawn, waiting for any break in the case that would send Patty's parents to the front porch with an update or a response.

What was especially notable about this period was that any given day on the front page of the *Chronicle* you might find stories about Patty Hearst, Zodiac, the Zebra murders, and the Watergate scandal in Washington, D.C.

On April 17, following the twelfth Zebra murder, San Francisco Mayor Joseph Alioto announced that in response to the growing list of victims, police would begin stopping large numbers of black men throughout the city for questioning. "This is an extraordinary situation and it calls for extreme measures," I quoted Alioto in my front-page article the next morning. "We are going to be stopping people in San Francisco who have a certain profile. We're going to stop a lot of people. We ask the cooperation of citizens and we want to assure them that we will be mindful of their constitutional rights." Chief Scott said the only persons who will be stopped will be those who match the description of a suspect in a police sketch based on descriptions "from surviving victims and witnesses." The unusual dragnet drew strong criticism from civil rights groups, but Chief Scott insisted the mass questioning of black citizens was required to bring about the arrest of "this rotten, rotten killer."

Alongside my article was one by Charlie Raudebaugh that law enforcement officials had issued four new felony warrants for suspected SLA members Angela Atwood, William T. Harris, Emily Harris, and William Lawton Wolfe.

With help from an informant, police arrested seven men on May 1 in connection with the Zebra murders. Four were later released for lack of evidence. Mayor Alioto said the killers called themselves "Death Angels," and were part of a Black Muslim conspiracy to kill whites. Again, I led the paper with that story, meaning my article appeared in the upper right corner of the front page, reserved for the day's biggest news.

Ultimately, four men were convicted in the sensational case and sentenced to life terms in state prison.

The hunt continued, meanwhile, for Zodiac and the SLA. Two weeks after the Zebra arrests, on May 17, authorities tracked down and cornered six members of the SLA in a house in South Central Los Angeles. They all died in the resulting shootout and fire, a savage gun battle in which some nine thousand rounds were fired by both sides and police propelled hundreds of tear gas canisters into the hideout. Patty Hearst was not at the house at the time.

Paul Avery was there, and I was stunned by it. First, I had no idea he'd gone to L.A., and second, it was still extremely rare for the *Chronicle* to approve travel outside the Bay Area. But Paul always seemed to know where the next big story would break. He had strong contacts in law enforcement, because of Zodiac and other cases over the years, and a keen instinct for breaking news.

Step by Step With 2 Detectives

They're Tracking Down a Killer

By Duffy Jennings

At 4:47 a.m. on a spring Friday, a 23-year-old laborer is shot to death on the sidewalk in front of a tawdry all-night hamburger joint on outer Mission street.

At 4:54 a.m., the telephone rings in a modest home on the Peninsula. San Francisco police homicide Inspector Bill Armstrong, already half-awake from a restless sleep, paws into the receiver.

Armstrong is jolted by the matter-of-fact voice of a police operator: "We have a double shooting. One man is dead, another is wounded," the communications cop says, and gives the address.

"OK," says Armstrong, "Roll the crime lab and a photo unit. We're on the way."

Armstrong hangs up, dials a number in the Sunset District of San Francisco, and repeats the information to his partner of seven years, Inspector David Toschi.

Toschi shuffles into the bathroom to brush his teeth, dresses hurriedly in green slacks, a yellow sweater, and dark brown suede boots.

He gulps a half-cup of lukewarm instant coffee, slips into a corduroy jacket, kisses his wife, and leaves. He will be gone 14 hours.

Homicide Inspectors David Toschi and Bill Armstrong in their office at the Hall of Justice.

By Clem Albers

The two detectives meet outside the hamburger joint shortly after 5:30 a.m. It is still dark, and Armstrong shivers beneath his red turtleneck sweater and black raincoat.

He stoops beside the victim. The body is crudely outlined in yellow chalk. Syrupy red liquid puddles beneath a pencil-sized hole in back of the man's head.

Armstrong's eyes narrow, his jaw stiffens momentarily. He is no stranger to violent death, yet once—with each new homicide—he draws up short, the cold finality of the act taking hold.

It's easy to become callous. Toschi will say later, "But we feel a responsibility for that body, any body, and to the victim's family. Every victim was once a little boy or a little girl; we try to remember that."

There is no time now, though, for grief, and Armstrong's thoughts turn automatically—defensively perhaps—to the ugly business that has brought him here.

"Probably a .38," he says. "Looks like the slug ripped here, behind the forehead." He points to a swollen purplish bulge just above the right eye.

A few yards away, Toschi scribbles notes on a lined yellow tablet while a patrolman tells him what is known about the killing. There is not much to tell.

"The way I get it," says the cop, "the beef went down inside."

He, too, kneels over the victim and three friends were having a late snack when a group of four or five young men, guzzling beer in bottles and acting tough, roamed in and picked a fight.

It began with verbal taunts of no particular dignificance, the blabs of numb young hoodlums not out bravely when in a group. Then someone's mother was called a whore.

Suddenly, a length of glittering steel appeared. As in an instant later a man was on the floor, slashed to the back. At the same time, another man produced a gun and fired three wild shots, one of them slamming into the injured man's arm.

"Teck they all ran out," says the cop, "and this guy here got it. Those vehicles were seen leaving the parking lot. We put out a description."

The stabbing victim is undergoing surgery. He will not be able to talk to the inspectors for several hours. Even then, he will say he was drunk and can't remember anything.

"This business has been over-glamorized by Hollywood," he says.

"It's not glamorous at all. Most of the time, it's boring, tedious work. You don't see Barry Kanna around checking dead ends, ringing doorbells, missing phone calls, and serving subpoenas all day, do you?"

In a strictly physical sense, Armstrong at times curiously belies the screen image of the square-jawed detective he is so quick to belittle, the one who shears single-handedly solve the crazed killer in the final reel.

He is properly tall, dark, and handsome, with sharp features and a touch of short silver hair, and confidantly favors tasteful business suits. But there's where the similarity ends.

His is otherwise much like any average 42-year-old father of three girls who's just had his teeth capped, frets over his wilting backyard garden, and rattles a mustache in over suburban dirt trails or warns Saturday afternoons.

"When I leave the office at night I forget the job completely," he says. "I never dream my work at home ... well, I can't really. I find other ways to unwind."

There have been exceptions, usually when the victims were children ("It's always tough when it's a kid"), and particularly when police officer Herman George was gunned down in the street one November night in 1969.

"I watched 10:30 a.m. die in my sleep for eight weeks," says Armstrong, flinching at the memory. "He died a very slow and painful death."

Toschi leaves the murder scene to interview a friend of the dead man at Ingleside Station, and a short time later Armstrong departs the Mission Station, where officers are holding a young man who was stopped driving a car that had been seen leaving the parking lot.

Toschi arrives at Mission just as Armstrong is concluding the interview. Armstrong talks him: "I buy this guy's story, Dave, I don't think he was involved. I'm going to cut him loose."

The two inspectors compare notes to this point, then walk outside and stand together on the front steps of the station house.

It is almost 8:30 a.m.

"Well, David," Armstrong says with a deep sigh, "it looks like another beautiful day on the boulevard of broken dreams."

However: Search for a killer.

A Way To Make Muni Drivers Smile

By Rick Carroll

The city's bus, trolley and cable car operators will begin the first "attitude improvement" program in the history of the San Francisco Municipal Railway system next month.

It is designed to teach Muni operators how to get along with others, especially passengers.

But it won't happen overnight. It will take at least three, maybe five years, and cost $25,000 in city and county funds for all 1502 Muni operators to complete the special training program.

The program is being developed by Anteiina Data Systems, a Mountain View firm which has reached bus drivers for Greyhound, the U.S. Air Force and two foreign countries.

"It's the typical Muni operator who meets the public two to learn—either through exposure or some program," said Ed Sass, Anteiina's training program manager.

One boxen will involve vi-deotaped "role-playing" so drivers can see how their facial expressions and body language create either a negative or positive response from their passengers.

The "role-playing" is an essential part of the program, Sass said. It will work like this:

"The driver will assume the role of a passenger who doesn't have the correct change, to take her work and fresh from a beef with his wife.

"He will encounter a bus driver with a fierce hangover who's worried about his family's big medical bills," Sass said.

What happens then will be videotaped, played back, and the reactions of each person in the drama will be critiqued by all the drivers in the room, Sass said.

A select group is now receiving training from Anteiina specialists who had their first frustrating brush with the Muni last week.

The first class of bus drivers arrived 14 Mountain View 20 minutes late.

Kidnap Report at Bay Airport

Oakland police were checking the possibility early today of the kidnaping of a man from the street in front of Oakland International Airport.

Police said they were tipped by an airport security guard at 11:30 p.m. last night who said an unidentified lieutenant reported seeing a man getting out of one car being grabbed by three other men who hustled him into another car and sped off.

The informant reportedly told the guard he had seen a woman with a baby get out of the man's car a few minutes before he was allegedly taken.

When police went to the airport, they found no trace of the woman or the man she had been with.

The California license plate reported on the car which sped off, police said, are from a car stolen a week ago in Los Angeles.

CHAPTER 32:
On Call with Homicide

As a crime reporter, I was in nearly constant contact with Zodiac investigators Dave Toschi and Bill Armstrong as well as other inspectors in the homicide bureau, including Gus Coreris, Frank Falzon, Eddie Erdelatz, Earl Sanders, Napolean Hendrix and others. I wanted to know more about their day-to-day work. I suggested to the city desk that I follow Toschi and Armstrong on call for a week, much the way I had embedded at the firehouse. All the SFPD homicide officers worked in pairs, and they rotated weekly, with a new team being on call twenty-four hours a day for seven days. When Toschi and Armstrong's turn came up in March, I spent the week with them.

I joined them in their office or out on casework during the days, and I asked them to call me anytime they were dispatched from their homes to a murder scene at night. I accompanied them to two murders, one of a man who was stabbed to death in the chest with a butcher knife in a dingy Hayes Valley hotel, and another where a man was shot on the street in the Mission District. I was there at crime scenes, during an autopsy, when they questioned a witness, and when they confronted a suspect. As much as I'd seen bodies and crime scenes, I never got used to it. I can't forget walking into that hotel room to see the victim lying naked on his back on the bed, his legs dangling over the end, the knife still buried in the center of his chest.

At the end of the week, I wrote these two pieces about the experience.

Part 1 – A Phone Call in the Night

At 4:47 a.m. on a spring Friday, a 22-year-old laborer is shot to death on the sidewalk in front of a tawdry all-night hamburger joint on outer Mission street.

At 5:04 a.m., the telephone rings in a modest home on the Peninsula. San Francisco police homicide Inspector Bill Armstrong, already half-awake from a restless sleep, yawns into the receiver.

Armstrong is jolted by the matter-of-fact voice of a police operator: "We have a double shooting. One man is dead, another is wounded," the communications cop says, and gives the address.

'"OK," says Armstrong. "Roll the crime lab and a photo unit. We're on the way."

Armstrong hangs up, dials a number in the Sunset District of San Francisco and repeats the information to his partner of seven years, inspector David Toschi.

Toschi shuffles into the bathroom to brush his teeth, dresses hurriedly in green slacks, a yellow sweater, and dark brown ankle boots. He gulps a half-cup of lukewarm instant coffee, slips into a corduroy jacket, kisses his wife, and leaves. He will be gone 14 hours.

The two detectives meet outside the hamburger stand shortly after 5:30 a.m. It is still dark, and Armstrong shivers beneath his red turtleneck sweater and black raincoat.

He stoops beside the victim. The body is crudely outlined in yellow chalk. Syrupy red liquid puddles beneath a pencil-sized hole in back of the man's head. Armstrong's eyes narrow, his jaw stiffens momentarily. He is no stranger to violent death, yet now—as with each new homicide—he draws up short, the cold finality of the act taking hold.

'It's easy to become callous," Toschi will say later. "But we feel a responsibility for that body, any body, and to the victim's family. Every victim was once a little boy or a little girl; we try to remember that."

There is no time now, though, for grief and Armstrong's thoughts turn systematically—defensively perhaps—to the ugly business that has brought him here.

"Probably a .38," he says. "Looks like the slug stopped here, behind the forehead." He points to a swollen purplish bulge just above the right eye.

A few yards away, Toschi scribbles notes on a lined yellow tablet while a patrolman tells him what is known about the killing. There is not much to tell.

"The way I get it," says the cop, "'the beef went down inside.'"

He tells how the victim and three friends were having a late snack when a group of four or five young men, guzzling beer in bottles and acting tough, roamed in and picked a fight.

It began with verbal taunts of no particular significance, the kinds of words young hoodlums spit out bravely when in a group. Then someone's mother was called a whore.

Suddenly, a length of glistening steel appeared. An instant later a man was on the floor, stabbed in the back. At the same time, another man produced a gun and fired three wild shots, one of them slamming into the knifed man's arm.

"Then they all ran out," says, the cop, "and this guy here got it. Three vehicles were seen leaving the parking lot. We put out a description."

The stabbing victim is undergoing surgery. He will not be able to talk to the inspectors for several hours. Even then, he will say he was drunk and can't remember anything.

Toschi and Armstrong, fondly referred to by co-workers as "The Zodiac Twins" for their part in that case, now begin the painstaking work for which they are each paid $1458 every month — homicide investigation.

"Time is important," Toschi says. "What we do in the first 24 hours is critical. We have to talk to as many people as we can while their memory is fresh."

For the next hour at the crime scene, witnesses are interviewed, physical evidence — blood, bullet fragments, shell casings, broken glass, hair — is examined, photographed, bagged and labeled, and rough charts are drawn to show the locations of each person and object involved.

The inspectors move about in a seemingly disorganized manner, but this is deceptive, for neither duplicates the work of the other; overlapping of chores in this or any other investigation is time-consuming and thus prudently avoided.

"We're really just information gatherers," says Armstrong, dispelling any notion that a homicide cop's life is one thrilling, dangerous moment after another. "We put each case together the best we can and lay it on the table for the courts to decide."

"This business has been over-glamorized by Hollywood," he says.

"It's not glamorous at all. Most of the time, it's boring, tedious work. You don't see Dirty Harry running around checking dead ends, ringing doorbells, making phone calls and serving subpoenas all day, do you?"

In a strictly physical sense, Armstrong at times curiously befits the screen image of the square-jawed detective he is so quick to belittle, the one who always single-handedly nabs the crazed killer in the final reel.

He is properly tall, dark and handsome, with sharp features and a brush of short silver hair, and customarily favors tasteful business suits. But there's where the similarity ends.

He is otherwise much like any average 45-year-oid father of three girls who's just had his teeth capped, frets over his wilting backyard garden and rattles a motorbike over suburban dirt trails on warm Saturday afternoons.

"When I leave the office at night I forget the job completely," he says. "I never discuss my work at home . . . well, I can't really. I find other ways to unwind."

There have been exceptions, usually when the victims were children ("it's always tough when it's a kid") and particularly when police officer Herman George was gunned down in the street one November night in 1967.

"I watched Herman die in my sleep for eight weeks," says Armstrong, flinching at the memory. "He died a very slow and painful death."

Toschi leaves the murder scene to interview a friend of the dead man at Ingleside Station, and a short time later Armstrong departs for Mission Station, where officers are holding a young man who was stopped driving a car that had been seen leaving the parking lot.

Toschi arrives at Mission just as Armstrong is concluding the interview. Armstrong tells him: "I buy this guy's story, Dave. I don't think he was involved. I'm going to cut him loose."

The two inspectors compare notes to this point, then walk outside and stand together on the front steps of the station house. It is almost 9:30 a.m.

"Well, David," Armstrong says with a deep sigh, "it looks like another beautiful day on the boulevard of broken dreams."

Part Two – A Slim Clue

Under the prying fluorescent lights in the coroner's autopsy room behind the Hall of Justice, the body of a young laborer lies naked on a sloping metal table, a bullet in his skull.

His flesh is milky, and cool from the 28-degree refrigerator in which he has lain on a gurney for four hours since being shot down on a San Francisco sidewalk.

Now the medical examiner stands alongside the slab and commences the autopsy, dictating into a microphone suspended from the ceiling.

"The body is that of a well-developed, well-nourished male ... he begins, "and shows a slight degree of rigor mortis in the lower extremities..."

Three floors above, homicide inspector Dave Toschi flips through a pile of notes on his desk.

"This is going to be a tough one," he says, thumbing the yellow sheets again. "A cast of thousands—and nobody saw anything, nobody heard anything. They're all afraid to talk, afraid of retaliation."

Toschi opens a box of animal crackers, chucks a tiger-shaped cookie into his mouth, and washes it down with coffee.

He and his partner, Inspector Bill Armstrong, have interrogated 13 persons so far in connection with the shooting at the hamburger stand.

They know now what the killer looks like, what his friends look like, where they hang out – but the inspectors have no names, no addresses, no gun. Nothing to make the pieces fit.

Toschi says: "What we need now is a good snitch."

He stretches backward in his swivel chair, and its springs whine shrilly. A brooding expression creases his usually ebullient face, and he gazes distantly out the window. Tonight perhaps, or tomorrow, he will take a leisurely drive down the coast highway alone, or a long walk through the neighborhood, as he does frequently to ponder a case. Or forget one.

Back home, he will throw a stack-of big band albums on the stereo and sink into an armchair with a Manhattan, absorbing the soothing effects of both.

Maybe he will sing lustily along, with the music, the way he did in high school, and later as a bartender on California street, just before he became a cop nearly 22 years ago.

He was 21 then, and joined the force the first chance he had. He always wanted to be a cop, and even now he balks at any suggestion that it might be corny to say so.

"For a while I thought maybe I could be a singer. I sang a lot at Galileo. Now it's mostly just in the shower."

Across the desk, Armstrong huddles with a deputy district attorney, discussing another case. It is one of a half-dozen cases Armstrong and Toschi are working simultaneously.

One or the other is almost always on the telephone, talking to witnesses, district attorneys, ballistics men, crime lab technicians, coroner's deputies, or relatives of murder victims, past and present.

"Our work doesn't stop when an arrest is made," says Toschi. "It just begins. We have to follow every case up to and through the trial."

But the work does stop when he goes home, for like most homicide cops, Toschi won't chit-chat over the pot roast at night about the kind of day he had, the way other working men do.

The inspectors go out to the Fillmore to see a witness in another case. On the way back, they stop at the home of a witness to the killing of the laborer. They think he may know more than he told them at the scene.

It is merely a hunch, but a good detective learns to trust his instincts. The young man is strangely reluctant to answer even the simplest questions.

Armstrong sets his eyeglasses on a small table and stares piercingly, silently at the man for several moments, then says: "If you know something about this, and you don't tell me now, you could later become an accessory. And the punishment for that is the same as for the one who actually did the shooting. So now is the time to tell the truth."

"O.K., O.K.," the young man says. "I, uh, I think I saw a guy they call the Snake in there. I don't know his real name."

The two detectives look casually at one another, managing to conceal their exhilaration at this key bit of information. Finally, they have a name. A nickname only, but a name. It is a start.

Presently the interview is concluded. The inspectors are enthusiastic during the ride back downtown.

"It won't take long to find him now," says Armstrong.

As of late last week. Toschi and Armstrong had identified at least two possible suspects in the case and were still attempting to identify another. None, however, was in custody.

It is almost 7 p.m. by the time the blue sedan glides into the Hall of Justice garage.

"Well, Deputy Dave," says Armstrong, "I think I'll go home, have a martini or two on the patio, and try to figure out what's killing my lemon tree."

CHAPTER 33:
Zodiac and Count Marco

Within three months after my homicide series ran, the newspaper received two new items in the mail from Zodiac, although he signed neither as such. Inspector Toschi showed them both to a documents expert who identified them within minutes as positively written by Zodiac. "He's trying to slip letters and cards into the *Chronicle* without being detected," Toschi said.

The first was a postcard from "a citizen" complaining about ads for a new movie. Postmarked May 8, 1974, in Alameda County, it had not reached the *Chronicle* until June 4. There was no explanation for the long delay. It was addressed to: "Editor, SF *Chronicle*, 5th + Mission, San Fran," in the familiar hand-printing style I knew well by then.

"Sirs," it began, "I would like to express my consternation concerning your

poor taste + lack of sympathy for the public, as evidenced by your running of

the ads for the movie 'Badlands,' featuring the blurb: 'In 1959 most people

were killing time. Kit + Holly were killing people.' In light of recent events,

this kind of murder-glorification can only be deplorable at best (not that

glorification of violence was ever justifiable) why don't you show some concern for public sensibilities + cut the ad? (Signed) A citizen."

The second was a letter mailed July 8 from Marin County, complaining about columnist Count Marco Spinelli, who gave outrageous advice to women for many years.

"Editor—Put Marco back in the hell-hole from whence it came—he has a serious psychological disorder—always needs to feel superior," said the letter. I suggest you refer him to a shrink. Meanwhile, cancel the Count Marco column. Since the Count can write anonymously, so can I—(Signed) the Red Phantom (red with rage)"

The *Chronicle* had not published a story about the postcard, but with the new letter it was deemed newsworthy enough to print a story on July 10 about the two items having arrived close together.

What was different this time, however, was that I was now the primary reporter assigned to the case. Paul Avery was working on the SLA and this was my first byline on a Zodiac story. I honestly don't recall exactly when or why Paul left for the *Sacramento Bee*, although there were suggestions his use of alcohol and cocaine contributed to his departure.

I saw Paul consume ample quantities of both on several occasions when we hung out on his Sausalito houseboat, yet it never occurred to me that he was any more of a drinker or user than some other reporters who were doing the same. Paul later wrote a book about the SLA, *Voices of Guns*, with co-author Vin McLellan, that Putnam published in 1977. After that he returned to his San Francisco newspaper career, this time with the *Examiner*.

Meanwhile, the buzz over the new Zodiac letter faded quickly within a few days, and I resumed my general assignment duties for the remainder of the year.

In July, I wrote a profile of the San Francisco Police Officer of the Year, patrolman Dan Hance. In August, I wrote about the cost of school supplies going up, bemoaning the unthinkable price increase for the venerated Pee-Chee folder from a dime to seventeen cents apiece. In December, I covered a bungled robbery at Petrini Plaza

Market at Masonic Avenue and Fulton Street, where two men were finally arrested peacefully after holding a number of employees and shoppers hostage for several hours.

I was pretty busy in the first half of 1975. I wrote a long piece in early February about the struggles people were facing in the small Northern California town of Covelo, where the sawmill had closed, leaving many jobless. Later that month I wrote about San Francisco's ambulance fleet in serious disrepair and a protest by women who shaved their heads at Synanon. Synanon was initially a drug rehabilitation program that evolved into an alternative community and ultimately became the Church of Synanon by the early 1970s. In March, I covered a student protest of Nazi speakers at San Francisco State University, the jury's visit to the scene of the Petrini Plaza hostage drama, the strangulation murder of a Walnut Creek woman who had moved from San Francisco to the East Bay suburb to be in a safer environment, and the opening of a new jail in Martinez. In October, the paper sent me to Napa to report on a head-on crash on Highway 29 that had killed six young men. In a rare assignment out of the Bay Area, I was sent to Los Angeles just before Thanksgiving to cover a major forest fire in the San Gabriel Mountains. I arrived on Wednesday and was there three days. On Thanksgiving Day, it rained, bringing welcome relief to the fire crews. My lead paragraph in the next day's paper was: "The thanks they were giving around this mountain refuge deep in the San Gabriel Canyon yesterday was more for the rain than the for the turkey, although there was plenty of both to go around."

CHAPTER 34:
New Home, Old Threat

By that time, Cheryl and I were living in the Greenwich Street flat where I grew up because my mother had moved out, first to a lofty Russian Hill condo with a wide view of the bay in a high-rise called The Summit at 999 Green Street, and later to a flat in the 2800-block of Sacramento Street near Divisadero Street.

Over the years, Club Dori grew in popularity, so Dori and George purchased a second gay bar and restaurant near Fisherman's Wharf. Jackson's, at 2237 Powell Street, was next door to the venerable Caesar's restaurant on the corner. George left my mom to manage Club Dori while he spent more and more time running Jackson's. Dori spiraled further and further into the depths of alcoholism. She was at her worst behind the wheel of her car. She often needed a ride home from the bar, but sometimes she refused a ride and insisted on driving herself. The consequences included two serious accidents, two DUIs that I know of, and several minor hit-and-run property damage accidents. I could tell from the damage to her car that she'd hit something, but when I asked her about it she couldn't recall any of the details.

One day after a week-long bender, she agreed to check into a Calistoga detox center named Duffy's, if you can believe it. I offered to take her, but she wanted to drive there on her own, saying she might need her car while there. It was a flimsy excuse, but there was no persuading her otherwise. Naturally, she stopped on the way to pick up a bottle of vodka she planned to hide in her room. But she drank half of it in the car and never arrived. Duffy's owner called me the next morning to ask where she was.

"What?" I asked. "What do you mean she's not there? She left yesterday to drive up there."

"Well, she never showed up," he said.

I dropped everything, jumped in my car, and headed north out of the city. Not knowing exactly where to go, I followed the route she should have taken, looking for her car in gas stations, at convenience stores, in winery parking lots or along the roadside. Finally, on the last mile of road leading to Duffy's, I noticed a section of tall grass, about the width of a car, that had been flattened on the side of the road. I pulled over and got out to have a closer look. Down in a culvert below the road there it was, front end down in the ditch, my mother's unmistakable lime green 1968 Dodge Challenger convertible, its top down, with its distinctive personalized license plate, "DORI," staring up at me. I scrambled down the slope. My mother was lying across the front seat, wedged in at an awkward angle, but visibly unhurt.

"Mom! Mom!" I cried. "Are you OK?"

"I'm cold," she mumbled. She had spent the night there in the Sonoma County rain but otherwise seemed fine. That was confirmed when I got her to a local hospital to be checked out. I drove her home and I had her car towed back to the city. Duffy's would have to wait.

One day not long after the Duffy's rehab fiasco, Dori was on the telephone muttering gibberish about taking her own life again, so I drove to the Sacramento Street place to find her smashed and holding a bottleful of pills she said she was about to swallow. She had written another odd suicide note that I found on her bedside. This one, scrawled in pencil on three-by-five-inch sheets of lime green notepaper, read:

"Dearest Duffy: Despite what I said yesterday, Pleeze take Jaxie (her mini poodle) to live with Nikki (our German shepherd). I know you really don't need him, but he needs somebody. What I am going to do—if you can keep it out of the news, good. But if not, it will be a one-day thing & people will forget, like Bob Bastian. (Bastian was a former *Chronicle* editorial cartoonist who committed suicide in 1970.) Now it's about our arrangement. My will is in the top drawer of my desk. I am sorry that it is not updated, so therefore George is still the executor. He now has other things on his mind, so I hereby designate you, D. Duffy Jennings, to be the executor. Which is silly, since there is no witness for this statement. Duffy, I love you, but I'm surely not showing it. Sell this house, take whatever cash there is and buy whatever you want. Please make mortgage payments. You remember you can sign checks at WF [Wells Fargo] & this will give you a month or so to pull things together."

I read the note and shrugged. My brother had been living in New Jersey for a year by then, so Dori looked to me to help manage her life. Or her death. I looked around her flat. Empty bottles, full ashtrays. It smelled of booze, cigaret smoke, and mildew. I knew she was looking for a way out, crying for help, but I didn't know how to help her.

A month later, out of a sense of guilt over her latest suicide ideation, my mother told Cheryl and me that we should move out of Greenwich Street and buy a house. Despite her unstable state, at times Dori could be quite insightful, and over the years she had invested in property wisely. She knew the value of ownership versus renting. Plus, she wanted to move back into Greenwich Street. She said she would help us with the down payment, so we started looking at homes in Marin County, where Cheryl's parents and all six of her siblings lived, several of them still at home. We looked at several houses, starting in Mill Valley and moving north until the prices were in our range. We finally found a brand new, three-bedroom, two-bath tract home on San Marin Drive in Novato, thirty miles from the Golden Gate Bridge. It had no fence and no landscaping, just a new house on a dirt lot, but we knew that with family help we could landscape it ourselves on the weekends.

Moving to Marin was a huge step for me. I had never lived outside San Francisco, but I figured it would be easier to start a family up there in a community with good schools, ample parking, shopping malls, and a safer environment than the city. I also knew it would take me farther away from Dori, so I wouldn't be tempted to come running every time she had a new crisis. At the time, Novato was the last suburban outpost for San Francisco commuters. Everything north of San Marin Drive was dairy farming country. Quite a few San Francisco police officers and firefighters had bought homes in Novato. The house we picked was priced at $57,000. Dori gave us $18,000 for the down payment, along with a note for the record that it was "an outright gift" with "no anticipation that it would be repaid." We closed escrow quickly and moved in December 1975.

CHAPTER 35:
City Hall Beat

A month after George Moscone's mayoral election, the *Chronicle* promoted city hall reporter Jerry Burns to chief political writer. Jerry had covered Mayor Joseph Alioto's administration for eight years and was both deserving of the new title and ready for a break from city hall. City editor Abe Mellinkoff asked me if I was interested in the beat. I saw it as a timely opportunity to take a welcome break of my own, from years of reporting on murders, fires, and other human tragedies.

"I would like that," I told Abe.

Working the city hall beat was a steady Monday-to-Friday, 9-to-5 gig, where the closest thing to violence was a boisterous protestor at the Board of Supervisors. From Novato, I could take a Golden Gate Transit bus to work and back without worrying about rush hour traffic.

The city hall press room, Room 247, was and still is directly opposite the Board of Supervisors suite of offices on the second floor. It was a large space shared by the *Chronicle* and *Examiner* reporters and used as a work station by other print journalists and radio and TV reporters who dropped in to make phone calls and take breaks. The *Chronicle* and *Examiner* each had a walled-off cubicle with an old-fashioned oak roll-top desk, telephone, typewriter, bookshelves, and a filing cabinet. In the center of the room stood a large old wooden table stacked with newspapers, scratch pads, pencils. I arrived at city hall to begin my new job Monday, January 5, 1976, four days before Moscone's inauguration.

Moscone's new press secretary, Corey Busch, started the same day. He was a Los Angeles native and UCLA grad who had moved to San

Francisco in 1971 to work in Moscone's state senate office and then remained on Moscone's mayoral staff.

Corey stopped by the press room that first morning to introduce himself to me and the *Examiner*'s bureau reporter, the slight, acerbic, and wiry Russ Cone. The fifty-four-year-old Cone was the reigning dean of the city hall press corps. During his twenty-two years on the beat he covered five mayors, starting with George Christopher in the 1950s. Cone was known not only for his reporting skill and good-natured cynicism but his quirky daily headwear as an offset to his stodgy gray business suits. One day he might sport a jaunty bowler and the next he'd wear his favorite, a Davy Crockett-style raccoon-skin hat, striped tail and all. Cone's first reaction at meeting Corey and me, both of us under thirty, was: "My God, my city is being run by children!"

Busch was convivial and politically savvy for someone so young. I liked him immediately. Within two months of joining the new Moscone administration, Corey was instrumental in changing the course of professional baseball for San Francisco. Giants' owner Horace Stoneham had put the team up for sale, accepted an offer from the owners of Labatt Brewery in Canada and a deal was struck to move the ball club to Toronto. But Moscone stepped in and went to court to halt the move. He helped local real estate magnate Bob Lurie to shape a new offer that would keep the team in San Francisco, but Lurie was looking for a partner to share the cost. It was Corey Busch who found another investor to join Lurie and the sale was confirmed with little time to spare. The Giants would stay put, and Moscone and Lurie were hailed for saving the team.

Over the next fifteen months I came to know Corey, Moscone, others on the mayor's staff, and most of the eleven city supervisors well. From time to time, I spent late afternoons talking city politics, news, or sports with Moscone and Busch in the mayor's back parlor, a small room behind his main office with large comfortable chairs, a TV and wet bar, where he went to relax at the end of the day. It was the room where he would be murdered just two years into his term.

By the middle of 1977 I missed the excitement and unpredictability of general assignment work, especially breaking crime stories. I asked to be transferred back to the city room. By then, Mellinkoff had moved over to the editorial department and longtime science editor David Perlman had taken over as city editor. He granted my request, and Tom Benet replaced me at the city hall bureau in May 1977.

Inside

One of the suspects in the brutal killing of four Indiana brothers said they were influenced by "Helter Skelter." Page 2.

After seven years as a fugitive, Mark Rudd of the radical Weather Underground appeared in court and was freed without bail. Page 2.

The death toll in the Kansas City flood rose to 22, with damage estimated running into the billions. Page 2.

Nighttime student patrols with walkie-talkies are part of a S.F. State security program occasioned by a brutal murder. Page 3.

A new book gives a behind-the-scenes look at the ordeal of the family of coma girl Karen Anne Quinlan. Page 5.

TOP OF THE NEWS

An eruption of Hawaii's Kilauea volcano sent lava flowing in all directions and caused a civil defense alert. Page 3.

Los Angeles has been selected as the site for a major Soviet trade and cultural exhibition in November. Page 6.

The Assembly approved a measure that would divide the state Health Department into five agencies. Page 9.

Former Secretaries of State Rusk and Kissinger declared it void for the Senate to ratify the Panama Canal treaties. Page 13.

Hundreds of Bert Lance's friends and neighbors turned out last night to give him a hometown rally. Page 16.

Pressure is mounting in Congress for passage of a law that would license mining combines to harvest mineral wealth from the seabed. Page 21.

G. Gordon Liddy bemoaned the "terrible damage done to the U.S. intelligence community" by public disclosure. Page 22.

The General Accounting Office declared that Americans are not being protected adequately from the hazards of radiation. Page 24.

Subliminal sex is part of advertising's pitch. Page 28.

The ability to cope with stress increases with the number of learned responses one develops. Page 30.

Heraldic banners depicting a real or imagined family crest are one way to advertise your roots. Page 30.

People with letter writer's block are turning to Maggie Shores to express their power and praises for them. Page 30.

Weather

Bay Area: Cloudy Thursday, with local drizzle. Partial clearing in the afternoon. Highs, 60s to mid 70s; lows, mid to upper 50s. Westerly winds to 25 m.p.h. Page 41.

San Francisco Chronicle

The Largest Daily Circulation in Northern California

113th Year No. 208   ★★★★   THURSDAY, SEPTEMBER 15, 1977   777-1111   20 CENTS

Growing Up

Class of '65

Song girls, yell leaders and senior class skits were the "in" things in 1965

How It Went In the Real World

By Duffy Jennings

On a warm afternoon in June 12 years ago, 600 capped and gowned members of Lowell High School's spring Class of 1965 walked triumphantly out of graduation ceremonies in the Civic Auditorium and ran smack into one of the most turbulent decades in American history.

Most of us perceived the morality inscribed diplomas we received that day as our express ticket to a rosy future, to success and happiness as we knew it — college, marriage, a career, a family.

Instead we clutched head-on with the Vietnam war, the draft, campus protests, the psychedelic

The students — where they are now — Pages 6 and 7

age, marijuana, rock music, black power, the sexual revolution, ethnic consciousness, the women's movement and Watergate.

And, most of all, with ourselves — our values, our attitudes, our goals.

As a cover story on America's teenagers in January of 1965, Time magazine told high schoolers were "on the fringe of a golden era." Turns then

were brighter, better educated and more affluent, motivated and independent than ever before, Time noted.

Yes, we had everything going for us. Or so it seemed. As it turned out, we may have been prepared for college, but not for society going topsy-turvy and, by the time things settled down again, not everyone from the Class of '65 had landed right side up.

During the past several weeks, I interviewed two dozen of my Lowell classmates — all of whom today are 30, or about to be — to see how they had coped with the upheaval of the late '60s and early '70s.

Almost all of them were eager to take part in the project, and many were astonishingly candid about themselves.

I listened in amazement, for instance, as

• Dennis Marcellino, the class poet, laughing-ly revealed that he broke into Lowell one night and stole $20,000 worth of band instruments.

• Read Dilmore, the drama student, talked openly about his homosexuality.

• Tony Shotwell, the cartoonist, spoke frank-

Back Page Col. 1

Permanent BART Tax Passed by Legislature

Brown's OK Expected

By Larry Liebert
Chronicle Correspondent

Sacramento

The Legislature voted final passage yesterday of a measure that would make permanent the half-cent sales tax for BART in San Francisco, Alameda and Contra Costa counties.

Governor Brown is expected to sign the measure when it reaches his desk.

The Senate approved the bill yesterday afternoon on a vote of 39 for to 4 against. Hours later, the Assembly, which had previously approved it, agreed to recent amendments by a vote of 67 to 4.

With it, the BART tax will go on forever — and that issue of permanence sparked the only debate on the measure.

"This bill is really a license to rape the taxpayers of Alameda, Contra Costa and San Francisco without their consent, without them having anything to say about it," charged Senator Milton Marks (Rep-S.F.). Marks and Senator John Nejedly (Rep-Walnut Creek) were the only senators from the Bay Area to vote against the tax.

Marks argued there should be a time limit of three years or so on the BART tax, forcing the transit system to come back to the Legislature for more money. Last week he persuaded the full Senate to amend the measure to include such a deadline. But the Senate reversed itself and dropped the time limit on Tuesday, after vigorous lobbying by the measure's author, Assembly Speaker Leo McCarthy (Dem-S.F.)

Supporting a permanent BART tax, Senator John Foran (Dem-S.F.) said all transit systems need a subsidy to stay in business. "There's no system in the world that runs out of the farebox," Foran said. "The issue isn't going to go away."

Foran acknowledged that voters who created BART had been promised that the sales tax would be temporary. "It was a nice thought," he said, "but it doesn't work."

As an extra incentive to legislators from outside the Bay Area, the measure barred by the entire issue, Foran said, "If you don't want to hear us debate this issue year after year, I suggest you vote for this bill."

In the past, BART got all of its $47 million a year collected from the half-cent sales tax directly. For three-fourths of the money but requires it to compete for the rest with San Francisco's Municipal Railway and the East Bay's AC Transit.

It also requires all three transit systems to collect at least 33 per cent of their revenues from passen-

Back Page Col. 5

Jody Powell Admits To Dirty Tricks

Washington

White House press secretary Jody Powell acknowledged yesterday that he tried to encourage the publication of damaging information about a senator who has raised critical questions concerning Bert Lance. He said his action was "inappropriate, regrettable and dumb."

Powell made a telephoned apology to Senator Charles H. Percy (Rep-Ill.) yesterday morning after The Chicago Sun-Times reported that, in "an apparent guerrilla offensive" against Lance's detractors, Powell had informed that newspaper of alleged improprieties by Percy.

The "allegations that Powell passed on to The Sun-Times Tuesday were that Percy had regularly flown on aircraft owned by the Bell and Howell Co., which the senator once headed, and that he had not fully reimbursed a Chicago bank for facilities used during his 1972 re-election campaign.

The Sun-Times reported that

Back Page Col. 1

JODY POWELL
'It was dumb,' he said

Conflicting Testimony On the Lance Probe

Washington

A Senate committee yesterday heard testimony in which John L. Stokes, the former U.S. Attorney in Atlanta, was pictured as having closed out an investigation of a bank headed by Bert Lance over the objections of his subordinates and at a time when he was hoping to save his job.

Two prosecutors who had been assistants to Stokes told the committee that they believed he had been wrong in ending a criminal investigation of the Calhoun, Ga., First National Bank one day before Lance was nominated to head the Office of Management and Budget.

During the same hearing a third former assistant prosecutor, Glenna L. Stone, testified that Stokes had told her he hoped the new administration would keep him in office long enough to qualify for a federal pension, and that after closing the case against the Calhoun bank he said "Jimmy and Bert to tell them what he had done."

Stokes, who was replaced as U.S. attorney last summer and who is now in private practice, took sharp issue with some of the statements by his former associates.

Back Page Col. 6

Crucial Vote On Property Tax Relief

By John Balzar
Chronicle Correspondent

Sacramento

A committee rushed together an elaborate property tax relief package yesterday — setting the stage for a last-chance vote on the floor of the Legislature today, the final scheduled meeting of the 1977 session.

The mood in the Capitol was tense with uncertainty over whether the complex scheme of redistributing tax dollars would find support from the two-thirds majority needed in both houses.

The bill represents a second attempt to pass a major property tax relief measure during the 1977 pre-election season. The Senate soundly defeated the previous proposal amid complaints that midsession discretion had homeowners were being shortchanged.

The new measure is a rewrite

Back Page Col. 4

Business Slump

Chinatown Group's Plea to Mayor

By Maitland Zane

The Chinese Chamber of Commerce plans to seek the help of the mayor and the Convention and Visitors Bureau in fighting Chinatown's fear-inspired economic slump, a spokesman said yesterday.

Chamber vice president Dennis Wong said, "If we're going to enhance the business climate, we will need the help of people in all walks of life."

Wong said a poll of merchants at a chamber meeting Tuesday night showed that all kinds of businessmen were hard hit economi-

cally after the slaughter of five persons and wounding of 11 others at the Golden Dragon restaurant on September 4.

One idea discussed by the chamber officials was for Mayor George Moscone to "walk through Chinatown late at night," as former Mayor Joseph L. Alioto did in the Tenderloin three years ago to calm the public's fears about the Zebra killings.

Another idea was for the Convention and Visitors Bureau to put out the word that the Golden Dragon massacre was an "isolated

incident," that Chinatown itself is not dangerous for tourists.

Wong said the public has every right to be "angry and disturbed" at Chinese youth-gang violence, where is harting tourists all over the city, not just on Grant avenue.

He said the response of city government and the police department to Chinatown's manifold problems has been "shameful."

Wong, a pharmacist and former president of the Chinese Six Companies, said city, state and

Back Page Col. 4

CHAPTER 36:
What Really Happened to My Class of '65

In 1976, Michael Medved and David Wallechinsky wrote a book about what had become of their classmates from Palisades High School in suburban Los Angeles ten years earlier titled, *What Really Happened to the Class of '65*.

The school had been the focus of a 1965 *Time* cover story on "Today's Teenagers," citing the upper-class Palisades kids as examples of American youth "on the fringe of a golden era," the vanguard of a new and better age.

Medved, who would become a prominent American radio show host, author, political commentator, and film critic, and Wallechinsky, the son of a Hollywood screen writer and now a populist historian and television commentator and the founder and editor-in-chief of AllGov.com, revisited thirty of their classmates for the book. It became a bestseller and later was the basis for a short-lived weekly television series by the same name.

As a 1965 graduate of Lowell High School in San Francisco, the title and positive reviews caught my attention. In summer 1977, now back from city hall, I read the book with great interest and found many similarities with my own classmates in the compelling individual stories. Like almost all of them, I also turned thirty that year. It was in July, and Cheryl organized a swim party for me at our house in Novato. We invited many of my *Chronicle* colleagues, who trekked from the city and other Bay Area communities out to the sticks of northern Marin County. I still have some memorable photos from the event, especially one with two of my favorite co-workers, assistant city editor Steve Gavin and entertainment columnist John Wasserman, seated together on the lawn by the pool. Sadly, Wasserman would die less than two years later in a drunk driving accident that also killed two other people. Gavin died in 2005 of a heart attack at sixty-eight.

Shortly after the party I proposed doing an article about my own Class of '65. I got the go-ahead and I spent the next few weeks tracking down and talking with some two dozen classmates to see how they had fared over the previous twelve years. My article ran on September 15, 1977, and featured separate profiles on nine of them. This was the lead article:

> On a warm afternoon in June 12 years ago, 608 capped and gowned members of Lowell High School's spring Class of 1965 walked triumphantly out of graduation ceremonies in the Civic Auditorium and ran smack into one of the most turbulent decades in American history.
>
> Most of us perceived the ornately inscribed diplomas we received that day as our express ticket to a rosy future, to success and happiness as we knew it — college, marriage, a career, a family.
>
> Instead we clashed head-on with the Vietnam war, the draft, campus protests, the psychedelic age, marijuana, rock music, black power, the sexual revolution, ethnic consciousness, the women's movement and Watergate.
>
> And, most of all, with ourselves — our values, our attitudes, our goals.
>
> In a cover story on America's teenagers in January of 1965, Time magazine said high schoolers were "on the fringe of a golden era." Teens then were brighter, better educated and more affluent, motivated and independent than ever before, Time noted.
>
> Yes, we had everything going for us. Or so it seemed. As it turned out, we may have been prepared for college, but not for society going topsy-turvy and, by the time things settled

down again, not everyone from the Class of '65 had landed right side up.

During the past several weeks, I interviewed two dozen of my Lowell classmates—all of whom today are 30, or about to be, to see how they had coped with the upheaval of the late '60s and early '70s.

Almost all of them were eager to take part in the project, and many were astonishingly candid about themselves.

I listened in amazement, for instance, as:

• Dennis Marcellino, the class punk, laughingly revealed that he broke into Lowell one night and stole $20,000 worth of band instruments.

• Read Gilmore, the drama student, talked openly about his homosexuality.

• Tony Shonwald, the cartoonist, spoke frankly about being an alcoholic.

• Lani Silver, one of the "Jewish princesses," told how she cast off the white gloves of a Kelly Girl to become a radical feminist.

Some of those I talked to either dived or fell into the whirlpool of social change. Others never so much as got wet.

Some are still searching for something that will bring stability to their lives — the right job, the best mate, more education, fewer pressures.

Some are only now concluding they frittered away a lot of valuable time and they're doing whatever is necessary to change all that — getting married, getting divorced, moving, quitting old jobs, getting new ones, going back to college, whatever.

Like the 900 sophomores entering Lowell this fall, we arrived at the Lake Merced campus 15 years ago excited, confused, eager, terrified.

The ideal Lowellite then had straight hair, straight teeth and straight A's. He or she came from an affluent home, wore the best clothes, often had plenty of spending money and probably owned a car.

The student population was predominantly white. They were the children of the middle and upper middle class Jewish and Protestant families who lived in the comfortable homes in the Sunset, Parkside, West Portal, St. Francis Wood, Ingleside, Stonestown and Parkmerced neighborhoods.

They were exemplified in our class by the likes of Paul Batmale and Nancy Motzer, the class sweethearts. Paul, an All-City basketball player, and Nancy, a song girl, never dated anyone else in high school.

Paul now owns Batmale's restaurant on West Portal avenue and Nancy works part-time as a registered nurse. They have three children and live in a cozy yellow house on a tree-lined street in San Mateo.

"We grew up together," said Nancy. "We've been together 15 years. Married for eight. As you grow together your needs change. You become different people, and you've got to adjust to that."

As an all-academic, non-district high school, Lowell also drew the brightest kids from Chinatown, the Mission, Bayview-Hunters Point and other districts.

Although minority students could compete scholastically, many felt out of place.

Terry Zachery, for example, had come to Lowell to cut his gang ties in the Hunters Point. But after one semester he wanted out.

"I felt so conspicuous," he said. "I had no friends. But Mrs. Brash took me to a meeting with the Superintendent of Schools, Dr. Spears, and we talked for about 45 minutes. I decided to stay."

Terry eventually became a star basketball player and popular rally commissioner, and as a senior was elected Student Body President in a landslide.

"I don't think it had anything to do with my being black," he said. "I think people just respected me." Today he is a sales agent for North American Van Lines in Van Nuys.

For song girl Barbara Quan, however, jumping headlong into the Lowell social scene brought hostility from her Asian classmates, who comprised barely ten per cent of the class and therefore avoided the mainstream of student activities.

"I just wanted to be in a white crowd to be accepted," said Barbara, now a substitute teacher who often works at Lowell, where the Asian percentage today is 42 per cent. "But it made me a banana — yellow on the outside, white on the inside. The Asian ethic was always to just study hard and become a professional. But I was a social butterfly.

"It took a long time for me to develop my own ethnic identity. That's why eight months after the ten-year reunion, Jeff Leong and I organized a kind of mini-reunion just for the Asian kids. We had about 30 people at a dinner party, with Chinese food and all that. It was really nice."

Several members of the class served with the armed forces in Vietnam, but it is not known whether any was killed. Two reportedly died in accidents — one a car crash, the other a drowning.

Of the more than 400 graduates contacted when the class reunion was held here in 1975, more than 300 attended.

At that time and again in recent weeks I had the opportunity to renew many old friendships — and make some new ones.

One thing was clear to me: No matter where they've been or where they're going, what they wanted or what they got, who they were or are — they've grown up.

The innocence is gone.

Class of '65, 22 Years Later

By the time we had our fortieth reunion in 2005, much had changed over the previous twenty-eight years. I was no longer working for the *Chronicle*, but I proposed a freelance piece catching up on the class as we approached our golden years.

I contacted several of the same classmates and some I hadn't reached before. I was moved by their stories of success, failure, joy, and tears. Even murder. Here's my article from October 2005.

> The leading-edge Baby Boomers of Lowell High School's graduating class of 1965, fresh from celebrating our 40th reunion last weekend in San Francisco, today are reflecting on four decades of turbulence, turning points, triumph and tragedy.
>
> Once the vanguard of our innocent Beach Boys-to-Beatles generation and now at the forefront of the maturing Boomer population, again we find ourselves facing a new age, in more ways than one. The Sixties, in other words, have taken on a whole new meaning.
>
> We were the pioneer class of sophomores when Lowell's shiny and spacious new $5 million Lake Merced campus opened in 1962, and we numbered 600-strong on graduation day three years later.
>
> More than 150 of us gathered in San Francisco last weekend to reconnect and ruminate about growing up, growing wiser and growing older. A certain denial remains, however, about the latter's impact on skin, hair, weight and eyesight.
>
> "Who are all these old people, and what am I doing here?" was a common remark heard throughout the celebration. "I still feel like I'm in my 30s."
>
> The events included a cocktail party at Tommy's Joynt on

Friday night, dinner and dancing at the Concordia Club on Saturday night, and a picnic at Lowell's Eucalyptus Drive campus on Sunday afternoon. The bash was planned and carried off by class member Roberta Bleiweiss, a longtime Bay Area event producer and a co-founder of Beach Blanket Babylon with her sister, Nancy, and Steve Silver, a 1962 Lowell grad.

"The turnout was a real testament to the closeness many of us still feel, even after all this time," said Bleiweiss. "For many in our class the memories of their days at Lowell are much fonder and more meaningful than their college days."

The camaraderie of the high school experience lives on at reunions, but over time the topics of conversation have changed from college, career, weddings and children to kids in college, retirement, multiple marriages and grandchildren. Not to mention aging parents, financial security, health care and even our own mortality. Illness and accidents have taken their toll. At least 16 of us are already gone.

Some in the Class of '65, befitting our generation's trademark iconoclasm, changed the world. And the world certainly changed many of us. Like any other cohesive group with 40 years of history, we've had our share of success and failure, hope and despair, love and heartbreak. Among those in our fold are:

-- Lani Silver, a political and social activist, longtime San Francisco State women's studies teacher and a 1993 KQED Woman of the Year who launched the first Holocaust Oral History Project, which led to her collaboration with movie director Steven Spielberg on gathering 53,000 Holocaust survivor histories for his Shoah Foundation for Visual History. (Lani died of brain cancer in 2009.)

-- Chuck Lindner, a Santa Monica attorney who helped Johnnie Cochran write the closing arguments for the defense in the murder trial of O.J. Simpson -- 30 years after Lindner tackled "The Juice" in a football game between Lowell and Galileo

High. But Lindner's football career came to an abrupt end -- a cancerous knee led to amputation of his left leg in college.

-- Randy "Gus" Koernig, a 57-year-old father of a class-record nine kids and a grandfather of 12 who, as a TV newsman in Montana, anchored the only nationally televised town hall meeting with President Bill Clinton, rode with the Blue Angels and reported from Russia on the collapse of the Soviet Union. And one day in 1991, while covering a fatal hiking accident in the Bear Tooth Mountains, he was stunned to learn that the victim was one of our classmates, Chuck Root.

-- Marilyn Sherman Ellis, a Southern California high school Spanish teacher who became a national advocate against drunken driving after a drunk driver killed her 22-year daughter in a crash eight years ago. More recently, Ellis has battled breast cancer.

-- Terry Zachery, the charismatic student body president who shot and killed a Los Angeles County deputy sheriff with the officer's gun after a routine traffic stop on the I-5 Grapevine in Gorman in 1978. Zachery was apparently under the influence of PCP when Deputy Arthur Pelino took him to the substation. When Pelino, who lived behind the substation, failed to come home for dinner, two of his children went to the substation, where they found their father dead on the floor and Zachery seated quietly in a chair. The children ran back to get Mrs. Pelino, who escorted Zachery into a cell and called for help. According to newspaper reports, Zachery pleaded guilty to involuntary manslaughter due to his mental state and served five years for the shooting.

-- Dennis Marcellino, a rock musician with Sly & The Family Stone, The Tokens and 3 Dog Night who turned from a near-suicidal period of abusing drugs, gambling and alcohol to Christianity when he "realized the Bible was true" and found inner peace.

-- Paul Batmale and Nancy Motzer, Lowell sweethearts who married at 21, had three children, divorced shortly before our

25th reunion in 1991, then remarried before the 30th. Today they have six grandchildren.

-- Tom Huff and Caren Bird, another pair of Lowellites who married young, had three children and were leading an idyllic life in Canada when Tom was diagnosed with cancer at 37. With surgeries, chemotherapy and radiation he lived 13 years before he died in 1998. "It's important to understand that Tom didn't 'lose his battle' with cancer," Bird says. "He won it."

In 1977, when we were turning 30, I profiled several of my classmates in a *Chronicle* article beginning with the premise that we perceived our Lowell diploma as our "express ticket to a rosy future, to success and happiness as we knew it."

Instead, we clashed head-on with the Vietnam War, the draft, campus protests, the psychedelic age, marijuana, rock music, black power, the sexual revolution, the women's movement and Watergate. And most of all, with ourselves -- our values, our attitudes, our goals.

Teens of the mid-1960s, according to a Time magazine cover story at the time, were "on the fringe of a golden era" -- brighter, better educated and more affluent, motivated and independent than ever before.

That came as no surprise to the Lowell community. The oldest public high school in the West -- Lowell turns 150 next year -- it has long ranked among the top academic schools in the nation and boasts some stellar alumni. Titans of business, government, medicine, law, education, science, public service, sports and the arts populate an alumni roster that includes:

Supreme Court Justice Stephen Breyer ('55), actress Carol Channing ('38), Yale University President Richard Levin ('64), former California Governor Edmund G. (Pat) Brown ('23), actor Benjamin Bratt ('82), *Chronicle* columnist Art Hoppe ('42), Pierre Salinger, network TV journalist and John F. Kennedy's presidential press secretary ('41), "Gorillas in the Mist" scientist Dian Fossey ('49), actor Bill Bixby ('52), author Irving Stone ('20), Bob Lee, three-time Minnesota Vikings Super Bowl quarterback ('63) and "Lemony Snicket" creator Daniel Handler ('88).

Many Lowell grads, encouraged toward independent thought by the times and the setting, were spurred to a philosophy of social change. At 20, when Lani Silver's priority in life was finding a husband and wondering "what color my brides-maids' dresses would be," her parents took her to South Africa, where the poverty and despair she witnessed in one short afternoon drive through Soweto transformed her.

"This morning I was a conservative," she told her mother and father at dinner that evening. "Tonight I'm a liberal."

In the 1977 article, Silver lamented a world "falling apart" with violence against women, pollution, unemployment, corporate indifference and injustice. Not much has changed, in her view.

"We're in a worse crisis today," Silver said. "The poor are getting poorer, the separation between the classes is growing, we're at war with half the world and we have the worst president ever."

Paul Batmale, a star basketball player at Lowell whose father, Louis Batmale, was the longtime chancellor of City College of San Francisco, and Nancy Motzer, a popular singer, personified the popular group in high school to which many adolescents aspire.

"I had a great time at Lowell, maybe too much fun sometimes," Batmale said. "It's a short period, but the times in high school are important developmental years where kids want to attach themselves to something."

Today the Batmales, the high school sweethearts who divorced and remarried, live in Auburn (Placer County), where he is an insurance broker with former 49ers quarterback Y.A. Tittle, and she is an executive with Kaiser in Sacramento.

For Marilyn Sherman, the post-Lowell path was predictable and happy -- for a time. A UCLA grad with a teaching credential, she met and married Sy Ellis, and they had two daughters, Kim and Amy. Then, on the night of December 9, 1997, their lives changed forever.

Kim, then a 22-year-old Pepperdine University law student on a break from finals, was driving on the Pacific Coast Highway when a drunk driver plowed head-on into her car, killing Kim and another young woman and injuring two other passengers. The driver, who had prior offenses, is now serving 18 years-to-life in prison.

Rather than cave in to debilitating depression, Ellis coped with her loss by forming a chapter of Students Against Destructive Decisions at her school, speaking at national conventions, organizing "Every 15 Minutes" drunken-driving awareness programs at schools, and supporting Mothers Against Drunk Driving events.

"When you lose your parents, you lose your past. But when you lose your children, you lose your future," said Ellis, who teaches Spanish at Sierra Vista High School. Her husband of 36 years is a mortgage banker.

Ellis has since overcome breast cancer and become a victims' advocate for MADD. "Without Kim, nothing is as joyful as it could be," Ellis said. "There will always be a big void, but life goes on. I stay involved to honor her. I try to keep busy and positive. My license plate frame says, 'Live Well. Laugh Often. Love Much.' "

That attitude typifies the outlook of many Baby Boomers today, the notion that life has been a collection of learning experiences, defining moments, rewarding work and precious memories. And that there is much more to come.

Some have retired while others are reinventing themselves and even now beginning new careers. Some are financially secure and others have failed to prepare adequately for their retirement years. Some married young, some often, some only recently. Some have grandchildren, some have infant children, some have no children.

One thing this particular group of Baby Boomers will always have in common, however, is their time together at Lowell.

Inside

The massive San Francisco public school redesign plan is to be voted on tomorrow night. Page 2.

A leading astronomer had some optimistic predictions about research in his field. Page 2.

The appointment of the new sheriff got "Amens" at a black church and criticism from Dianne Feinstein. Page 3.

Residents of an area in Los Angeles were advised to flee as new rainstorms began pounding the region. Page 3.

Environmental design critic Allan Temko described what's in store for Alcatraz Island under Park Service plans. Page 6.

A former U.S. ambassador said the government may drop the charges against the International Telephone and Telegraph Corp. Page 7.

A study released by Senator Edward Kennedy says that increases in defense spending cost the jobs of many Americans. Page 7.

President Sadat's appeals to U.S. Jews have divided a part of the community's organized leadership. Page 8.

Syrian and Lebanese leaders agreed on measures to end fighting between Syrian troops and Christian militia. Page 8.

Ousted U.S. Attorney David Marston tried to kill a probe of political corruption, a former aide said. Page 9.

A study showed that taxpayers earning more than $80,000 account for one-third of the tax breaks taken each year. Page 10.

South Africa's foreign minister cut off talks with Western nations on the future of Southwest Africa. Page 14.

Somalia's president said his hopes for help in the war with Ethiopia have been shattered by U.S. refusal of aid. Page 14.

James Bryant Conant, eminent educator who also served as adviser on the atomic bomb project, died at 84. Page 17.

Feminist artist Judy Chicago resents her work being classified as vaginal art. Page 21.

Allison Laland, who views parties as an art form, is the new Perle Mesta of Washington. Page 22.

Despite West Germany's prosperity, at least one city is a poverty pocket with ten percent joblessness. Page 30.

Weather

Bay Area: Showers likely Monday morning, clearing in the afternoon. Highs in the 50s, lows in the upper 30s and 40s. Winds to 30 m.p.h. Chances of rain, 6 in 10. Page 26.

San Francisco Chronicle

The Largest Daily Circulation in Northern California

114th Year No. 24 ★★★★ MONDAY, FEBRUARY 13, 1978 777-1111 20 CENTS

Disco Fever Sweeping Bay Area

These dancers at the Arthur Murray Dance Studio have been hit with the newest craze—disco fever—inspired by the smash hit 'Saturday Night Fever,' which stars disco king John Travolta and his boogying partner, Karen Gorney (at top)

Everybody Loves Saturday Night

By Duffy Jennings

The Fever is here and the Bay Area's got it bad.

It's not a virus or a disease in the normal sense, but disco fever — a phenomenon sweeping nightclubs, theaters, record shops, radio stations, dance studios, schools, parties and homes.

It's music and dancing, Latin satin and sweat. It's youth, energy, power and sex.

Makes you wanna snap your head back and strut. Wear slinky clothes and laugh, laugh . . . LOVE!

It's a fun fever, a happy fever. A work-all-work-and-then-bust-loose fever.

The afflicted got it from "Saturday Night Fever," the blockbuster film about Tony Manero, a 19-year-old Brooklyn kid who works in a paint store and leads an empty life except for Saturday night, when he reigns as king of the local disco.

The movie, starring John Travolta and featuring disco tunes by the Bee Gees, is grossing $1.5 million a week nationally. It pulled in $22,000 at the Regency II theater in San Francisco last week.

The soundtrack album has sold more than three million copies nationwide in 12 weeks, 100,000 in the Bay Area

alone, according to Jeff Trager, promotion manager for the distributor, Phonodisc. Local record industry experts say any album that sells 10,000 to 15,000 copies in the Bay Area is a monster hit. "This is incomprehensible," said one.

Dancing schools and instructors all over the region report that since the movie opened in December the number of people wanting to learn disco dancing has doubled or tripled. Many schools have had to hire new teachers and schedule extra classes exclusively for disco.

Some fever-wracked applicants have

Page 4, Col. 3

Tough Tone

Israel Assails U.S. Stand on Sinai Outposts

Jerusalem

The government of Prime Minister Menachem Begin yesterday sharply expressed its "regret and protest" over comments made by Secretary of State Cyrus R. Vance that Israeli settlements on the occupied bank of the Egyptian Sinai Peninsula "should not exist" because they violate international law.

A statement read by Begin to newsmen after a 2½-hour cabinet meeting was the strongest criticism of U.S. policy since Begin came to power nearly nine months ago.

The consensus statement of the cabinet, which clearly bore Begin's imprimatur, questioned the U.S. role as an impartial intermediary in the Egyptian and Israeli peace talk attempts.

It clearly reflected a growing concern here that the United States was moving towards the Egyptian position only a few days after talks at Camp David between President Carter and President Anwar Sadat of Egypt.

American officials here were presumably forewarned of the tough Israeli response to Vance's remarks when Begin met Saturday night with Ambassador Samuel W. Lewis. The normally communicative ambassador declined to comment to waiting newsmen after the meeting.

Members of the diplomatic community were a bit surprised at the tone of the Israeli response, since they said that Vance's remarks at a Friday news conference about Israeli settlements on lands captured from the Arabs during the 1967 war were not really new. The United States has long maintained that the settlements were "illegal" and constituted an "obstacle to peace."

But Vance's remarks that "they should not exist" were seen by a stronger than normal refutation of the Israeli position. In addition, the timing of Vance's comments so close after Sadat's visit may have prompted the strong response from Israel, which is hypersensitive to what it perceives as shifts in American support.

Some diplomats said that they felt the Israeli reaction comes also from a growing feeling that support for the Israeli stand in the current round of efforts for a Middle East peace may be eroding.

Back Page Col. 1

More Rain Heading For Bay Area

By Jack Lynch

Another fast-moving storm drenched the Bay Area yesterday morning, causing a number of automobile accidents on the Bay and Golden Gate bridges and an earthslide on Telegraph Hill before moving east to dump new snow in the Sierra.

Showers are forecast through this morning. And while skies are expected to clear later today, two

Back Page Col. 6

Diplomats Escape Fatal Hotel Bomb

Sydney, Australia

A bomb planted in a trash can exploded early today outside a hotel where 12 Asian and Pacific heads of state were gathered for a regional Commonwealth conference. Two Sydney sanitation men were killed.

Police reported six other persons were injured in the blast that was heard as far as buildings from the luxury hotel. A police spokesman said some of the conference delegates was injured.

He said an anonymous telephone caller warned of the bomb three minutes before it went off. He declined to speculate on the individual or group that might have been responsible for the bombing.

Police Superintendent Reginald Douglas said the bomb was planted in a trash can outside the main entrance of the Hilton Hotel on George street, a main Sydney

Back Page Col. 3

Deadly Sandstorm Hits Arab Nation

Abu Dhabi

A sandstorm lashed the United Arab Emirates this weekend, killing four people and uprooting power lines, the semi-official Al-Ittihad newspaper reported.

The gale-force winds, which started a string of minor fires, were followed by sporadic heavy rains in the emirates of Dubai and Sharjah. Scores of road accidents were reported.

Reuters

Mine Union Council Officially Rejects Pact

Washington

The bargaining council of the United Mine Workers union overwhelmingly rejected a proposed settlement of the nationwide coal strike yesterday, ordering UMW president Arnold Miller to begin new negotiations with the soft coal industry.

The action came in the 69th day of the strike, one day after the Carter administration ordered that plans be drawn up for emergency movement of coal to areas that are running critically short of fuel

needed to produce electric power.

Actually, yesterday's action was only a reaffirmation of the council's initial, unofficial rejection Friday of the three-year pact. At the time, the council conducted a straw vote, in which 33 of 36 members voted against the contract. Because Miller was not present for the session, yesterday's formal vote had to be taken.

The strike of about 160,000 miners — the longest coal strike in U.S. history — is threatening some Midwestern and Appalachian states

with critical fuel shortages.

"It's just too bad," said a dejected Miller, who had refused to attend Friday's session in a protest over what he called pressure tactics by miners who massed in the lobby of the union's headquarters here, demanding that the pact be voted down.

Miller, who had been pressing for approval of the contract offered by the Bituminous Coal Operators Association and signed last Monday, made little effort to conceal his

feelings about the latest development.

"I did not enumerate it," he said, when asked to give the vote by which the council rejected the pact. "It doesn't mean anything anyway."

On Saturday, Miller said he feared for his life. "I'm not going to present this contract to the council under conditions of mob rule," he said at the time.

Harrison Combs, general counsel of the UMW, said the contract

Back Page Col. 4

Index

Comics	46
Deaths	26
Entertainment	45
Finance	56
People	20
TV Radio	44
Weather	26

© Chronicle Publishing Co. 1978

CHAPTER 37:
Disco Fever

The film *Saturday Night Fever* opened in December 1977, whipping the Bay Area and the rest of the nation into a disco frenzy. I was among the throngs at local bars and music halls, buzzed on shots of tequila and toots of blow, trying to dance "The Hustle" like John Travolta to the music of the Bee Gees, Donna Summer, Gloria Gaynor, and Chic. The city editor said, "This disco thing is taking over. Go find out what it's all about and why everybody is so crazy about it." My front-page story ran the day before Valentine's Day, February 13, 1978.

The Fever is here and the Bay Area's got it bad.

It's not a virus or a disease in the normal sense, but disco fever — a phenomenon sweeping nightclubs, theaters, record shops, radio stations, dance studios, schools, parties and homes.

It's music and dancing, Latin satin and sweat. It's youth, energy, power and sex. Makes you wanna snap your head back and strut. Wear slinky clothes and tingle, laugh . . . LOVE!

It's a fun fever, a happy fever. A work-all-week-and-then-bust-loose fever.

The afflicted got it from "Saturday Night Fever," the blockbuster film about Tony Manero, a 19-year-old Brooklyn kid who works in a paint store and leads an empty life except for Saturday night, when he reigns as king of the local disco.

The movie, starring John Travolta and featuring disco tunes by the Bee Gees, is grossing $15 million a week nationally. It pulled in $22,000 at the Regency II theater in San Francisco last week.

The soundtrack album has sold more than three million copies nationwide in 12 weeks, 100,000 in the Bay Area alone, according to Jeff Trager, promotion manager for the distributor, Phonodisc. Local record industry experts say any album that sells 10,000 to 15,000 copies in the Bay Area is a monster hit. "This is incomprehensible," said one.

Dancing schools and instructors all over the region report that since the movie opened in December the number of people wanting to learn disco dancing has doubled or tripled. Many schools have had to hire new teachers and schedule extra classes exclusively for disco.

Some fever-wracked applicants have even demanded to be taught the precise solo routine Travolta performs in the film.

Many of these new students are men taking lessons secretly to surprise their wives and girlfriends.

"I think they feel threatened by Travolta's image as the new American sex symbol," suggested one Peninsula instructor. "He's young, lean, tough, sensitive and gorgeous. And he can dance.

"Guys come in here and say, 'Teach me to dance like him. I want to look like that on the dance floor'."

The movie, the record and the publicity have given the public a new awareness of the disco scene.

Disco dancing is bringing specific steps, courtship and sexuality back on the nation's dance floors after a generation of formless, individual expression in response to music.

Disco music is a more complex, more sophisticated and somewhat sweeter form than the hard-edged, brassy style of rock music. It is characterized by some changes and breaks, a tighter beat and longer instrumental passages.

This leads to longer tunes in general — six to ten minutes compared with three to four minutes for rock songs — and thus to longer periods on the dance floor.

Discos have been in existence here for about five years, and even longer on the East Coast, expanding steadily as an outgrowth of the Motown-style sounds and steps of the '60s. Now disco dancing has exploded.

There are an estimated 2000 discos in the United States today, with more opening everywhere there's room for a dance floor, a mirrored ball on the ceiling and some loudspeakers.

"Disco is finally hot," said Karen Lustgarten, who pioneered disco dance instruction here and still teaches it at The City disco in North Beach. "The movie definitely raised the public consciousness of disco."

She predicted that disco fashions popular in New York — shimmery, silky dresses and high heels, expensive shirts and elegant slacks — will soon be replacing T- shirts and jeans on Bay Area, disco dance floors.

The combination of the fleshy, flowing clothes, the upbeat and polished music and the moderately complex, structured dances that require more touching, turning and individual flourish appeals to people of all ages and cultures.

Also, with the evolution of the liberated '70s — not to mention Travolta's peacock-style primping and prancing on screen — men have a greater desire to look better, dress better and dance better than they have in many years.

The disco is also an economical form of entertainment, both for the proprietor and the customer.

By paying a lone disc jockey to play records rather than hiring an entire band, the owner saves enough overhead to be able to keep admission and drink prices remarkably low.

Admission averages $1 to $2 for most Bay Area discos, with drinks ranging from 75 cents to $1.25.

Lessons in the various styles of the Hustle (L.A., New York, Latin, Spanish, Rope and Tango, among others) along with other disco dance steps, average $4 to $5 per hour. They're given at formal dance schools, private studios and discos.

"We've signed-up 50 people in the last three weeks,' said Sharon Wroten at Schumacher's School of Dance in South San Francisco.

"Most of them aren't sure what to call it when they come in, but by the time I get through talking with them I find out they wanted to learn to dance like John Travolta."

She said the new students range in age from 16 to about 40, and that the school had to hire new teachers and schedule new classes for disco.

LaVonia Herrington, an instructor at Dance City in Oakland, said disco dances are appealing because they're based somewhat on the swing, jitterbug and cha cha dances of yesteryear, which draw's older students, yet they feature more footwork, turns and abrupt movements that younger dancers enjoy.

Bambi Lander at Arthur Murray's studio in San Francisco said nine out of ten new students ask for disco lessons.

Disco dancing routines are also being taught in junior high and high school P.E. classes-throughout the Bay Area as part of courses in modern dance or jazz dancing.

These classes are filled mainly by adolescent girls, but some boys are taking lessons, too, in apparent defiance of long-established, taboos among pubescent boys.

But it's definitely the girls among the teenagers who are the most swept up by the fever, or at least by the magnetism of Travolta.

"He's, so cute," said one enamored tenth-grader. "All anybody talks about around my school is Vinnie Barbarino (the character Travolta plays in "Welcome Back Kotter" on television) and his black bikini underwear."

Inside

Three San Francisco boys who ordered mid-morning tea were taken off the cruise ship Oriana, thwarting their plans to stow away. Page 2.

The state attorney general's office has filed suit against a firm, charging it sold thousands of fake diplomas. Page 2.

A self-portrait by Vincent Van Gogh was slashed and badly damaged in Amsterdam. Page 3.

A TV show has brought to the fore the debate between believers and disbelievers in the mind's power to move objects. Page 4.

Southern Pacific is trying a new tack in its efforts to abandon Peninsula passenger train service. Page 5.

TOP OF THE NEWS

Close scrutiny suggest that the attorney general's job is more varied and less jazzy than being the state's "top cop." Page 6.

There is an internal struggle in the state attorney general's office over environmental laws. Page 6.

Senator Ted Kennedy denied rumors that he and his wife of 20 years, Joan, have split up. Page 8.

Columnist Jimmy Breslin found some interesting answers to questions about John Mitchell's furloughs from prison. Page 9.

Italian officials issued warrants for the arrest of nine suspected kidnapers of Aldo Moro. Page 10.

Soviet sources said Moscow ordered Soviet fighter pilots to fire missiles at the Korean airliner to force it down. Page 10.

The Supreme Court outlawed pension plans requiring women to contribute larger portions of their salaries than men. Page 11.

A $4 million center for treatment of sickle-cell anemia victims in the Bay Area was unveiled. Page 14.

Some Bay Area household pets earn their keep by modeling for advertisements and TV commercials. Page 17.

Hollywood is betting that American audiences are ready to pay to see movies about the Vietnam war. Page 18.

It's possible to change cooking measurements to the metric system without making conventional cookbooks obsolete. Page 20.

In the second heaviest trading in history, the stock market moved up 7½ points. Page 27.

Weather

Bay Area: Partly cloudy and clearing Wednesday. Lows, upper 40s to mid 50s; highs, 60s. Winds westerly to 20 m.p.h. Page 35.

A New Zodiac Letter

See Below

San Francisco Chronicle

The Largest Daily Circulation in Northern California

114th Year No. 81 ★★★★ WEDNESDAY, APRIL 26, 1978 777-1111 20 CENTS

Emotional Plea by Carter For $25 Billion Tax Cut

U.S. Studies Closing of The Presidio

The Defense Department has begun a study aimed at the possible closing of the Presidio of San Francisco and Letterman Army Hospital and possible cutbacks at the Alameda Naval Air Station, Senator Alan Cranston (Dem-Calif.) disclosed yesterday.

Cranston said seven California military installations have been targeted for cutback or "closing" studies, which may take six to eight months to complete.

If the cutbacks or closings are carried out, he said, it would result in a reduction of 11,720 military personnel in the state, 3338 of whom are civilians.

Mayor George Moscone took the news in stride, saying "the closing of the Presidio has been rumored many times before and a final decision is still a long way off."

Nevertheless, the mayor said, he has asked director of planning Rai Okamoto to begin a study of possible uses for the Presidio's 1480 acres in the northwest corner of the city.

The land, should the Defense Department abandon it, would automatically be transferred to the Department of the Interior and become part of the Golden Gate National Recreation Area.

Dianne Feinstein, president of the Board of Supervisors, sprang to the historic Presidio's defense.

She said she will introduce a resolution Monday urging Congress to keep the Presidio open as a military post.

"I will do everything I can to keep it open. I will lobby with the Congress and with the President to gain a reprieve," she said.

The Presidio was originally fortified as a military base by soldiers of King Charles III of Spain in 1776 and has continuously served as a military base since then.

It currently employs 3300 military personnel, with 7000 dependents, and 3489 civilian personnel, including those who work at Letterman Army Hospital.

Under the Defense Department's study plan, Cranston said, Letterman Army Hospital would be closed and its patients and personnel would be transferred to the Oakland Naval Hospital.

Before this could be done, the Oakland hospital would have to be reinforced for earthquakes at a cost of $30 million.

Representative John Burton (Dem-S.F.) said the House Governmental Operations Committee, at his request, has been investigating for some months the financing and

Back Page Col. 5

Patty at Home

Patricia Hearst was caught off guard by a television camera as she walked into her parents' home on the San Francisco peninsula yesterday. In San Francisco, meanwhile, her attorney, Albert Johnson, was trying to get her bank robbery sentence reduced. In a meeting with U.S. District Judge William H. Orrick and U.S. Attorney William Hunter in the Federal Building, Johnson asked that her sentence be either modified or revoked. The three will meet again today.

Zodiac Ends Silence— 'I Am Back With You'

By Duffy Jennings

Zodiac, the cryptic and boastful killer who stalked the Bay Area in the late 1960s and was last heard from more than four years ago, wrote a new letter to The Chronicle yesterday, proclaiming: "I am back with you."

The random slayer of at least six persons, who delighted in teasing police with coded messages to news media after each cold-blooded murder, claimed no new victims and made no threats in the note, but surfaced nevertheless in Zodiac's typical bold fashion.

"This is the Zodiac speaking," the letter began, exactly like the first message Zodiac sent The Chronicle in 1969. "I am back with you."

The letter, postmarked Monday in San Francisco and hand-printed in Zodiac's familiar style with a blue felt-tipped pen, was addressed simply, "Dear Editor."

He sent greetings to Chronicle columnist Herb Caen, taunted San Francisco police homicide inspector David Toschi, who has pursued Zodiac nearly nine years, and said he was waiting for a Zodiac movie.

"Tell herb caen I am here. I have always been here," he wrote. "That city pig toschi is good but I am smarter and better he will get tired then leave me alone."

"I am waiting for a good movie

Back Page Col. 2

Gay Rights Law Repealed in St. Paul by a Large Margin

St. Paul, Minn.

Voters repealed the city's four-year-old "gay rights" law yesterday in the nation's first major test of such legislation since Dade county, Fla., threw out its homosexual rights ordinance last June.

With returns counted from half of the city's 161 precincts, the vote was 23,680 in favor or repeal and 11,075 against it.

The Baptist-led Citizens Alert for Morality crusaded to repeal the St. Paul ordinance. The St. Paul Citizens for Human Rights, which also included some clergy, fought to keep the law.

They disagreed on what was at issue. The repeal forces said the issue was morality. Their opponents said it was human rights.

The law was enacted in 1974 as part of the city's human rights

Back Page Col. 2

Warning On Jobs

Washington

President Carter pleaded anew yesterday for passage of his tax cut, saying congressional failure to approve it would cost each American family $800 and swell unemployment rolls by a million people.

Carter insisted that his proposal for a net income tax reduction of $25 billion would not fuel inflation, a possibility raised by congressional Democrats who are seeking a smaller cut.

In a nationally televised news conference, Carter also:

- Delivered an emotional defense of his proposals for revising the laws governing the collection of taxes from U.S. citizens. He cited as an example a $14,000 deduction claimed by a surgeon to entertain fellow doctors on a yacht. "Most Americans don't even have a yacht," Carter said.
- Rejected Soviet President Leonid Brezhnev's offer to forego production of a Russian neutron bomb if the United States will do likewise. Carter said the idea was "of no significance" because the weapon would be of no use of to the Soviets anyway.
- Repeated his insistence that Congress approve the all-or-nothing sale of U.S. fighter jets to Egypt, Saudi Arabia and Israel. Carter said, "I am completely convinced that the Saudis want the planes to protect their own security." The sale has been opposed by some who fear the Saudis would use the U.S.-supplied F-15 planes in any offensive against Israel.
- Said he has found dealing with the federal bureaucracy "worse than I anticipated," and called for prompt congressional action on his legislation to overhaul the civil service system.

The President said that he has no intention of scaling down or delaying the effect of his tax-cut proposal, due to take effect at the beginning of fiscal 1979 on October 1.

"I hope that the Congress can act rapidly enough to make the reduction effective then," Carter said, adding:

"The last quarter's results in the growth in our national product showed some leveling off. It needs

Back Page Col. 1

Brezhnev's Pledge On Neutron Bombs

Moscow

Soviet President Leonid I. Brezhnev promised yesterday that the Soviet Union will not build neutron warheads unless the United States eventually decides to produce the controversial weapons.

President Carter's decision to defer production of neutron bombs was "at best a half measure," Brezhnev said in a televised speech to the Young Communist League.

"But I can inform you that we have taken the President's statement into account and that we, too, will not begin production of neutron arms so long as the United States does not do so," he said. "Further developement will depend on Washington."

In Washington, President Carter told a televised news conference the Russians have no need for a neutron weapon, because the warhead is primarily an anti-tank weapon and the Russians have more tanks in Central Europe than NATO forces do.

Carter suggested a more res-

Back Page Col. 6

South Africa OKs West's Namibia Plan

Cape Town, South Africa

South African Prime Minister John Vorster announced yesterday that his government has accepted a Western-sponsored plan to bring independence to the disputed territory of Namibia by the end of the year.

Vorster's decision to accept the Western formula for ending 58 years of South African rule over the mineral-rich territory seems likely to bring strong international pressure to bear on the guerrilla group that has been battling South Africa, the South West Africa People's Organization.

If SWAPO can also be persuaded to accept the Western plan — which calls for an end to the guerrilla war, introduction of a U.N. peace-keeping force and free elections for a constituent assembly — a transition to majority rule will prove possible without the kind of civil war looming in Rhodesia.

In New York, where the U.N. General Assembly is holding a debate on the Namibian situation, SWAPO leader Sam Nujoma declined immediate comment on Vorster's statement.

U.S. officials, however, expressed hope that SWAPO will decide to accept the plan.

The independence plan, drawn up during the past year by the United States, Britain, France, Canada and West Germany, envisages a phased withdrawal of the 20,000 South African troops now based in Namibia by the end of the year.

In announcing South Africa's acceptance, Vorster indicated that the final breakthrough to agreement came in a Western "clarification" that some South African troops could remain in Namibia if asked to do so by an interim administration.

This seems likely to make the

Back Page Col. 6

Younger Challenges A-Plant Law

By John Balzar
Chronicle Correspondent

Sacramento

In an act with as much political as practical impact, Attorney General Evelle Younger issued a formal opinion yesterday that California's much-proclaimed nuclear safeguards laws are unconstitutional.

Younger is a Republican candidate for governor and a strong advocate of continued nuclear development in the state.

His opinion has legal significance, but by itself does not have the force of overturning the landmark 1976 safeguards laws.

Governor Brown's administration spurned Younger's action yesterday as "just one lawyer's opin-

Page 6, Col. 6

Unique Tax Relief Package in Colorado

Denver

The Colorado Legislature, invoking a new law that limits the growth of state spending, is giving residents a $101 million tax break.

The law requires that excess revenue be returned to the state's 2.2 million citizens in the form of tax relief.

The reductions will mean a saving of at least $53 for a family of four with an income of $18,000 when that family pays state taxes on its 1978 income, state officials say.

The tax relief will take this form:

- A $35 million appropriation to increase state financing of public schools, in effect reducing local property taxes by that amount.
- A nine-bill tax-reduction

Back Page Col. 2

Index

Comics........32
Deaths........36
Entertainment........53
Finance........27
Food........20
People........17
TV-Radio........52
Weather........35

CHAPTER 38:
Zodiac is Back...Or is He?

Four years had passed since Zodiac's last letter to the *Chronicle* in 1974, but a sample of the killer's printing was still pasted to the counter atop the mail slots, so copyboys could be on the lookout for anything new from him when sorting the mail. Early on the afternoon of April 25, 1978, copyboy Brant Ward was sorting mail when a hand-printed letter addressed to the editor caught his attention. Brant, an outgoing kid with straight, white-blond hair and a youthful face, was a friend of Cheryl's oldest brother, and I had helped him get the job. He had a keen eye for images that later helped him become a prize-winning *Chronicle* photographer, a job he held for thirty-one years. Brant took the letter to office manager Mike Duncan, who brought it right to me at my desk. "This looks like Zodiac's printing," he said.

"It sure does," I said. I showed it to the city desk, then we opened it carefully and removed the letter with care not to get any fingerprints on it. "This is the Zodiac speaking," it began. "I am back with you." A cameraman came out to photograph the envelope and the letter before we slipped it into a plastic bag and then into a manila envelope. When I couldn't reach Dave Toschi by phone, I took the bus over to the Hall of Justice. He was out working on a case when he got word on his police radio to call in. Toschi went to a nearby police call box and was told that I was waiting for him.

"This is the real thing, Dave," I said. "I have to get back to write the story. Let me know what you think when you see it."

Toschi took the letter to questioned documents expert John Shimoda, director of the United States Postal Inspection Service Western Region Crime Laboratory in San Bruno. After examining the letter for thirty minutes, Shimoda looked at Toschi.

"I'd say he's back," Shimoda said.

"Are you sure?" Toschi pressed.

"That's your man," he replied.

Sherwood Morrill, the retired questioned documents expert for the State Bureau of Criminal Investigation and Identification, who had verified all the previous Zodiac letters and notes, corroborated Shimoda's finding. As soon as Toschi returned from seeing Shimoda, he called me at the paper and told me the new letter was genuine. "It's been a long four years," he said. We talked a bit more before I hung up, inserted his comments into my story and finished in time for the first edition.

This was my article that ran on April 26, 1978:

> Zodiac, the cryptic and boastful killer who stalked the Bay Area in the late 1960s and was last heard from more than four years ago. wrote a new letter to The *Chronicle* yesterday, proclaiming: "I am back with you."
>
> The random slayer of at least six persons, who delighted in teasing police with coded messages news media after each cold-blooded murder, claimed no new victims and made no threats in the note but surfaced nevertheless in Zodiac's typical bold fashion.
>
> "This is the Zodiac speaking," the letter began, exactly like the first message Zodiac sent The *Chronicle* in 1969. "I am back with you."
>
> The letter, postmarked Monday in San Francisco and hand-printed in Zodiac's familiar style with blue felt-tipped pen, was address simply, "Dear Editor."
>
> He sent greetings to *Chronicle* columnist Herb Caen, taunted San Francisco police homicide inspector David Toschi, who has pursued Zodiac nearly nine years, and said he was waiting for a Zodiac movie.
>
> "Tell herb caen I am here. I have always been here," he wrote. "That city pig toschi is good but I am smarter and better he will get tired then leave me alone.

"I am waiting for a good movie about me. who will play me. I am now in control of all things."

He signed the note. "Yours truly," as he did in his last message to The *Chronicle* in January 1974.

Below that was drawn Zodiac's now infamous logo—a circle with a cross through it—and the notation "SFPD-O"—his customary method of reminding police that they have not caught him.

"It has been a long four years," Toschi said late yesterday after a handwriting expert "positively confirmed" the printing as Zodiac's first communication since he wrote to criticize the film, "The Exorcist," in 1974.

Zodiac is known to have killed at least six persons and wounded two others between 1966 and 1969, mostly in random shooting attacks on couples alone in remote Bay Area settings.

Included in the slayings were the shooting of a San Francisco cab driver in the Presidio Heights district in 1969 and the 1966 throat slashing of a young woman student at Riverside City College.

In his last letter in 1974, however, Zodiac claimed a total of 37 victims, then disappeared and was not heard from again until yesterday.

"I could feel the excitement in my body as soon as I saw it," Toschi said after the letter was turned over to him for examination.

Toschi said he was so rattled by the development, in fact, that he picked up a cigarette and started smoking for the first time in three years.

"But I put it out right away as soon as I realized what I was doing." said the detective, his voice trembling with nervous excitement.

Toschi said he has talked to more than 5000 persons since he was assigned to the Zodiac case in 1969.

"I have always felt that he was alive and out there, somewhere," Toschi said of Zodiac's self-imposed 51-month silence. "I still don't know where he is, but at least now I know that all our work all these years definitely has not been in vain."

Zodiac's latest reference to a movie of his exploits is in keeping with his apparent affinity for show business, particularly films and theater.

In his previous messages, he often quoted from Gilbert and Sullivan's operetta, "The Mikado," and, in addition to his harsh review of "The Exorcist," he panned other movies as well.

A movie about him, titled "Zodiac," was, in fact, produced and shown here at the Golden Gate Theater in 1970.

The low-budget film, starring two unknown actors in the title role, ended without clearly identifying either one as the killer but a narrator hinted to the audience that he "may be the man behind you in the theater."

Zodiac first came to public attention in October 1969, when he mailed a note and a piece of cab driver Paul Stine's bloody shirttail to The *Chronicle* a few days after Stine was murdered in his cab at Washington and Cherry streets.

In the letter, Zodiac heckled police for not catching him at the scene of the killing and said he was "the same man who did in the people in the North Bay Area," referring to four other murders in Vallejo and Lake Berryessa during the previous year.

At the time, witnesses to and survivors of Zodiac attacks described their assailant as a husky white man wearing glasses and a crew cut. The descriptions served as the basis for a composite drawing circulated widely at the peak of the hunt for him.

The case drew worldwide attention – and thousands of tips from persons believing either that they knew the killer or had broken the code of the peculiar cryptograms in his messages.

But the elusive Zodiac remained free and unidentified other than by his self-chosen astrological nickname.

He continued to write letters and bizarre messages to this newspaper and others until 1971, when he abruptly stopped all communication and kept silent for three years until the so-called "Exorcist" letter of 1974.

But there would be a surprising development about this letter that no one expected. Although Toschi said two experts had verified its authenticity, suspicion arose that Toschi may have written the letter himself to generate new attention to the case—and to himself—after four years of silence since the 1974 letter.

An investigation ensued in which Toschi admitted writing anonymous fan letters to *Chronicle* writer Armistead Maupin about his ongoing series, "Tales of the City," in 1976, but he denied writing the newest Zodiac letter and it was never proven that he did. Nor was it determined that Zodiac was the author, either.

Because of the fan mail to Maupin, Toschi was removed from the homicide detail—and the Zodiac case—and reassigned to the robbery squad. He remained on the force for another nine years before retiring in 1987 after thirty-four years, including twelve in homicide.

CHAPTER 39:
A Detective's Search for Answers

For years after I left the newspaper, I went out to the Sunset District at least once a year to have coffee or lunch with Dave Toschi just to keep in touch. He always wanted to meet at his favorite place, the Copper Kettle on Taraval Street, around the corner from his house. He would show up in his trench coat, pulling back one flap just enough so I could see that he still carried his small revolver in its upside-down shoulder holster under his left armpit. "You never know," he would say, closing his coat again. He explained it by reminding me he was working as a part-time security guard for a downtown hotel, but even after that ended he still never left the house unarmed.

When we last met, in early October 2009, the conversation turned to the upcoming fortieth anniversary of the Zodiac killer's last known murder, the shooting of cab driver Paul Stine.

Over coffee that morning, Dave told me that every October 11 for the previous forty years, if he was healthy and in town, he would drive across the city to Washington and Cherry Streets in Presidio Heights, where Zodiac killed Stine.

"I always park exactly where I parked the radio car that night," he said. "I look around the intersection and I wonder what the heck happened. Did we cover all the bases? Did we miss anything at the scene? Why didn't we get this guy? I ended up with a bleeding ulcer over this case. It still haunts me. It always will."

Toschi still recalled that night in precise detail. He and his partner, Bill Armstrong, had been on call all week and had already worked three murders, including one the night before.

"I was exhausted," said Toschi. "I went to bed around 8 o'clock. The phone rang at 10:15. I remember exactly what the dispatcher said:

'You've got a sloppy one near the Presidio. Cab driver shot in the head.' I got dressed and went to pick up Bill in Parkmerced.

"There was blood everywhere. We thought it was a robbery from the beginning. We had witnesses, we had a description, we had fingerprints – we just figured we're gonna get the guy. I will always wonder if he really was watching us, like he said in his letter."

Toschi worked on at least a hundred murder cases during his career, including the Zebra killings and others with notoriety, but none as compelling, frustrating, or infamous as Zodiac.

Toschi gained notoriety of his own for his trademark upside-down shoulder holster, his bow ties, his tan trench coat, and the ever-present animal crackers he snacked on. Steve McQueen was said to have modeled his SFPD detective character in the acclaimed film, *Bullitt*, after Toschi. McQueen wore a tan trench coat and shoulder holster in the movie.

Actor Mark Ruffalo portrayed Toschi in the 2007 feature film, "Zodiac," based on a book by former *Chronicle* editorial cartoonist Robert Graysmith. Anthony Edwards of television's *ER* fame played Armstrong, who retired from the police department in 1977. Armstrong died several years ago.

Also in the film, Jake Gyllenhaal played Graysmith and Robert Downey Jr. played the part of Paul Avery.

"I thought Ruffalo did a good job," said Toschi, who still watched the film from time to time. "I enjoy it, but it depresses me. After I watch it I get angry at myself because I couldn't close the case."

Graysmith's book and the film focus on one man, Arthur Leigh Allen, as the prime suspect in the case. Toschi said Allen was the "best suspect" he ever investigated. But Allen was ruled out by fingerprints, handwriting samples, and DNA and was never charged in connection with any Zodiac killings. He died in 1992.

Toschi's health continued to decline over the years and on January 6, 2018, he died peacefully at eighty-six at home with his wife of sixty years, Carol, and his family by his side. He never once referred to Carol in any conversation with me by anything other than "my bride."

Dave's daughter, Linda Toschi-Chambers, asked me to help with notifying the Bay Area news media about her father's passing. "Mom wanted me to tell you that my dad considered you a friend and always respected you and your work," she said.

CHAPTER 40:
A Reporter's Search for Adam Goldberg

In 2006, I received an e-mail from my son, Adam, himself a budding young Los Angeles actor at the time, who had seen an online casting notice for the part of Duffy Jennings in director David Fincher's upcoming Zodiac film. "Hey, Dad," he wrote. "Check this out." It called for a "30-ish male, blond, slightly chubby."

"What the hell?" I said to Adam. Sure, I'd been a little overweight from time to time, but I was miffed about the "chubby" reference. What's more, I had no idea they were making a Zodiac movie. All was forgiven later when I learned that the role had gone to Goldberg, then in his mid-thirties, who looks nothing at all like me but at least was a fellow of average weight.

A few months later, in conjunction with the movie's debut in March 2007, the *Chronicle* had asked me to write a freelance piece for its Sunday Datebook section about the atmosphere at the newspaper during the Zodiac years. I asked the editor, Leba Hertz, if I could also interview Goldberg about playing me for a short sidebar article. She agreed, and I set out to contact him.

I was curious to talk to my new alter ego to find out how he planned to bring me to life on the big screen. Goldberg's profile on the Internet Movie Database Web site begins with the pithy observation that he is "an actor with a talent for mining the neuroses of his characters for both comedic and dramatic effect."

This gift doubtless served him well for his role as Sol in the Oscar-winning film *A Beautiful Mind* and multiple appearances as Russell Shultz on the TV series "Head Cases." Like everyone else, I have a few neuroses, but I wasn't sure how I felt about having them "mined" by a Hollywood actor for comedic or dramatic effect. Never mind about the chubby part.

How, I wondered, could he tap into the nuances of my inquisitive personality, my unique facial expressions, the precise timbre of my voice on that morning thirty years earlier when I shouted into the phone to Inspector Toschi: "We just got another Zodiac letter!"

When I told my daughter, Danielle, that Goldberg had been cast as me, she asked if he had contacted me to ask any questions. No, I told her. "Can he do that? Just play you in a movie without calling you?" she asked "Doesn't he have to get your permission or something?"

I guess not, I told her. And it's not as if I didn't try to reach him.

Over the course of nine months after hearing about the casting notice, I left messages chasing Goldberg through two talent agencies ("I'll let him know you called") and three PR firms ("We used to represent him, but not anymore").

I finally connected with his then-publicist, Rene Ridinger, who returned my call on the third voice mail.

She apologized profusely, citing recent duties at the Sundance Film Festival and a subsequent cold, and said Goldberg had been traveling.

"Adam is back but had a ton of meetings today," she said in an e-mail. "He's going to call me tomorrow, so we can get a time figured out. I will call or e-mail you as soon as we have connected tomorrow."

But then, nothing. More waiting and no further contact from her, or him. In the end, Goldberg proved as elusive as Zodiac, who was never found either. But at least Zodiac called the media and wrote to the *Chronicle* when we were looking for him.

I told Leba Hertz about my futile efforts to reach Goldberg and said I wouldn't be able to write the sidebar about him. "But that's even a better story about how hard it was to find him," she said. "You should definitely write about that."

Fortunately, my character's part in the film was so minuscule that it escaped the attention of all the critics except the harshest ones—my family and friends—who said it wasn't a big enough role.

In a city room scene, Jake Gyllenhaal, as Robert Graysmith, sees a new reporter unpacking his belongings at what had been Paul Avery's desk. Jake walks over to him.

"Hi, we haven't met," he says with an outstretched hand. "I'm Robert Graysmith."

"I'm Duffy Jennings," Goldberg replies, returning the handshake. Then he sits down, pulls a tape recorder from his box and places it on the desk.

"Nice to meet you," says Gyllenhaal. "You got a great desk. Guy who used to work here was a great reporter."

"Oh, yeah? I'm sure he was," says the Duffy guy. "I mean, it's an honor to leave the *Chronicle* and go work for the *Sacramento Bee.* Dare to dream, right, Robert?" He lights a cigarette and ends the conversation with, "Nice to meetcha."

I never said such a snarky thing about Paul Avery, to Graysmith or anyone else. A script writer's license, it was. And that was it for my character, save for another couple of lines a bit later in the film when the new 1978 Zodiac letter arrives. (Graysmith told me later that he insisted on having my character in the story to explain why Avery was suddenly gone from the paper.)

CHAPTER 41:
Do Something

One February morning in 1979 Dave Perlman called me up to his desk. "Bill German [the managing editor] and I want you to cover the Dan White trial," he said. "We think you've earned it, and you know the case and all of the key people better than anyone else."

I was both surprised and gratified. First, it was something of a redemption for not getting the lead story assignment the day of the Moscone-Milk murders. I had covered parts of other trials before as a fill-in, including the Patty Hearst and Golden Dragon cases, but never a complete trial. I was hoping to get the assignment but there were other longtime trial veterans on the staff and I knew this would be the city's biggest story of the year up that point. As Perlman said, I was very familiar not only with the crime, but with the board of supervisors, the city's homicide detectives, and the prosecution team.

As much as I wanted to cover the trial, though, I couldn't bring myself to ask directly for it. Among the traits the adult child of an alcoholic learns is the reluctance to ask for what you want. It made me uncomfortable to impose on someone else with my own needs, and I feared they might say no, leaving me feeling rejected. At the same time, I was struggling with other personal issues. I had been separated from Cheryl for several months and was missing work, owing to my mother's declining health, my depression, and late-night partying.

Only a couple of weeks earlier, I had written a letter to Ed Roseborough, a high school buddy who lived in Vail, Colorado. I sent him letters often with updates on my work, family, and social life. Cheryl and I had visited him to ski in the past and we were talking about another visit. He knew we'd been separated quite a while, but he wasn't aware how bleak the situation was. Partly because I kept telling him I hoped she and I would get back together. Now I spilled out the truth.

"I sure as hell never expected to be telling you this," I wrote, "but the reason I haven't told you if Cheryl and I are coming out there to ski this year is because I'm not too sure we'll still be together a month from now. Or a week from now, for that matter. I guess a lot of it comes down to boredom, for me especially. For her, success in her career finally surpassed me in importance in her life. I guess I want a change. I've been in the same job and with the same woman for 12 years, and now I want a family and more of a domestic situation, but she's not ready for that, and even if she says she is, I know she's not being honest with herself. It's the damnedest situation I've ever heard of, Eddie, and I'm so fucking confused right now that I really don't know what will happen in the next few weeks.

"It all started really about six months back, just after our trip to Colorado and Cheryl got her new job. She worked six days a week for two months, then went on all nights and has been doing that since. I got so I didn't want to go home after work and I had difficulty dealing with her new fame and recognition. It was overwhelming, how everywhere we went all anybody talked about was how great she was and how exciting it was to see her on TV. I encouraged it, of course, and supported her all the way, and I don't ever regret that. But at the same time, I was having my own identity crisis because she was getting something I'd worked years for and never saw. Shit, I can't tell you how many parties we went to and after all the attention she got, people would turn to me and ask things like, "And what do you do?" or "Are you in broadcasting, too, Duffy?" I realize that I dealt with all of it badly, but just the same I couldn't help it. And Cheryl worked, and worked and worked, assuming I was fine all the time, as usual. What she didn't know, and I didn't want to tell her for fear it might put too much pressure on her to give up something she worked so hard for, was that I wanted her home more, and I wanted children.

"The upshot of all this for right now is that I think I'm on the brink of moving out, at least for a few weeks, just to see if the old spark will be rekindled, because there's sure no evidence of it when we're together. I haven't really decided yet, or told Cheryl I'm even thinking about it, but it's only a matter of days, I think, before I do something. That's the whole point. I've got to *do something*, even if it turns out to be the most fucked up move I ever made. I could regret it for the rest of my life, but what I'm afraid of is that I might regret it even more if I don't do something different with my life right now. And certainly, the way things are now is no fun for her, either."

In a 2007 interview with the *Marin Independent Journal*, Cheryl talked about the effect on us of her working both the radio and television jobs—days at K101 and nights at KPIX-TV—for about a year. "Let's just say the demands of my career were hard on the relationship," she told the IJ reporter. Sitting home alone at night while she worked reminded me too much of being home alone in high school. But to be fair, while I blamed our separation on her long work hours, that also became a convenient excuse for my own failures in the relationship. I know my behavior caused her a lot of pain. I never really understood this until many years and two more marriages later.

Meanwhile, my mother was in Mount Zion Hospital for treatment of the first stages of liver disease. Complicating her condition was the fact she spent hours in bed every day, watching TV, needlepointing, and drinking. She had no desire to do anything. She had poor circulation, high blood pressure, bedsores, and difficulty walking a block or climbing the one flight of stairs to her flat. She was discharged from the hospital after two weeks, and two months later was arrested for a hit-and-run accident. I don't recall the details after all these years, but it further added to my worries and frustration over her. I didn't know what to do, how to help her. I was angry, frustrated, confused, and feeling guilty.

Within a month of my letter to Ed, I moved out of the Marin house and into a Cow Hollow flat on Filbert Street with two of my *Chronicle* colleagues, sports copy editor Bill Regan and copyboy Brant Ward. Most of my co-workers knew I'd moved out, but I doubt many were aware of the depth of my funk. For weeks I had questioned my abilities to concentrate and perform at a high level. This trial assignment, however, was exactly the shot of confidence I needed.

CHAPTER 42:
The Dan White Trial

On April 21, 1979 I wrote a long advance piece about the upcoming trial, a "scene-setter," we called it, outlining the people who would be involved, the prosecution and defense strategies, the political environment behind the killings, and Dan White's background. It began:

> Daniel James White, a single-minded political neophyte in a city of widely varying social and political values, goes on trial for his life next week, charged with the murders of San Francisco Mayor George Moscone and Supervisor Harvey Milk in city hall last November 27.
>
> For White, a fierce competitor who calls himself 'a believer in the American dream that a person can do anything he wants when he puts his mind to it,' this will be the toughest of all his personal battles.
>
> And for the city, the trial of the 32-year-old former supervisor for killing two popular elected officials will be a test of its own ideals – that government can function objectively even when torn asunder from within."

The article noted that security at the trial would be inordinately tight. Reporters were coming from around the nation and everyone entering the courtroom would pass through a metal detector and be patted down by county sheriff's deputies.

A thick shield of bulletproof glass would separate the gallery from the forward arena occupied by the judge, prosecutors, attorneys, defendant, and the jury. Prosecutor Thomas Norman said he expected to call some twenty witnesses, while White's lawyer, Douglas Schmidt (who had represented one of the Golden Dragon restaurant shooters) planned to call twice that many. The trial was expected to last four to six weeks.

Judge Walter Calcagno had reserved two wooden chairs inside the glass shield for reporters from the city's two daily newspapers— me and my colleague from the *Examiner*, the highly respected Jim Wood. The remaining press were to sit in the gallery behind the glass or in an overflow auditorium down the hall, where three twenty-one-inch, closed-circuit TV monitors were set up to view the proceedings.

On April 25, I reported to Department 21 of the Superior Court at the Hall of Justice at 850 Bryant Street for the first day of jury selection.

From my seat inside the glass and just behind the prosecution table, I could see White's face clearly, as well as those of defense attorney Schmidt and assistant DA Norman and, later, all the members of the jury. A television camera was bracketed to a front wall, pointing at White, the prosecutor's table and the gallery. Another was affixed on a rear wall, facing diagonally across the courtroom toward the judge and the jury box.

A list of more than one hundred potential witnesses read to prospective jurors included the names of two congressmen, a state senator, an assemblyman, the mayor, thirteen present or former supervisors, the district attorney, the city attorney, the sheriff, and several well-known city hall staffers.

Judge Calcagno announced the jury would be sequestered in "a top flight, first class hotel" for the duration of the trial, which he expected would last three to four weeks.

Two hundred twenty-six registered voters summoned for jury duty reported to a large waiting room at the Hall of Justice, then were brought into the courtroom in groups of twelve for questioning. They were asked whether they had a conscientious objection to the death penalty, whether they supported or were affiliated with any groups dealing with homosexuality; whether they had campaigned for

Moscone, Milk, or White; whether they had been to a psychiatrist; and about their views on psychiatry.

No jurors were seated the first day, but by Friday, April 27, a jury of seven women and five men was sworn in for the trial. The panel included a former San Francisco policeman, three insurance company workers, an auto mechanic, a printer, a retired printer, a mattress saleswoman, the wife of the chef at the county jail, a construction company executive, and a housewife. None was homosexual.

The trial began Tuesday, May 1. In his opening statement, Doug Schmidt said White's defense would center "not so much on what happened, but rather why those tragedies happened." Dan White, said Schmidt, had "cracked" under the burden of "manic depression" when he shot and killed Moscone and Milk. The young attorney said his client was mentally ill due to a "biochemical change" in his brain when he went to city hall to see Moscone the day of the killings. "He had no intent at that time to harm anyone, much less to kill the mayor or to kill Harvey Milk," Schmidt declared.

Prosecutor Norman said in his opening statement that the evidence would prove White was guilty of first-degree murder with special circumstances. If such a verdict was returned, White could receive the death penalty.

On Wednesday, May 3, the jury heard testimony from the coroner, Moscone's appointments secretary and a volunteer aide of Milk's who was with him when Dan White appeared at the office door and said, "Say, Harv, can I see you a minute?"

On the third day, White wept quietly when Mayor Dianne Feinstein testified how he confided in her that his financial burdens and political innocence drove him to resign from the board of supervisors. It was the first public display of emotion by White since the city hall murders.

Feinstein testified for thirty-five minutes. She said she had seen White hurry into the supervisors' offices that morning and called out to him from her desk, but he went past her office, saying, "I have something to do first."

"I heard him go down the hall and I heard the door close," Feinstein said. "Then I heard the unmistakable shots. After the first shot, I thought he had shot himself. Then I heard additional shots and I knew something was wrong. I was trying to force my brain and my body to function together. I got up and saw Dan. I went into the hall and smelled gunpowder."

Feinstein testified she went down the hall to the office White had used when he was a supervisor. She opened the door and saw Harvey Milk lying on the floor.

"I tried to get a pulse, but I couldn't because of the blood," she testified. "I felt that he was dead. Then I closed the door and secured the area."

Feinstein's testimony and Dan White's taped confession to homicide investigators were the dramatic highlights of the trial. While the prosecution worked to establish White's premeditation for the killings, Doug Schmidt countered with a parade of five psychiatrists who testified to White's "diminished capacity" to understand his actions.

As a longtime police reporter familiar with murder cases, together with my close working relationship with Moscone, I was convinced early on, as were many other reporters and trial observers, that White was undoubtedly guilty of first-degree murder.

For the next two weeks, I observed the proceedings, taking extensive notes. We did not have the luxury then of using small handheld tape recorders or other ways to hear the testimony repeated, so it was crucial to have clear and all-inclusive notes. (I still have my notebooks from the trial today.) During breaks I waited in the nearby press room with other reporters. Often, they asked Jim Wood and me questions about things they might not have been able to hear or see from their vantage points in the gallery or on the closed-circuit TV down the hall.

At the end of each day's testimony, around four-thirty p.m., I drove the six blocks back to the *Chronicle* offices and wrote my account for the next morning's paper. It took me about forty-five minutes to write five or six triple-spaced pages, or some fifteen hundred words, for the first edition. For later editions, I added more material and cleaned up my earlier work.

Most nights when I got off work I got together with a new group of friends I had met. On any given night, there were as many as eight to ten of us who gathered around a huge table in a house on Clay Street in Pacific Heights. My friend Jack Paul was renting the house from the owner, coincidentally a member of the Thieriot family, which owned the *Chronicle*. We talked, drank beer, and partied well into the early morning. Everyone there was fascinated by the day-to-day details of the trial.

There were days I arrived at the Hall of Justice in the morning on just a few hours' sleep, and occasionally with none. I don't know how I was able to muster the energy to get up, shower, put on a suit and tie, and make it out the door.

The case went to the jury at 10:02 a.m. on Wednesday, May 16. They deliberated five hours before retiring to dinner and then to their hotel. The deliberations continued through the weekend.

On Monday, May 21, the jury foreman sent word to the judge that they had reached their verdict.

VERDICT ON DAN WHITE

San Francisco Chronicle

The Largest Daily Circulation in Northern California

115th Year No. 108 ★★★★ TUESDAY, MAY 22, 1979 777-1111 20 CENTS

It's Voluntary Manslaughter
— Maximum Penalty 8 Years

Four police cars went up in flames in front of City Hall during last night's rampage following the Dan White verdict

Several Jurors Weep in Court

By Duffy Jennings

Dan White was convicted by a jury of two counts of voluntary manslaughter yesterday for the killings of San Francisco Mayor George Moscone and Supervisor Harvey Milk in City Hall last November 27.

White, 32, who faced a possible death sentence if convicted of first-degree murder, could now receive a total maximum prison term of seven years and eight months for the manslaughter convictions and related charges.

With good behavior, he could be eligible for parole in about five years.

The former city supervisor, fireman and policeman dropped his head and rubbed his eyes as the verdicts were read in a locked, emotion-charged courtroom at the Hall of Justice at 5:28 p.m.

Several jurors — many of whom had cried listening to White's anguished taped confession on the third day of the trial May 3 — wept openly while court clerk Anne Barrett read the verdicts.

DAN WHITE
Ex-supervisor

White's wife, Mary Ann, cried with joy and embraced White's sister, Nancy Birkel, as Superior Court Judge Walter F. Calcagno polled each juror individually to confirm the verdicts.

It was the climax of six days of jury deliberation that began last Wednesday following the 11-day trial.

Defense lawyer Douglas R. Schmidt who called five mental health experts to testify that White was mentally ill from severe depression, reacted to his major victory with subdued elation.

"There's nothing I can say that will help the families of the victims, but the verdict is just," Schmidt said in a Hall of Justice corridor that was jammed with reporters and television equipment minutes after the verdicts were announced.

"It was a tragedy," Schmidt said of the shootings that stunned San Francisco nearly six months ago. "Now it's behind us."

He and White, who walked expressionlessly out of the courtroom to return to his jail cell after the verdicts, was "guilt-ridden and filled with remorse."

"He's in very bad condition at the moment," Schmidt said.

A stern-faced District Attorney Joseph Freitas said the jury's conclusion was "somewhat of a tragedy."

"I don't think justice was carried out," Freitas said. "I'm very, very disappointed. There were two charges of first-degree murder and the evidence was there to

Back Page Col. 1

City Officials Shocked by The Verdict

By Marshall Kilduff and Eugene Robinson

News of the voluntary manslaughter verdict in the Dan White trial went through City Hall yesterday like an electric shock, bringing gasps of astonishment and furious denunciations of the jury.

Mayor Dianne Feinstein, her eyes glistening with tears, reacted to the verdict with "disbelief."

"As far as I'm concerned, there were two murders," she said 15 minutes after the jury announced its decision. "This raises the question of who gets what kind of penalty and why."

Feinstein, who discovered the bullet-riddled body of Supervisor Harvey Milk on the day of the killings, issued a call for unity in the city.

"I think it's important that this town pull itself together again," she said. "We've gone through a physical bloodbath and now we are going through a mental one."

The mayor was asked if the verdict appeared to her to be a

Back Page Col. 5

A Bloody Protest at City Hall

Some enraged demonstrators smashed the doors at City Hall

Verdict Angers Gays

By Katy Butler

In a long night of looting, burning and chaotic fire vengeance, more than five thousand demonstrators, many of them gay, rampaged through Civic Center and nearby neighborhoods last night in a violent protest of the manslaughter verdict against Dan White.

It began in a quiet march of shocked and grieved gays from Castro and Market Street at about 7 p.m. But the mood quickly became disorganized and chaotic as demonstrators arrived at City Hall and night fell.

For four hours, Civic Center Plaza was a virtual battlefield. In the eerie, smoky fires of trash barrels. Waves of police, dressed in riot gear and swinging batons, tried again and again to drive demonstrators away from the besieged City Hall and out of the plaza.

They finally succeeded shortly after midnight, driving bands of looters and demonstrators north

Back Page Col. 1

Index

Comics 50
Deaths 39
Entertainment 38
Finance 46
People 15
TV-Radio 36
Weather 37

© Chronicle Publishing Co. 1979

CHAPTER 43:
The Verdict

I returned to my seat in the courtroom for the conclusion of the trial. What we heard stunned the courtroom, the media, and the entire city.

When everyone was seated, Judge Calcagno asked the jury foreman, Bechtel company executive George Mintzer, if the jury had reached its verdicts.

"Yes, it has, your Honor," Mintzer replied. He handed the papers to the bailiff, who gave them to the judge. After reading the verdicts in silence, the judge gave them to the clerk to be read aloud.

"We, the jury, find the defendant guilty of the crime of voluntary manslaughter in the death of George Moscone," she read. Nearly everyone in the courtroom, spectators, and journalists alike, gasped audibly. Almost no one, except perhaps Doug Schmidt, expected this outcome. Voluntary manslaughter was the lightest possible conviction the jury could return. It delivered the same verdict for the killing of Harvey Milk. White faced a maximum sentence of seven and two-thirds years. With time served and good behavior, he could be free in five.

Judge Calcagno thanked the jury, said the city owed them a "debt of gratitude," and excused them.

I dashed out of court, ran into the nearby press room and called the office to relay the stunning verdict. Then I returned to the newspaper building, composing my lead paragraphs in my head on the way. I sat at my desk, still feeling the adrenaline rush of the verdict much the same way I felt when Feinstein had announced the murders at city hall six months earlier. I collected my thoughts, reviewed my notes from the courtroom and wrote the verdict story for the first edition. Much of it was pre-written during the jury deliberations to

have the background already in type if the verdict came in close to
deadline. Other reporters helped by calling people involved in the
trial for comments, which we inserted into the story. I then joined
other *Chronicle* reporters covering the riot.

The shocking verdict plunged the city into chaos and violence and
what became known as the White Night Riot. Some five thousand
angry protestors infuriated by the decision poured out of the predominantly gay Castro District and other neighborhoods, converged
on the Civic Center and rampaged well into the night. They broke
windows at city hall, set police squad cars on fire, threw tear gas stolen from police cars and disrupted public transit.

Here's my story of the verdict that ran on the front page, May 21,
1979:

> Dan White was convicted by a jury of two counts of voluntary
> manslaughter yesterday for the killings of San Francisco May-
> or George Moscone and Supervisor Harvey Milk in city hall
> last November 27.
>
> White, 32, who faced a possible death sentence if convicted of
> first-degree murder, could now receive a total maximum pris-
> on term of seven years and eight months for the manslaugh-
> ter convictions and related charges.
>
> With good behavior, he could be eligible for parole in about
> five years.
>
> The former city supervisor, fireman and policeman dropped
> his head and rubbed his eyes as the verdicts were read in a
> packed, emotion-charged courtroom at the Hall of Justice at
> 5:28 p.m.
>
> Several jurors — many of whom had cried listening to White's
> anguished taped confession on the third day of the trial May
> 3 — wept openly while court clerk Anne Barrett read the ver-
> dicts.
>
> White's wife, Mary Ann, cried with joy and embraced White's

sister, Nancy Bickel, as Superior Court Judge Walter F. Calcagno polled each juror individually to confirm the verdicts.

It was the climax of six days of jury deliberation that began last Wednesday following an 11-day trial.

Defense lawyer Douglas R. Schmidt, who called five mental health experts to testify that White was mentally ill from severe depression, reacted to his major victory with subdued elation.

"There's nothing I can say that will help the families of the victims, but the verdict is just," Schmidt said in a Hall of Justice corridor jammed with reporters and television equipment minutes after the verdicts were announced.

"It was a tragedy." Schmidt said of the shootings that stunned San Francisco nearly six months ago. "Now it's behind us.'

He said White, who walked expressionlessly out of the courtroom to return to his jail cell after the verdicts, was "guilt-ridden and filled with remorse "

"He's in very bad condition at the moment." Schmidt said.

A stern-faced District Attorney Joseph Freitas said the jury's conclusions were "somewhat of a tragedy."

"I don't think justice was carried out," Freitas said. "I'm very, very disappointed. There were two charges of first-degree murder and the evidence was there to support that verdict.

"It's a wrong decision. The jury was overwhelmed by emotion. I don't think the jury analyzed the evidence properly. I think the jury was struck by his wife, his background and the politics of the case.

"I don't like it and I think the people of San Francisco will be disappointed," Freitas said.

Assistant District Attorney Thomas F. Norman, who had said earlier that he put on a flawless case for the prosecution, was downcast and grim.

"There's little that I can add," Norman said. "Tragically, there are so many people who feel great sympathy for Dan White."

Mayor Dianne Feinstein, who was appointed to replace Moscone after the killings and whose testimony at the trial reduced the stone-faced White to tears, greeted the verdicts with "disbelief."

"As far as I'm concerned, these were two murders," she said.

Gina Moscone, the mayor's widow. declined any comment on the results of the trial, according to a family spokesman. She did not follow the trial in the news media, he said.

Harvey Milk's brother, Robert Milk of Long Island, said he thought the verdict "would be something more severe," but that he had not wanted White to die in the gas chamber.

The jurors, who had been sequestered at the Jack Tar Hotel since the beginning of the trial, collectively decided not to discuss their deliberations publicly.

Although they were obviously exhausted by the experience and some cried with the reading of the verdicts, at least one juror wore a broad smile as he entered the courtroom.

Jury foreman George Mintzer, a Bechtel executive, handed the written verdicts to a bailiff, who gave than to Calcagno. The judge read them silently, then handed them to Barrett to be read aloud.

White, dressed in a tan sports coat and brown slacks, remained seated at the defense table with Schmidt and associate defense lawyer Stephen J. Scherr beside him. White did not look at the jurors, but stared straight ahead as he had throughout the trial.

Freitas, Norman and homicide inspector Frank Falzon sat at the prosecution table, closest to the jury.

As Barrett began to read the verdicts, Schmidt's chest heaved and courtroom spectators perched stiffly on their seats, craning for glimpses of White and the jurors through the bullet-proof glass partition.

The jury found White guilty of voluntary manslaughter and of using a firearm in both killings.

The only state of mind required for voluntary manslaughter is intent to kill. By its verdicts, the jury determined that White could not have premeditated, deliberated or harbored malice — the elements necessary for a murder conviction.

The penalty for voluntary manslaughter is two, three or four years in prison.

Under sentencing laws, White would receive four years on the first conviction for voluntary manslaughter, half the minimum — or one year — for the second conviction, and an additional two and two- thirds years for the gun-use finding.

After each verdict was read, Judge Calcagno asked each juror if that was indeed his or her verdict.

One by one, they replied: "Yes, your honor."

The judge set a pre-sentencing report for June 19, then thanked the jurors profusely for their "very, very hard work" and said, "the people of San Francisco owe you a debt of gratitude."

Jurors Helga Soulie, Patricia Powis and Darlene Benton were still wiping tears from their cheeks as the panel left the courtroom.

Schmidt and Scherr stood to shake their hands and thank them, while the prosecution team remained seated — stunned and motionless.

The dramatic highlight of the trial came when the prosecution played a 24-minute tape recording in which White was heard confessing to the slayings of Moscone and Milk.

His voice anguished and halting, White was heard saying there was a "roaring" in his ears as Moscone calmly asked how White's family was reacting to the controversy over his failure to gain reappointment.

White wept during the confession, as did his wife, one of his lawyers and a number of courtroom spectators. "I just shot him," he said of the Moscone slaying. "That was it. It was over."

Calmly reloading his gun, White then headed toward the supervisors' offices, where Milk was encountered. "He just kind of smirked at me . . . and then I got all flushed and hot and shot him," White said.

During the trial, the defense portrayed White as a fundamentally decent man who had, however, a rigid and unbending view of morality.

This inflexibility and inability to compromise led to a growing inner torment as White watched with disgust the horse-trading normal to politics, the defense contended.

Pressures built on White — financial, family and political — until they brought him to the breaking point, defense lawyer Schmidt contended.

The tip-offs were the spells of withdrawal and the recourse to junk food by the fitness-conscious former cop and fireman, he said.

The seeds of the tragedy were sown November 10 when White resigned his supervisorial seat, complaining that the $9600 salary was too low to make ends meet. The city attorney earlier had ruled that White had to resign his job as a fireman because of conflict of interest.

White and his wife had a new baby and she had quit her teaching job. A new restaurant at Pier 39 was making excessive demands on his time and energies, White said.

But no sooner had he resigned than his political supporters brought pressures to bear to have White withdraw the resignation. Finally, be buckled and five days later asked for the seat back.

"A man has a right to change his mind," Moscone told reporters when he appeared determined to reappoint the supervisor.

But behind the scenes, a campaign was waged by board liberals led by Milk to deny White reappointment to a seat he had come to regard as his own.

"I no longer feel duty-bound," the mayor concluded at last, "to reappoint Dan White." Those words were to seal Moscone's doom.

Moments before Moscone was to announce that he had appointed Don Horanzy to the District 8 seat held by White, White sneaked into city hall, using a window to avoid the metal detectors at the door.

Moscone was killed by four bullets, including two fired into his head as a coup de grace. Moments later, Milk was cut down in another fusillade.

Schmidt succeeded in persuading the jury that the killings were not the work of a coldly rational killer, but the unpremeditated outburst of a man who had been pushed over the edge and no longer, able to weigh the factors involved in the act.

"These were two cold-blooded, premeditated executions, and that's all they were," responded prosecutor Norman. In the end, though, the jury did not accept this explanation for White's actions.

The key to the denial of the prosecution's reconstruction of the events of that tragic day was the testimony of four psychiatrists called by the defense. Together, they established a reasonable doubt that White was sane on the day of the crimes.

REPORTER'S NOTE BOOK

Psychiatrist George F. Solomon testified, "It's inconceivable for Mr. White, who couldn't even tell off someone who stepped on his toe in a line, say, to plan something heinous.

"Good people — fine people with fine backgrounds — simply don't kill people in cold blood," was the way lawyer Schmidt put it.

"The mental illness, the stress and emotion of that moment, simply broke this man," he told the jury. "He was honest and fair — perhaps too fair for politics in San Francisco."

CHAPTER 44:
"I Knew What I Had to Do"

On Saturday, May 18, while the Dan White jury was still deliberating, I found this two-sentence note on my desk from Managing Editor Bill German:

"Duffy: The Dan White trial coverage has been precise, lucid and rich in extra insight. The *Chronicle*—in particular, [publisher] Dick Thieriot, [city editor] Dave Perlman and I—say thanks for an arduous reporting job well done. Sincerely, William German."

In the weeks after the verdict, the *Chronicle* submitted my trial coverage for the Pulitzer Prize as well as the San Francisco Press Club and San Francisco Bar Association annual media contests. I won none of them. Over the summer I covered a variety of stories—a walkout by the state's water system workers, the layoffs of more than three thousand workers at the GM plant in Fremont, a string of assaults on the Municipal Railway.

In early September, I spent several days covering the murder of an eighteen-year-old San Francisco girl, Catina Salarno, by her boyfriend on her first day of classes at the University of the Pacific. The boyfriend, Steven Burns, the son of Lowell High School football coach Ed Burns, shot her in the head outside her dormitory because she had broken up with him before leaving for college. After that I wrote about the end of the "The Treasures of Tuthankhamun," exhibit at the M.H. de Young Memorial Museum in Golden Gate Park, which had drawn 1.3 million visitors during its four-month run.

In October, my assignments ranged from a San Francisco teachers' strike, a sniper firing from the sixteenth floor of a building at Ninth and Market Streets, and the grand jury dropping a cam-

Duffy with Senator Dianne Feinstein at the Chronicle, 2017.

paign finance case against District Attorney Joe Freitas to a Golden Gate Bridge jumper and a foiled mass escape from the county jail by nine inmates who had dug a tunnel under a wall and were on the brink of busting out when sheriff's deputies discovered the passageway.

November brought the first anniversary of the city hall killings, the one-year mark of a day no one wanted to relive.

I went to city hall to ask Mayor Feinstein to reflect on the events of November 27, a year later. The media loves anniversary stories, and this was a big one. In the mayoral election three weeks earlier, Feinstein had earned a runoff spot against Supervisor Quentin Kopp and was awaiting a December vote. We talked briefly about memorial events she was planning for the Moscone-Milk anniversary and a few other routine items on her schedule. Then she came around from behind her desk, settled into a visitors' chair next to mine, and lit a cigarette—a moment of relaxation she rarely allowed herself in public. I asked if it was hard planning the memorial events and the painful memories they would revive.

"Yes, it was hard," she said. "It's still very disturbing, to me and to a lot of people."

Because she had been the first to find Harvey Milk's bullet-riddled and lifeless body and because she assumed the office of mayor the same day, the year since had been as eventful, significant, and troubling for her as much as anyone. She had also undergone a difficult day of testimony at the Dan White trial in May, weeping as she recounted her actions while White sat in front of her in the courtroom.

"I'm a victim of circumstances," she said to me. "I've always believed in the old saying that when you fall off a horse, you get right back in the saddle again. I function best in a crisis.

"It still hits me at the strangest times. For a long time, I had nightmares about finding Harvey's body and the acrid smell of gunpowder. And I get an odd feeling sometimes when I go back in that room," she said, gesturing toward the small, private sitting room adjacent to the mayor's office where Moscone was killed. "I'll never sit in that chair."

She recalled the moment she made the announcement on the day of the shootings, how she stared into my eyes for a long time before speaking, and how she got through it. "You wake up one morning and you're a supervisor, and when you go to bed that night you're the mayor. I felt a little like a mini-Lyndon Johnson. But in the last ten years I've seen a lot of death and a lot of blood. I knew what I had to do."

Feinstein conceded that "a lot of people are disappointed that I'm not George Moscone," who had been a champion for many in the city. "They might be thinking they worked hard to put the man in office, voted for him and hailed his victory, then suddenly someone takes it all away."

She was reluctant to delve much beneath the surface of her own psyche in the wake of the murders, but when I pressed her she acknowledged having undergone certain psychological changes, ones she categorized as "growing" and "positive."

"I have a greater heightened sense of time," she told me. "I realize more than ever that we're here for an instant in eternity and that instant is measured by what you accomplish while you're here. My motivation to achieve has increased and I've changed from a fragile individual to a much stronger person."

From the moment of her abrupt ascension to the mayor's office, Feinstein said, she was determined that "the bullets are not going to interrupt the orderly course of government."

"I can't change my personality overnight. I can only be what I am and do what I think is right. I can live with myself that way. I've become more philosophical than I was before. I just take every day as it comes. And there's always another day..."

Two weeks after our conversation, on December 11, 1979, Feinstein defeated Kopp with fifty-four percent of the vote, the first woman elected to the post in the city's history. She was inaugurated January 1, 1980.

CHAPTER 45:
Don't Talk, Don't Trust, Don't Feel

I had my own emotional scars from the Moscone-Milk murders and the Dan White trial, both from the events themselves and from the concurrent unraveling of my personal life over the year that I covered them. By mid-April, my mother was back in the hospital, the fourth time in a year. Her liver disease had worsened, but the doctor wasn't calling it cirrhosis yet. She also had emphysema, bronchitis, and circulatory problems. She was unable to walk because her leg muscles had atrophied from her being so sedentary. The doctors seemed to think that once she got dried out, back on a regular diet, and started physical therapy, she would regain the use of her leg muscles. I knew better after all the years and hospital stays. The only ray of hope, I convinced myself, was that this was the first time she had decided to go into the hospital herself. She was clearly scared. At sixty-five, she began to realize she could die if she didn't take better care of herself.

By then, Cheryl and I had been separated for fifteen months. In March and April of 1980, we spent eight weeks in counseling in a last-ditch attempt to restore the marriage but came out of it back at square one. Still, we couldn't pull the plug on the marriage. Six months earlier, KPIX-TV had let Cheryl go in a ratings shuffle. Two days later she was hired by KGO-TV, where she soon signed a five-year contract. (Cheryl rose to local stardom as a Channel 7 news anchor and remained there for the next thirty-five years.)

I was distraught at the stigma divorce would bring. My own parents divorced. My father divorced three times. It wasn't supposed to happen to me. Almost no one in our generation ever got married thinking it wouldn't last. Cheryl and I had no awareness or knowledge that our marriage was at risk before we took the vows. By now studies have shown that sons of divorced parents have a thirty-five percent higher chance of divorce than other adult males, sons of an alcoholic parent are forty percent more likely to divorce, and the average length of a first marriage that ends in divorce is eight years. But Cheryl and me? No way. The perfect couple, everyone called us. No couple is perfect, but it's easier to pretend the flaws aren't there when everyone around you can't see them. Many children of alcoholics don't know how to discuss difficulties in a relationship openly, honestly. If we ignore them long enough, they'll go away and there won't be an uncomfortable confrontation. Don't make waves. Don't break the rules of the dysfunctional family: Don't talk, don't trust, don't feel. Bottling it all inside, however, eventually leads to a lopsided explosion of emotions and frustration. This had been my pattern.

One way to deal with the conflict is to ignore it and numb it with alcohol and drugs. I was spending a lot of time out at night with my friends at bars in the Marina and the Financial District. The Balboa Café, Pierce Street Annex, and Camelot in the so-called Bermuda Triangle at Greenwich and Fillmore Streets were popular hangouts for young, single professionals. Other so-called "fern bars" and restaurants like Perry's on Union Street, Henry Africa's at Polk and Broadway, the Royal Oak on Polk and Thomas Lord's, a Victoria Station restaurant at Union and Buchanan, were drawing big crowds.

Inside

An afternoon of entertainment will precede San Francisco's fireworks show on Friday night. Page 2.

Firefighters battled desperately to contain an unpredictable blaze in Colorado's timberland. Page 2.

A powerful earthquake jolted Tokyo and neighboring cities, startling slides and disrupting train service. Page 3.

The number of felons sent to California prisons has doubled in eight years but their stay has dropped. Page 4.

Full-scale venting of radioactive gas began at Three Mile Island, with renewed assurances of safety. Page 5.

Admiral Rickover tried to stop a Navy contractor's party as a potential conflict of interest headache. Page 6.

Over 150 Brown for president supporters lived out a few fantasies at a fund-raiser at Hugh Hefner's Playboy Mansion West. Page 6.

President Carter is planning to resume public communion on the hostages in Iran, after six weeks of relative silence. Page 14.

A House report said the Soviet Union's denial that a germ weapon accident occurred is "incomplete at best." Page 17.

An American hostage accused of seducing an Iranian woman will be tried no matter what. Page 14.

Iranian President Bani-Sadr took the offensive against his opponents in an appeal to Ayatollah Khomeini. Page 12.

Gerald Ford worried about what would happen if the presidential election is thrown into the House Page 10.

Up-to-date couples pick what wedding traditions they like and skip the rest. Page 21.

Wonder Bread is being put through the legal ropes by five women who say the company discriminates against females. Page 23.

Chrysler's K-body compact car, now undergoing testing, is literally carrying the company's future. Page 37.

Ford's chairman asked for government help to curb foreign auto imports. Page 37.

Weather

Bay Area: Partly cloudy Monday with chance of sprinkles. Highs, near 60 to low 60s; lows, 50s. Afternoon westerly winds to 30 mph. Chances for rain: 2 in 10. Page 18.

McCovey A Hero as Giants Split
See Sports

San Francisco Chronicle
The Largest Daily Circulation in Northern California

116th Year No. 142   ★★★★   MONDAY, JUNE 30, 1980   777-1111   20 CENTS

Inside Singles Bars

How Lonesome Lovers Meet

By *Duffy Jennings*

Some people might say Jack has it all.

At 34, he is a goodlooking, well-paid, well-dressed, fit, polished and articulate copywriter in a major San Francisco advertising agency.

He lives by himself in a 2500-a-month, leather-and-chrome, one-bedroom Pacific Heights apartment, owns part of a Lake Tahoe condominium and drives a 1978 Porsche 911.

He belongs to a health club, skis in the winter and plays a wicked game of backgammon.

He is fond of Russian vodka, Italian cuisine, French wine and Peruvian cocaine.

1980
THE STATE OF SEX

This is one of a series of articles exploring the current sexual scene in San Francisco.

Above all, Jack loves the women he meets in various San Francisco singles bars, where he spends the better part of three or four nights a week filling his address book and emptying his wallet to keep from sleeping alone.

In the past year, he's man-

aged to do both with uncommon regularity. He says he has slept with more than a dozen women he's met in singles bars during the past year, thanks to an enormous attitude and a persistent itinerary.

On a typical night, Jack leaves his financial District office and drops by the Royal Exchange or the Holding Company for his first cocktail and an early look at the menu.

If no one catches his eye by

Back Page Col. 5

30,000 Marchers

A Quiet Gay Freedom Parade

By *Paul Liberatore*

For the sixth time in as many years, gays took to the streets of San Francisco yesterday to celebrate their sexuality, protest their oppression and display their unity in the face of their diversity.

They came from the familiar haunts of Castro and Polk streets and from as far away as Amsterdam, Vancouver and Hawaii.

Despite the outward look of solidarity, yesterday's Gay Freedom Day Parade held undercurrents of political rifts in the gay community and differences of opinion among parade organizers on the success of the annual gathering.

Some organizers called it the biggest Gay Freedom Day Parade of all, drawing more than 30,000

marchers and 200,000 spectators along Market Street from the Embarcadero to the Civic Center.

Others said it fell far short of the 300,000 predicted and was only about half as large as last year's

event.

There was no violence. Police information officer Henry Friedlander, who estimated the crowd

Back Page Col. 1

19 More Die in Southwest's Heat

Dallas

The heat wave continued in the Southwest yesterday, claiming 19 more victims over the weekend and raising the total of heat-related deaths to 28.

Temperatures rose past 100 degrees for the seventh straight day in several cities in Texas. The high was 113 degrees in Wichita Falls.

breaking the daily record there for the sixth straight day, and forecasters see no relief.

Twenty-three of the heat deaths this week were in Texas. In Oklahoma, where the heat caused four deaths, officials said a portion of Interstate 40 exploded as it expanded in the sun, leaving large chunks of concrete in the road

might mile east of Okemah.

In Arkansas, one man's body temperature was 108 when he died of cardiac arrest.

Infants, the elderly and the infirmed are most affected by the heat, doctors said. A 96-year-old woman was found dead of a heart.

Back Page Col. 4

Administration Fears A 'Hasty' Tax Cut

Inflation Is Still Top Priority

Washington

The Carter administration, fearful that any hasty action will upset its anti-inflation efforts, is trying to hold the line against a congressional stampede toward a pre-election tax cut, Secretary of the Treasury G. William Miller said yesterday.

However, if Congress produces a "conscientious and thorough" tax-relief program before the November general election, President Carter most likely will approve it, Miller said.

"I have a deep concern about any hasty action," Miller said. A tax cut "should not be done for political reasons, it should not be done to mislead the people or to buy their votes."

Miller said the White House is willing to cooperate with Capitol Hill in formulating tax-cut strategy, but Carter's No. 1 fiscal priority still is to curb inflation and cancel federal spending.

He said premature enactment of a tax cut would undermine administration pains in bringing down interest rates and consumer prices.

"We must not lose three gains through some hasty, hip-shooting action," he said.

Miller said it would be a miracle if Congress enacted an acceptable tax-cut proposal before ending its legislative session this year. But he said Carter probably would not veto such a measure, if Congress was successful.

Miller termed as irresponsible the $26 billion tax cut proposed last week by GOP presidential candidate Ronald Reagan. The secretary said the administration prefers a program that is better targeted to help the economy.

He said the administration favors credits against Social Security taxes for individual taxpayers and tax reductions for business that would stimulate investment and boost productivity.

Miller predicted the economy would begin recovery from the recessionary slump by the end of the year, although he expects that unemployment, now at 7.8 percent, will continue to rise.

The secretary of the Treasury made his remarks on the ABC-TV program "Issues and Answers."

Los Angeles Times

CIA Radio War Against Iran

Washington

American officials have acknowledged that the United States was responsible for clandestine radio broadcasts aimed at undermining the Iranian rule of Ayatollah Ruhollah Khomeini.

The programs, broadcast in Persian from transmitters in Egypt, one believed to be near Alexandria and the other near the Suez Canal, appear to have begun in the middle of May, the officials said, and were set up by the Central Intelligence Agency.

Spokesmen for the CIA and other intelligence agencies refused to comment.

The idea for the project,

one of a number conducted by the CIA's "unconventional broadcasting" section, was described by the officials as having come up during the winter. Egyptian President Anwar Sadat, who inherited a large radio-transmitting capacity from his predecessor, Gamal Abdel Nasser, is said to have authorized the use of time for the broadcasts.

American correspondents who were in Tehran in mid-May said that the nightly broadcasts featured music by Gogoosh, a popular female singer from Iran, and news broadcasts aimed at undermining Khomeini's government.

The non-entertainment

Back Page Col. 3

The Vietnamese Free 4 Western Civilians

Bangkok

Vietnam yesterday released four Western civilians, including two Americans, held prisoner for four days in the rain-soaked jungles of western Cambodia.

They said they had been well-treated but had been warned they would be shot if caught trying to escape.

The captives said their four-day ordeal ended when they were blindfolded by Vietnamese officers and trucked to a wooden bridge separating Cambodia from Thailand, where they were turned loose.

"They gave us cigarets — they even gave us toothbrushes," said Richard Franken, 33, of Miami, a commercial photographer and co-owner of the Leemage Agency in Bangkok.

Franken and his partner, George Liemsenan, 31, of Los Angeles, were taking pictures for a U.N. photo album on refugee children when they were captured by Vietnamese troops at the Nong Chan camp on the Thai-Cambodian border Thursday.

Captured with them were Red Cross officials, Robert Ashe, 36, of England, and Dr. Pierre

Back Page Col. 1

Israelis Kill Informant in Agent's Death

By *Dial Torgerson*
Los Angeles Times

Jerusalem

Israeli troops shot and killed an Arab informant suspected of killing an Israeli agent, an army spokesman said yesterday. The army said investigating the car bombings of two West Bank Arab mayors Jerusalem said here.

Israel Radio said that three government Cabinet ministers had held an expectors that Moshe Golan, an agent of the Shin Bet, was shot to death while attempting to learn details of the bombing attack. Jone 5 that left two Arab mayors maimed.

After a four-day search, other Israeli agents found the killer of Golan Saturday and shot him to death in an exchange of gunfire, military sources said. They said that the gun used to kill Golan was in his possession.

The Arab informant, Bassam Mohammed Habash, 21, apparently forced Golan to a meeting on the pretext of giving him information

Back Page Col. 4

Index

Bridge 22
Business World 37
Chess 23
Comics 40
Deaths 26
Entertainment 46
People 20
TV-Radio 44
Weather 18

° Chronicle Publishing Co. 1980

270

CHAPTER 46:
Inside Singles Bars

"Hey, Duffy," the city editor said to me one day. "Let's do a piece on these singles bars. Go out and talk to the people spending their time there. Find out who they are, what's attracting them, why they go there."

Okay, I said. But I was at a such a low point emotionally and psychologically that I froze at the prospect of walking up to strangers at bars with awkward questions about sex. My self-esteem had hit bottom and I couldn't muster the journalistic fortitude needed for the assignment. It was too much like looking into a mirror. I bullshitted the city desk for a week or two that I was out at night doing interviews. But I wasn't. And I had no legitimate reason for spiking the idea altogether.

Twice before in my career I had a turned down assignments or lied about why I couldn't do them. The first was in 1974, and it was my idea in the first place. There were stories about a so-called "Hippie Bus" that traveled intermittently from New York to San Francisco filled with counter-culture vagabonds in search of the groovy California lifestyle. "This would make a great story," I told Abe Mellinkoff. "I'd like to make this trip undercover. Just sign on as one of them. I'll bet the stories will be amazing." I was quite sincere about it at the time, though I had short hair and still looked more like a Marine than a Moonie. He was reluctant at first. The *Chronicle* rarely sent someone out of state on assignment, let alone to New York, because of the expense. I'm sure part of my motivation about the trip was the chance to see my brother for the first time in a couple of years. Finally, Abe agreed. I waited until I learned the next departure date for the Hippie Bus and hopped a plane to New York. Once I got there, I balked at the prospect of making the bus trip. I was afraid something bad would happen but didn't know what. Yet I couldn't shake the fear. Looking back on it after all these years, I can only guess that my fear was related to an uncertain time in my life. Most likely it was related to my mother's health, or my marriage, or both. Whatever it was, I froze up. I stayed in New York for a day or two visiting my brother until the bus left for the West Coast. Terrified, I called Abe. "I can't believe this," I lied, "but I missed the bus. It left the day before I got here." Abe was furious, angrier than I'd ever heard him, and he could intimidate reporters with his scowl more than anyone I ever worked for. "Okay," he said begrudgingly, "get the next plane back."

The only other time I couldn't do my job was September 25, 1978. A Pacific Southwest Airlines jet on approach to San Diego Airport collided with a small private plane and nosedived into a neighborhood near the airport, killing one hundred and forty-four people. "Get on the next flight to San Diego," the assignment editor said to me. I went out to San Francisco Airport and bought a ticket on PSA to San Diego. Before the flight could board, something came over me. I was gripped in fear. I called the desk. "I don't know how to explain it," I said, "but I can't get on this plane. I've got a lot going on at home and I just don't think I can fly right now." The editor tried to convince me it was only because a plane had crashed, and I would be alright. But when I pushed back, he relented. "Fine, I'll send someone else."

I know other reporters who squirmed at the prospect of questioning victims of tragedy in their darkest moment. It's horribly invasive and never feels right. We shrug it off as "part of the job," but no one with a conscience is ever devoid of feeling. On the day of the Moscone-Milk murders, one of my colleagues was sent out to Dan White's supervisorial district to interview his neighbors and local business owners about White. Was he hot-headed? Did he ever say anything about his anger with Moscone or Milk? That sort of thing. At one point, the reporter walked into a novelty store and approached the woman behind the counter. "Excuse me," he said, "I'm from the *Chronicle*. I'm out here talking to people about Dan White. Maybe you heard he shot the mayor and Harvey Milk at city hall this morning." The woman quickly brought a finger to her mouth. "Shh," she whispered, tilting her head in the direction of a woman at the other end of the store. "That's his mother right over there." The reporter, one of the paper's best, knew he had a major scoop just a few steps away. "I've never told anyone this before," he said to me. "But I couldn't bring myself to go up to her in that situation. I just walked out."

Finally, I came up with a plan for the singles bar piece. I decided to focus on one guy's story as a representation of what so many young professional men were thinking and doing in the hip bars all over the city. But he wasn't quite real. He was more of a composite of several guys, including myself. Much of the information in the piece was accurate, and some of it reflected my own situation, but I did embellish it to make the piece work. I didn't tell the city desk about this before I turned it in. No one ever questioned it, and it ran on page one June 30, 1980. This was one of my final bylined articles for the paper.

Inside San Francisco's Singles Bars

Some people might say Jack has it all.

At 34, he is a good-looking, well-paid, well-dressed, fit, polished and articulate copywriter in a major San Francisco advertising agency.

He lives by himself in a $500-a-month, leather-and- chrome, one-bedroom Pacific Heights apartment, owns a Lake Tahoe condominium and drives a 1978 Porsche 911.

He belongs to a health club, skis in the winter and plays a wicked game of backgammon.

He is fond of Russian vodka, Italian cuisine, French wine and Peruvian cocaine.

Above all, Jack loves the women he meets in various San Francisco singles bars, where he spends the better part of three or four nights a week filling his address book and emptying his wallet to keep from sleeping alone.

In the past year, he's managed to do both with uncommon regularity. He says he has slept with more than a dozen women he's met in singles bars during the past year, thanks to an uncommon attitude and a persistent itinerary.

On a typical night, Jack leaves his Financial District office and drops by the Royal Exchange or the Holding Company for his first cocktail and an early look at the action.

If no one catches his eye by the simultaneous conclusion of the rush and happy hours, Jack climbs in his Porsche and heads west through the Broadway tunnel for the singles bars clustered along the Van Ness-Union-Fillmore scene or that zigzag through the Cow Hollow neighborhood.

Moving by whim, or by set plans to eat dinner or meet a friend, he may stop at Lord Jim's or Henry Africa's, or go directly to Perry's or the Balboa Cafe.

Wherever he happens to be, Jack's eyes constantly sweep the bar for an interesting-looking woman, alone or with other women, who returns his glance in a courting ritual characteristic of the singles scene, commonly referred to as "eye contact."

It is one of the small paradoxes of the liberated, feminist society that, with a few exceptions, the man's role as the pursuer hasn't changed much.

Jack understands this, and besides, he hasn't had very many women come on to him first so he takes the initiative — with a twist.

"When I hit on a lady in a bar," he says, "I come on with the standard lines and all the phony charm, mostly because it's easier to deal with the rejection if she doesn't want anything to do with me.

"But, as soon as she shows she's interested, I end up turning off a lot of that and start taking a real interest in who she is.

"I guess that's what helps me a lot. I really want to know more about her than the superficial crap. In fact, a lot of times we end up talking about why the hell we're both in this bar, and pretty soon we decide to get the hell out of the place and go somewhere we can really talk one-on-one.

"Well, after a while we're both so glad to find out that we're not the only ones stumbling around in this mixed-up life that we start hugging just for the comfort of being close to someone. Then, one thing leads to another and we end up in bed."

Only two people know for sure what happens in his bedroom or hers that night, but bartenders and regulars at Jack's favorite San Francisco singles saloons confirm that he comes in alone and leaves with a woman most of the time.

"He gets lucky more than anyone I know," said one Cow Hollow bartender. "It's amazing, considering the competition."

Some people might say Jack has it all — but he's not one of them.

"To tell you the truth," he whispers over his 100-proof Stolichnaya, "I'm lonesome as hell."

Like countless single men of his generation — especially those living in the morally capricious, sexually liberal, anything goes social climate of San Francisco — Jack's full life is full of conflict and confusion, and little else.

Under pressure from a modern society, Jack bombards himself with so many questions about changing values, role models, his identity and goals — and just about everything else he says or does — that he becomes the victim of an aggravating irony.

"There aren't any goddamn answers," he says, growing more frustrated because he can't direct his anger at any particular person or thing.

"It's not fair. I followed all the rules. I got good grades and stayed out of trouble in school, joined the Army, went to college, got a good job, married my high school girlfriend, bought a house in Marin — everything you were supposed to do back then to be 'successful and happy.'

"Then, bang, they changed the rules. No, they threw 'em out altogether and told you to make your own. Everything changed so fast I'm still not sure what hit me. "My marriage broke up, I moved into the city and suddenly my life's back at square one.

"On our anniversary after I left home my wife sent me a card that said it all: 'Well, we didn't make Who's Who this year, but I think well be listed in What Was That?'"

Jack stopped and sat back in his chair, a defeated expression on his face. He got up and went to the bathroom. When he returned, a tiny spot of unmistakable white powder underlined each of his nostrils. He lit another Marlboro and took a sip of his cocktail. Recharged by the coke, he resumed talking at a quicker pace.

"It's just not fair. Our parents never had to question anything about their lives, their relationships. Everything was just understood. And I bet our kids will grow up with a fairly dear set of values, too. But we're caught in the middle.

"I can't fall into that trap and let things pass me by again. Even if I'm not crazy about the life I'm living now. it's all I've got, so I might as well get something positive out of it, the bad as well as the good. So I'm going for it."

Specifically, women. As with the other facets of his life, Jack's approach toward women is loaded with contradictions.

He readily acknowledges a stubborn adherence to certain sexist or chauvinist attitudes, by today's standards. At the same time, he knows the key to the puzzle of his life is developing better relationships with women, and that's where he is channeling much of his introspection.

This, he says with conviction, has forced his most troublesome shortcomings to the surface and produced the most significant compromises to his fragile machismo.

"Everybody wants companionship, and anyone who says they like being alone is a liar," he says. "All this stuff that makes up the so-called 'good life' isn't worth a damn without a good woman, as far as I'm concerned.

"If I'm going to have that kind of relationship again, it's going to have to be a 50-50 situation in terms of what we each put into it, and that means I've got a lot of work to do on myself.

"Sure, I've learned how to move around in the bars, how to talk that talk and play that game. But it's all bull. The whole scene is a cliché ... the bars, the rap, the 'single life,' all of it.

"You put so much energy into 'finding out who you are' and trying to be an individual but, ironically, you end up looking and sounding like everyone else."

Men like Jack who are seeking a balance between old values and new requirements for a fulfilling relationship end up looking for it with two faces instead of one.

Jack says he feels trapped by the desire to approach a woman honestly and the fear that no matter what he says first it'll sound like a line.

He usually ends up taking the easy way out with a hackneyed opener but, if she doesn't tell him to buzz off and he shifts out of the stereotype to his "up front" style, he sometimes finds himself explaining later why he started out with a line in the first place.

Jack says many women have told him they slept with him simply because he was as sensitive to their feelings as he was to his own, even when they both knew their time together would end faster than a room gets dark when the light's turned out.

"Most women don't want to get laid," he says. "They want someone to make love to them.

"I know I probably won't find a lasting relationship in a bar, but it's a good place to learn what single women my age are looking for. So when I find one who's looking for the same thing I am. I'll know it."

As he talked, his eyes kept darting toward an attractive young woman who had strolled into the bar a few minutes earlier and was trying to catch the bartender's attention to order a drink.

Jack stubbed out his cigarette and stood up, signaling with a jerk of his head where he was going.

"Nice talking to you," he said, and headed off in her direction.

Most of my friends recognized some of me in the piece, but everyone else said they thought they knew who "Jack" was because it sounded like so many guys. I even got letters from women who wanted to meet Jack. It would have broken their hearts to know he didn't really exist.

CHAPTER 47:
Softball Question

A year before the city hall murders, Corey Busch had quit his job as George Moscone's press secretary and returned to Los Angeles. He decided to leave after Moscone surprised him with the news that he did not have long-term plans in politics. "We were sitting in an airport waiting for a flight," Busch recalls. "George told me he was going to run for re-election, but after that he wanted to pursue other interests—in business or professional sports, perhaps. That got me thinking that I was only in politics because of him. I knew it wasn't going to be my career. If I was going to make a change, I decided it was better to do it then than to wait another six years for him to leave office. So, I went back to LA, but leaving George was not easy. I loved the job and I loved George."

Busch had become personally close to Moscone's family over the years he worked in George's state senate and mayoral offices and had kept in touch with George and his family during the year he was back in Los Angeles. The day Moscone was killed, Busch flew to San Francisco to comfort his widow, Gina, and to help her and Moscone's four children cope with the tragedy in any way he could.

In addition to being among the pallbearers at Moscone's memorial service in the city hall rotunda, Busch helped the family arrange for honorary pallbearers as well. Corey suggested to Gina that one of them be Bob Lurie, the real estate tycoon who had purchased the San Francisco Giants with help from Moscone and Busch in 1976. Lurie and Moscone were friends for some time even before the Giants deal and had remained so during Moscone's mayoral term. Busch had also kept in touch with Lurie, occasionally meeting for lunch or dinner in Los Angeles when Lurie was in town with the team for games against the Dodgers. When Corey called Lurie, the Giants's owner readily agreed to the solemn funereal duty.

By early 1979, three years into his ownership of the baseball team, Lurie was still splitting his workday. He spent mornings at the Lurie Company office downtown before going out to Candlestick Park in the afternoon. Most weekday games were at night and Lurie stayed until the end. He often returned to his Cow Hollow home around 11 p.m. or midnight. One afternoon over lunch with Corey Busch, Lurie mentioned being stretched thin managing both businesses. Busch suggested Lurie find someone to help ease the load, which prompted Lurie to ask Busch himself if he'd be interested.

Busch was intrigued. He hadn't yet figured out where his career was headed after leaving city hall, but the idea of returning to San Francisco appealed to him. What's more, he had grown up a big baseball fan, albeit for the Dodgers, and the notion of working in baseball was one he couldn't pass up. A few days later, Bob and his wife, Connie, and Corey met to discuss the idea in more detail, after which Connie encouraged her husband to bring Corey aboard.

Corey went to work for Lurie on April 1, 1979, dividing his time at the Lurie Company and Candlestick for a short time to become familiar with both organizations before moving to the stadium full-time.

Once Busch was back in the Bay Area, he and I re-established our relationship, but this time it was entirely social, unfettered by the adversarial one we knew as journalist and mayoral press aide. Over the next year, we often got together for drinks, dinner, or at ball games. I got to know a widening circle of his colleagues and friends and he got to know mine. In early 1980, I moved out of my temporary digs with Bill and Brant and rented a house on Chestnut Street near Van Ness Avenue with my friend Jack Paul and his big, loveable black Labrador, Sullivan. Our house soon became a gathering spot for ten to fifteen regular guys and girls to hang out, listen to music, watch sports on TV, play cards or backgammon—and tell stories into the night.

Corey knew of my longtime passion for baseball. I had played baseball through high school and was on Sunday league teams in the city into my late twenties. I was co-captain of the *Chronicle*'s Media League softball team, which had just finished its fourth season.

"The Lurie Company softball team could use you," he said to me one day in early 1980. "It's co-ed and very low key but we have a lot of fun. Would you like to play with us?"

"Love to," I replied. Soon Corey gave me a jersey with the team name, "Grunts," screen-printed across the chest in familiar Giants-style script, and I joined the team for their games at what is now James P. Lang Field at Gough Street and Golden Gate Avenue. Eventually I was invited to Giants games at Candlestick, sitting in Lurie's luxury suite with Corey.

CHAPTER 48:
The New Yorker

By late 1979 into early 1980, I was at a low point, emotionally and psychologically. I was out often and late, partying to forget my marital problems and Dori's illness. At times I was thoughtless and spiteful to Cheryl when my anger over our situation and my own guilt about it bubbled over. I knew what I was doing wasn't healthy for either of us, but I didn't care.

Medical professionals and studies have identified a series of traumatic and stressful life-changing events that can lead to anxiety, depression, drinking, drug abuse and other self-destructive behavior. They include the death of a loved one, severe illness or injury, marital separation and divorce, changing jobs, and a change in living situation. Within a six-month period, I would experience all of them, save an injury. What's more, in the middle of all that Cheryl and I even had to put down our eight-year-old German shepherd with incurable hip dysplasia. I bawled like a baby the day I left Nikki at the vet. One thing piled onto another. When I wasn't missing work, I was late and was either buzzed through my shift or sleeping at my desk. I was a wreck, without a clue about how or when it might change.

At the time, Bill Regan was dating city editor Jerry Burns' assistant, a New York girl named Sharon Jacobs. One day in early June 1980 Sharon came by my desk and told me that a childhood girlfriend of hers had moved to San Francisco from Long Island. "I think you'd like to meet her," said Sharon. "Her name's Faye Zimmerman. She's a nurse. She's really cute and she's lots of fun. We're having an anniversary party for Bill's parents at Bill and Brant's place next Sunday. Faye will be there. Why don't you come?"

I showed up at the party late on the afternoon of Sunday, June 8, said hi to my former roommates, and congratulated Bill's folks on their anniversary. When I went into the living room, Sharon was there with a girl who had short black hair, big eyes, and a welcoming smile. Sharon was right. She was very cute. Sharon introduced us, and we talked for a while about her making the big move from coast to coast. She grew up in Oceanside on Long Island with her parents and two brothers, one older and one younger. She had graduated with a nursing degree from the University of Bridgeport in Connecticut and worked at Mt. Sinai Medical Center in Manhattan before moving west. I was immediately captivated by this woman and her distinctly New York accent. Even at twenty-three, nine years younger than me, she looked more like a teenager.

At some point during the party, the Tony Awards telecast came on TV, live from New York. Faye, who grew up going to the theatre, was delighted to see a connection to her hometown and giddily plopped into a chair to watch. I sat beside her and made some offhand remark about liking the Tony Awards.

"What do you know about the Tony Awards?" she challenged me.

I must have I mentioned some of the plays and actors in the running for Tonys and I said a thing or two about the New York theatre scene. She was impressed that a California guy knew anything about Broadway. Later, I was equally impressed to see her in the kitchen voluntarily doing the dishes at a complete stranger's house. Hmm, interesting girl, I thought. So helpful, and funny. I was infatuated by her infectious laugh and energy. We started dating right away.

It was a lightning courtship. Within a month I filed for divorce from Cheryl and barely two months after that I proposed to Faye. She accepted immediately, and we set a wedding date for July 4, 1981.

CHAPTER 49:
Giant Changes

One night Corey told me that after being at the Giants for over a year he could see where some of the weak spots were in the front office team. He told Bob Lurie that the ball club needed a publicity director with the right combination of people and writing skills, journalism and sports knowledge and local connections. Furthermore, he said the current publicist, Stu Smith, was reluctant to travel with the team, which Corey thought was vital to maintaining good relationships with the beat writers and national media in other cities. Bob agreed.

"Would you be interested in coming over to the Giants?" Corey asked me. "I know it's a big change from the newspaper and you've been there a long time."

Corey knew I'd been talking about leaving the paper for some time. I just didn't know what would be next. In my wildest dreams I never imagined it would be baseball.

"Seriously?" I replied. "I'm definitely interested."

It was early November when Corey arranged for me to meet with Bob Lurie about the Giants' publicity director job. I went to the Lurie Company office on the top floor of the fifty-five-story Bank of America world headquarters on Montgomery Street. Lurie's personal office had floor-to-ceiling picture windows that looked out over the northern half of the city and bay. The Embarcadero, Coit Tower, the Golden Gate Bridge, Marin County, and the blue waters of the bay lay in a panorama before me. There were photos of Lurie with ballplayers on the walls and baseball mementoes on Lurie's desk. But the most compelling thing about the office, to me, was a giant tan leather chair in the shape of a classic old baseball glove, with the pocket of the glove as the seat and the individual fingers sticking up from it as the back.

Lurie, the city's best known and most successful commercial real estate magnate, entered the office wearing a dark suit and necktie. He was warm and welcoming, with a friendly smile and a firm handshake. Corey was also in the room. Lurie, who had been a *Chronicle* copyboy himself and taken journalism courses at Northwestern, asked me about my background, my interest in leaving the newspaper, my willingness to travel extensively with the ball club, and my salary needs.

At the time, as a reporter with more than six years' experience—the maximum pay level under the Newspaper Guild rules—I was earning $29,000 a year, not including overtime. I hadn't been in a formal job interview since Abe Mellinkoff made me a copy boy. I told Lurie that money wasn't that important, that I was confident the compensation would be fair. He said they were considering a couple of other candidates and would be in touch as soon as a decision was made.

I left the interview feeling confident, but I was concerned that having no experience in baseball, or public relations, was a problem. In fact, the idea of being a publicist and catering to journalists was a complete reversal of everything I knew about the media business. I'd been on the other end of it for so long that I knew what journalists needed and what PR people did. I knew that in a private company like the Giants I would not only deliver news but would have to withhold information from reporters—and the public—at times. The Giants weren't like any typical company that attracted media attention only occasionally, if ever. A baseball team was in the public eye constantly. The Bay Area was in the country's top five media markets and was a two-team region to boot. The media presence was enormous. What other business has thirty to fifty journalists sitting in its "office" every day, observing events minute-by-minute, asking probing questions of the executives, scrutinizing every detail, reporting every action, every decision? Not to mention columnists and commentators expressing their opinions about the organization, good and bad, daily. I wasn't at all sure how I would adjust to it.

Bob called me the next day. "You impressed us yesterday," he said. "We'd like you to join the Giants organization. I'm prepared to offer you a salary of $33,000. I know it may not seem like a lot, but we are struggling financially, as you know, and it's more than we're paying our current publicity director. If this is acceptable to you, Corey will be in touch later today to talk about the details."

"I'm thrilled!" I told Bob, without mentioning that based on our interview I believed he would only be able to match my *Chronicle* pay. "I accept. This is very exciting. Thank you so much." After some more pleasantries, I hung up. Corey called me a few minutes later.

"You did it, DJ!" he exclaimed. "When can you start? We'd really like it if you could be on board in time for the annual baseball Winter Meetings the first week of December. They're in Dallas this year."

"I can do that," I said. "I can give the paper two weeks' notice and be ready to start December 1." It didn't occur to me until much later that eleven years earlier December 1 had been my first day as a reporter.

I submitted my resignation to the *Chronicle* in a note that said I was leaving for "another opportunity." I couldn't say what it was because the Giants wanted it kept quiet until the team could make the announcement to the media and the baseball industry. My resignation also noted I was leaving "with bittersweet feelings." There was regret for leaving a job I loved, my friends and colleagues at the paper and my experiences over thirteen years. Another part, which I never mentioned to anyone at the paper, was that I had hoped to become city editor, but now realized that wasn't in the cards.

Over my last couple of years at the *Chronicle*, the city editor entrusted me to fill in on the city desk as the assignment editor or night city editor when the regular assignment editor took vacations or days off or the paper was short-staffed. Eventually I spent entire weeks in the job. In this role, I came to work in the morning or late afternoon and dispatched reporters to cover news events. At the time, there were about four dozen reporters on the city staff. Half of them had regular beats, while the other half were general assignment reporters available for whatever the day would bring. This was a big responsibility for someone in his late twenties, but I was very comfortable with it. I knew the staff, the types of things we covered and who was best suited for each story. And no one openly resisted me as their supervisor, at least not to my face. "You carried your weight in spite of your age," one former reporter told me. "You had the respect of the staff."

It seemed like I would be in line for city editor eventually, but I never got a sense from anyone in management that they might be thinking about me for it. And, of course, my upbringing kept me from asking anyone about it, or telling the managing editor of my interest. Believing I wasn't destined for city editor helped to make my decision to leave easier. What's more, I was in the midst of other big changes in my life—divorce, engagement, another move—so it seemed like a good time to upend my career as well.

CHAPTER 50:
Rookie in the Desert

I left The *Chronicle* in late November 1980 to take my new job with the Giants. After a few days on the job, I flew to Dallas for the Major League Baseball Winter Meetings at the Loew's Anatole Hotel, where I met all the other baseball public relations directors and many baseball executives and officials. It was baptism under fire for me when Lurie fired manager Dave Bristol a few hours before I arrived, and the next day general manager Spec Richardson traded pitcher Bob Knepper and outfielder Chris Bourjos to the Houston Astros for infielder Enos Cabell. I didn't have the first clue what to do. The only news releases I had issued for the Giants up to that point was one I did for my own appointment to the front office and another announcing a player move. I didn't know to make these personnel announcements to the Bay Area baseball writers in attendance at the Winter Meetings but Ralph Nelson, the traveling secretary, walked me through it. We typed up a release and summoned the writers to my room. They had already heard about Bristol. I gave them the release anyway and then made copies that I took to the press room for all the other media covering the meetings.

Then it was back to San Francisco to learn more about the team and the business of baseball and wait two more months for Spring Training to start.

By mid-February, when players began reporting to Spring Training, I was anxious to get to Arizona and my first experience in the Cactus League. On Sunday morning, March 1, I stopped by my mother's house on the way to the airport to say goodbye. I let myself in and went back to her bedroom, doing my best to ignore the fetid, stale air that hung in the hallway. She was in bed reading the *Chronicle*.

On her nightstand, a half-smoked cigarette smoldered in the glazed ceramic ashtray I'd made for her in eighth grade shop class. Next to it sat a glass of Chablis. She coughed in hoarse, raspy jags and was semi-coherent.

"Hi, Mom," I said, sounding as upbeat as possible. "That cough sounds awful. Can I get you anything for that?"

"No," she replied. "I'm having a little trouble breathing, but I'll be fine."

"You know I'm leaving for Arizona today, right? Spring Training? The Giants?"

"That's today?" she replied with a quizzical look. "I forgot. Sorry, I'm not really with it. Are you excited? I'm very happy for you."

"Yeah, Mom, I am excited. I'll be back in a month. You need to take care of yourself. I left a note on the kitchen table with my hotel and office phone numbers if you need to reach me. I'll call to check in on you whenever I can."

The plane's tires screeched on contact with the tarmac in Phoenix shortly after 1 p.m. I picked up my suitcase and walked out of the terminal. It was eighty degrees, nearly double the temperature in San Francisco that morning. I had never been to Arizona. I liked it right away.

I rented a car and drove southeast, out through Tempe and Mesa, passing mile after mile of strip malls, Circle K convenience stores, golf courses, and homes with Spanish tile rooftops and Saguaro cacti poking up through the otherwise barren front yards carpeted in beige rock. Gradually the city fell away to suburbs, then to the open desert.

Interstate 10 was a shimmering two-lane ribbon of dark asphalt lined on both sides by vast meadows of clay, scrub brush and red dirt. Afternoon gusts carried the fragrance of the creosote bushes and sent tumbleweeds rolling across the desert like infield grounders.

After an hour, I turned off the highway toward Casa Grande, a small town where Giants owner Horace Stoneham had built the team's training complex in 1962, four years after the club moved west from New York.

The Giants trained there for three weeks each spring before moving to Phoenix Stadium when the Cactus League schedule opened in early March.

Plunked in the middle of the Sonoran Desert between Phoenix and Tucson, Casa Grande was designed as a completely self-contained training facility, with four practice fields fanning out around a central observation tower, a 3000-seat stadium, its own seven-story Francisco Grande Hotel and adjacent motel, bat-shaped swimming pool, dining hall, 18-hole championship golf course – even an airstrip.

There was no highway in the region when Stoneham invested $2 million on the complex, but speculation was that the new interstate would cut right through Casa Grande, turning the town into a prosperous resort destination. Ultimately, I-10 ended up seven miles away, leaving Casa Grande as a forsaken pit stop.

"Welcome to Spring Training!" travel director Ralph Nelson called out as I parked the car in front of the hotel. He walked right up to me, casually tossing a baseball in the air over and over in his right hand, the red seams spinning in all directions.

"Do you know what this is?" he asked.

"Sure," I replied. "It's a baseball."

"NO!" he said, pausing for emphasis as the ball smacked into his palm. "This," he said, gripping the ball tightly and shoving his fist forward, "... this is what we're all here for. This is what it's all about."

Corny, but I loved it.

I spent the first couple of days at Casa Grande acclimating to the camp routine, meeting players and coaches, talking with the reporters in camp and enduring my share of rookie ribbing and pranks from all quarters.

It was a historic spring for the ball club. Owner Bob Lurie had signed a new manager, Frank Robinson, making him the first black manager in the National League. And this was to be the team's last camp at Casa Grande before moving to Scottsdale permanently.

Robinson's coaching staff included Jim Davenport, Jim Lefebvre, Don McMahon, John Van Ornum, and Vern Benson. Joe Morgan had signed as a free agent, joining Darrell Evans, Johnnie LeMaster, and Enos Cabell on the infield. Jack Clark, Larry Herndon, and Billy North would be the Opening Day outfield, but Chili Davis and Jeffrey Leonard were in the wings. Milt May was the starting catcher. Vida Blue, Doyle Alexander, Fred Breining, Greg Minton, and Gary Lavelle headed the pitching staff. All of them seemed larger than life to me.

Camp buzzed with the sounds and smells of baseball – spikes clicking on the pavement, balls cracking off bats and smacking into gloves, infield chatter, coaches shouting directions, fans calling out for autographs, the odor of pine tar, liniment, chewing tobacco, bubble gum.

And the grass, everywhere the intoxicating fragrance of freshmown grass.

Casa Grande may not have been close to any place else, but for me it was as close to heaven as anywhere I had ever been.

CHAPTER 51:
Thirty

The morning of my third day in Arizona, Ralph Nelson came to me on the field. "There's a phone message for you in the office," he said. "It was your mother's doctor. He said it was important."

In the office, I dialed Doctor Lake's number and waited while his assistant went to get him. *Jeez, what now? Shit, I thought I would get a break from her down here, for a while, at least.*

"Hello, Duffy?" he said when he came on the line. "It's Doctor Lake. I wanted you to know that we had to admit your mother to the hospital last night. She's quite ill. Her organs are starting to shut down. It's very serious. I think you'll want to get here as soon as you can."

He told me that her emphysema and chronic bronchitis had severely compromised her lungs and that advanced cirrhosis was accelerating liver failure. She also had just contracted pneumonia, he said, and her overall decline was likely irreversible.

I called Faye to let her know I was coming home. I explained the situation to Spec Richardson, quickly packed my things, drove back to Phoenix, and caught the first available flight to San Francisco. I couldn't think of anything else but my mother on the flight. I know I just wanted it all to be over, for my mother's sake more than mine. When I arrived, Faye picked me up and we went straight to Presbyterian Hospital.

I found my mother in the intensive care unit, breathing heavily and barely conscious. Her eyes were closed. I spoke to her, and she mumbled something, but I'm not certain she understood me or even knew who I was. I stayed by her bedside until Doctor Lake came by with an update. It was grim.

"We're doing what we can to keep her comfortable," he said. "Why don't you go home and get some rest. We'll call you if there's any change."

A couple of months earlier, Faye and I had taken an apartment that happened to be just a few blocks from the hospital. We left, planning to return first thing in the morning. We weren't back at the apartment very long when a nurse called from the hospital.

"Hello, Mr. Jennings," she said in a soft voice. "I'm so sorry to tell you that your mother expired a short time ago."

"Thank you," I said, "please hold on a moment." I put my hand over the mouthpiece and looked over at Faye.

"She's gone," I said. I took a deep breath and got back on with the nurse.

"What now?"

"She'll need to be taken down to the morgue until the funeral home can pick her up. We can wait to move her if you'd like to see her first," the nurse said. "When you come in we need you to pick up her things and sign some papers."

"I don't need to see her," I said. "She made arrangements some time ago with the Neptune Society to be cremated. Can you please notify them? I'll be over as soon as I can to take care of the paperwork."

I hung up and looked at Faye, who had a knowing expression on her face. "Well, she's out of pain now," I said. Just as it was when my father died twelve years earlier, I felt some sadness but no strong emotion. There were no tears, just relief.

"I'm really sorry," Faye said. We hugged for a long time in silence.

It was Thursday, March 5, 1981. Dori was sixty-six years old.

I notified my brother and Dori's sister, the Giants, George, and a few other people I thought would want to know. In keeping with my mother's wishes—spelled out in her will, previous suicide notes and several conversations—no services were held. Without a memorial, my brother stayed in New Jersey while I spent the next two days taking care of the most urgent personal affairs. I did not, as I had anticipated for years, write her obituary because I was no longer with the newspaper.

The *Chronicle* did run a short obit on Dori and on March 11 I received a note from Mayor Feinstein. "I just want you to know that you have been very much in my thoughts since I learned of the loss of your mother," she wrote. "It's terribly sad for you now but the memories of the happy times you had together will see you through. I know, I've been there. Call on me if there's anything I can do."

The Board of Supervisors, upon a joint motion by John Molinari and Harry Britt, adjourned its meeting of March 16 in Dori's memory.

Two days after my mother died, Faye and I, needing a break from our melancholy state, went to the second annual Bay Area Sports Hall of Fame dinner at the Fairmont Hotel in the city. The inductees were former Forty-Niners quarterback Frankie Albert, the late Major League Baseball star and San Francisco Seals manager Francis "Lefty" O'Doul, former San Francisco Seals and major league pitcher Vernon "Lefty" Gomez, the legendary tennis star Helen Wills Roark, and two-time Olympic decathlon champion Bob Mathias. We sat at the Giants table with other front office executives, who were sympathetic and supportive.

The next day, with no other immediate matters to take care of in San Francisco, I flew back to Phoenix, taking Faye with me this time. While I was away, the Giants broke camp in Casa Grande and moved into their Scottsdale hotel to prepare for the Cactus League schedule at Phoenix Stadium.

When we landed, the Arizona sky was cloudless, and the temperature was eighty-two degrees. In homage to Dori's lifelong fondness for convertibles, we rented one, a blue Ford Mustang.

We put the top down and we drove to Scottsdale with the desert sun warming our faces.

Epilogue

I'd like to report that this blissful, Hollywood-style denouement—my new life ahead of me and Dori on to the next one—signaled the end of my issues with personal relationships, that I was finally able to confront problems openly with honest communication, express my feelings and needs without fear of rejection, react reasonably to minor slights, and accept love and support without guilt.

Yes, I'd like to report that, but I can't. Before I had a real grasp on those issues, it would take another twenty-five years, a second divorce, and a new life partner who understood what a "normal" marriage and family life was. She called me on my bullshit and had the patience to help me learn, change and grow. The simple truth is that we are all a blended product of our parents. We carry their best and worst traits, share aspects of their triumphs and failures, and hope to mold our own life into one we and others around us can live with.

There were good years, of course. Faye and I had two wonderful children, Adam and Danielle, in the early 1980s. We raised them on the Peninsula while I worked in baseball and beyond. During a typical season I put in 70-80 hours a week, including most every weekend, with a handful of days off between February and October. I was gone on eight to ten road trips a year that lasted between a week and ten days. That left Faye to deal with schools, activities, doctors, and babysitters as well as her own nursing schedule, an unfair burden for any working mom.

The baseball world was unlike the newspaper world, or any other world, in every respect. Now I was on the "dark side," as the journalist community refers to publicists, whose job it is to withhold almost as much information from the press as to announce. It was a rough transition at first, switching from reporting to being adversarial with reporters. I knew what they wanted and needed but I couldn't always provide it, owing to the sometimes-secret operations of a private business in a very public eye. Plus, I was an arrogant jerk at first, still with the haughty assertiveness of a reporter along with my personal emotional shortcomings.

Within a few months, the beat writers demanded Bob Lurie fire me because I wasn't the all-accommodating team spokesman they were accustomed to, either with Giants' PR folks in the past or on other teams. Baseball was such a collegial environment. On road trips, reporters and broadcasters traveled with the team regularly, rode the team bus, stayed in the team hotel, drank in the same bars, ate in the same restaurants. It's a close-knit society. But Bob said no, I was his guy.

Over my twelve years with the ball club, I again found myself at the center of some of San Francisco's biggest news stories, none as big as the 1989 Loma Prieta earthquake, a 6.9-magnitude temblor that rocked Candlestick Park minutes before the start of the first World Series game in San Francisco in twenty-seven years. There were more than a thousand media in the ballpark—reporters, broadcasters, photographers, crew. It was my job to make sure they all had credentials, assigned locations, electricity, phone connections, transportation schedules, and food. Suddenly, all the power was out for computers and telephones (no cell phones then). Fortunately, no serious injuries occurred at the stadium and it wasn't until reports came in from the collapsed Cypress Structure of Interstate 880, the fallen section of the Bay Bridge and the fires consuming the Marina District that we began to fully understand the deadly impact of the quake. The Series was postponed for ten days. When it resumed, the Oakland A's, who had taken the first two games of the series in Oakland, quickly dispatched the Giants in the first two games at Candlestick to complete a four-game sweep.

My time with the Giants also included PR duties associated with hosting the 1984 All-Star Game at Candlestick, the 1987 and 1989 Division and League Championship series, respectively, the tragic story of Dave Dravecky's battle with cancer in his pitching arm, working with Willie Mays, Willie McCovey, other Giants legends, and many other memorable events.

When Bob Lurie sold the Giants in 1993 and the new owners' group brought in its own senior staff, I was suddenly out on the street, unemployed for the first time in my life at the age of forty-five. It was crushing to leave that job. So much of my personal identity was wrapped up in the Giants, much as it had been at the *Chronicle*. However, I did not want to return to the newspaper nor did I want to leave my hometown. But leaving the Giants wasn't like leaving a software company, with the chance of finding work at any one of dozens of others in the Bay Area. There was only one other Major League team in the Bay Area, and the A's had their PR team in place.

I began to explore other options in public relations or communications. Despite my background and extensive Bay Area connections, employers couldn't fathom how my baseball experience would serve their company interests and goals. Over the next two years I applied for more than one hundred jobs, had a handful of interviews, and came up empty. This was a strain on me emotionally and on my family financially.

I opened my own public relations consulting business in 1995 and did that until retiring from PR altogether. I paused along the way to take full-time jobs for a year or two—vice president of public relations for online sporting goods retailer Fogdog.com from 1998 to 2001 and vice president of strategic communications for the Silicon Valley Leadership Group in 2007. For the next ten years after that I served in a consulting role as vice president of communications for Joint Venture Silicon Valley.

My marriage never recovered from the impact of losing my Giants job and the struggle to recover financially and professionally. Faye and I divorced in 2005 after twenty-four years of marriage. Within several months and with the help of a great therapist, I finally began to understand and deal with those longtime lingering issues that were holding me back.

I had never really come to terms with the way alcoholism impacted me, even long after the alcoholic was gone. I always made excuses for my mother—that she worked hard to support her boys, that she had a relentless disease, that I couldn't help her to change. Nor had I faced my feelings about my father. For so long I subconsciously lived in fear of ridicule by those in authority and in fear of my own success as measured against his, especially as a journalist.

I was more ashamed of divorcing a second time than going back to therapy at fifty-seven to figure out why. My therapist, the late Tom Samuels, often told me: "You will never rid yourself of these demons until you face your fears," he said. "Keep telling yourself: If I can't, I must."

Among those fears was risking rejection in search of a new relationship. I was renting a house in San Mateo in March 2005 when I posted a profile on Match.com and something magical happened. I got a note from a woman in Los Gatos who said she found my profile interesting and that she liked writers. She was a senior-level executive at a tech firm in Cupertino and had a bachelor's degree, a Master's, an MBA, and a doctorate in education. Way out of my league on several levels.

Bonnie Becker had grown up in Berkeley and Menlo Park, graduated from San Jose State University, and taught in high school and community college. Then she went into high tech and did her doctoral research with the University of San Francisco just as the field of e-learning, or distance learning, was opening up with the explosion of the web.

When we met, Bonnie was the senior manager of worldwide learning and development at the networking company Packeteer in Cupertino. She had worked previously for several other big networking companies, including Brocade, Ascend, and Commerce One. She also had a two-year stint living in Paris as Cisco's global program manager for learning and development in Europe.

Bonnie was smart, sophisticated, worldly, attractive, and funny, with short brown hair, hazel eyes, and a passion for learning. She was an incurable Francophile, a gourmet cook, and a voracious reader who loved hiking, wine tasting, travel, and politics—none of which I had in common with her. She couldn't care less about sports, although her late father was a baseball fan and she could rattle off the starting lineup of the 1962 Giants from memory. Bonnie had been married twice and had a grown daughter, Stacy, a lawyer living in San Francisco.

After an exchange of emails and a phone call, Bonnie and I met for coffee at a cafe next door to Kepler's bookstore in Menlo Park on April 12, 2005. When you know your life has changed, you remember the day, time and place. Dates followed. Love flourished. A year later I moved into her condo. A year after that I proposed over dinner at Le Petit Zinc, her favorite restaurant in Paris, and in June 2008 we were married in a small ceremony at the California Café in Los Gatos. Mindful of my father's poor marriage record, I waited three years before plunging in again, but for the first time in my life I honestly understood those who believed that when you know, you know.

It's impossible to describe how much Bonnie changed my life. She grounds me when I revert to my old ways. When I mention something I've been putting off, her common refrain is, "What are you waiting for?" She inspired me in our first year together to lose forty pounds that have stayed off ever since. At the rate I was going, I soon would have been at risk for heart disease, high blood pressure and other ailments. She helped me repair strained relationships with my children, react appropriately to criticism and mistakes without malice or spite, and to speak up when something is bothering me, before it escalates in silence. I also tapped into her passion for travel, cooking, politics, and a healthy lifestyle. And learning.

With so much education, being with a man who hadn't graduated from college went against all of her values and beliefs. One day Bonnie asked me if I had ever thought about going back to finish school.

"Not really," I said. "What's the point now? I've had a full life and career. It's not like I need a degree now."

"But it would be a big personal accomplishment," she persisted. "Why not at least look into it? You have the time."

She was right about that. I contacted the journalism department at San Francisco State University, where I'd taken my last class in 1974 and had accumulated nearly three years of credits toward a bachelor's degree before dropping out because I already had a job at the *Chronicle*.

Journalism department chair Venise Wagner was caught off guard at first by my inquiry but was pleasantly encouraging and said she would do what she could to help. After reviewing my old records and my *Chronicle* career and consulting with admissions officials, she said the department would give me enough credits for my work history to bring me within twelve units of graduation, but that I would need to attend school for those. In the fall of 2008 I signed up for two three-unit classes and added two more in the spring semester. The unexpected bonus was that these classes cost only three dollars each per semester because I was over sixty years old. (That senior tuition plan has since been discontinued in favor of ElderCollege, where students over age fifty may attend any class on a space-available basis with instructor approval for fifty-five dollars per semester.)

I made the one hundred-mile round trip from Los Gatos to S.F. State twice a week that winter and spring. My instructors included Don Menn, a former editor of Guitar Magazine, who teaches journalism history, and Peter Richardson, an author and humanities instructor who teaches California culture. Because of my background, I ended up making special presentations in both classes about my *Chronicle* experiences and have maintained my connection to both of them.

In May 2009, at the age of sixty-one, I graduated with my bachelor's degree in journalism, erasing a lifelong regret and keeping my promise to Abe Mellinkoff after 39 years.

With Bonnie as my life coach, I also became a City Brights blogger on the *Chronicle* website for a time, freelanced articles for the newspaper, took classes in creative writing at Stanford, became a certified oral historian through the Bancroft Library at UC Berkeley, co-founded and later sold Los Gatos Magazine, took up hiking and biking, traveled to several countries in Europe and Asia for the first time and even started French classes.

Now you are holding in your hand evidence of my other long-delayed goal: I can add Author to my résumé. And this time I had a plan.

I wonder what Dori and Dean would say.

ACKNOWLEDGEMENTS

Having published my first book as a septuagenarian, I could easily roll out another one simply acclaiming the time, effort, encouragement, and care shown by all those who, in ways large and small over the past seven decades, helped to bring both me and the book to this outcome. Journalism co-workers and writing colleagues, newsmakers, mentors, classmates, teachers, teammates, friends, and family—hundreds of you are woven throughout my story, whether you are specifically mentioned in these pages or not. I won't, of course, devote another 300 pages to express my gratification to everyone, but there are those without whom I could not have brought this memoir to life who deserve to be acknowledged.

My foremost thanks go to Daniel David, Don Ellis, and Mike Monson of Grizzly Peak Press for their belief in my work and its appeal to readers interested in the tumultuous 1970s, Bay Area journalism in general, and the unique place that the San Francisco *Chronicle* holds in Northern California history. You three, along with copy editor Paul Samuelson and designer Sara Brownell, have my deepest appreciation.

Nor could I have imagined this tome without my *Chronicle* family. I am particularly indebted to three late newsroom decision-makers—city editor Abe Mellinkoff, news editor Bill German and managing editor Gordon Pates—for their early and lasting faith in me. Hats off as well to former Datebook editor John Stanley and the late assistant city editors Dick Hemp, Bill Chapin and Steve Gavin for plum story assignments and writing mentorship; to former city editor David Perlman for his leadership during the city hall tragedy and the Dan White trial, for his amazing longevity and for offering his ever-wise input to my story at the young age of one hundred; to the late Paul Avery for sharing Zodiac case duties and crime reporting tips with me; to former colleagues Carl Nolte, Jerry Jay Carroll, Marshall Kilduff, Robert Graysmith, Julie Smith, Mike Brown, Bill Pates and others for sharing invaluable anecdotes, feedback and advice. Special thanks go to library director Bill Van Niekerken for his unselfish time and support and for alerting me to the invaluable Newsbank archive of *Chronicle* content.

I especially want to thank three other *Chronicle* hands—Bruce Jenkins, the ridiculously talented and venerable sports columnist, for his gracious, flattering foreword and four decades of "Hey, now!" friendship; Joel Selvin, the newspaper's esteemed former rock music critic and author of sixteen books that make him the undisputed national historian of rock and roll, for his typical smartass publishing pointers and brotherhood; and current star cityside reporter Kevin Fagan, the keeper of the Zodiac file that we both hope will someday be closed, for his collegial assistance to an ink-stained guy from another era.

Beyond the *Chronicle* world are others who helped shepherd this memoir through, either during its formative years or more recently. I am especially grateful to U.S. Senator and former San Francisco mayor Dianne Feinstein for her public acknowledgement of our moment in time and its impact on her. Thanks, too, to her former state director Sean Elsbernd, for his assistance. I will always remain indebted to the late San Francisco police homicide detective David Toschi for his candor, honesty, and friendship during and long after our crime-fighting/crime reporting days. Nor will I ever forget the men of Engine Company 21 who welcomed me into their private world behind the firehouse doors in 1972 for the experience of a lifetime. I have enormous respect for your service and sacrifice.

I also want to single out my former *Chronicle* Question Man colleague and current Our American Stories business partner, Kristin Delaplane, for her gentle encouragement and publishing guidance, and my former Giants colleagues Bob Lurie, Corey Busch, and Pat Gallagher for their support. A shout-out also goes to webmasters extraordinaire Hal Klopper of New Montage Media and Jill Minnick Jennings of Joint Venture Silicon Valley for their keen eyes and graphic vision.

Friends who've been there along the way to lend support, read the manuscript and offer valuable insight include Faye Jennings, Rick Schaefer, Jeff Raleigh, Robin Carr, Keith and Janice Inman, Russell Hancock, Alejandro Ciudad-Real, Jack Paul and Becky Boyer. Thank you all.

Finally, and most important of all, is the gratitude I have for my family, who have lived this story in part or in whole and who shared in its telling.

My late brother, Dorn, provided lengthy notes of his memories of our childhood in the months before he passed away and I think of him both fondly and with sadness at every turn through this journey. My nephew, Jeffrey Edward Mindham, was instrumental as the unofficial Jennings family historian. Thanks, Jeff, for all your research and feedback.

Whether they realized it or not, my children, Adam and Danielle Jennings, both served as catalysts for a written history of the Jennings family that preceded them. I wanted them to have a greater understanding of their heritage and the paternal grandparents they never met, and the roles that alcoholism and divorce played in their life. Love and gratitude to you both from a proud dad.

My step-daughter, Stacy Salvi, has been a force of support, advice and love as if she were my own child. Both on a personal level and as a lawyer, she provided some of the most important creative and legal direction I received. Her feedback changed the course of the narrative entirely, and for the better, and her contractual advice was spot on. Not to mention that she and her husband, Kevin Ernst, created the two grandsons who give me so much joy.

Finally, how do I find the words to thank my remarkable wife of ten years and best friend, Bonnie Becker? Bonnie changed my life in ways I may not even yet understand and made this ambitious project possible. Even before this memoir, she was the one who motivated me to a discover a normal and blended family dynamic, a healthy lifestyle, a passion for travel and learning, and true joie de vivre I had never known. It was Bonnie, with a lifetime hunger for learning that compelled her to earn a doctorate in education and succeed in high tech, who inspired me to return to college after a thirty-five-year hiatus and finally obtain my bachelor's degree in journalism at sixty-one. And it was Bonnie who asked me one day, in her deftly persuasive way, if I was ever going to finish the book I'd talked about for years. "I don't know," I replied. "Well," she persisted, "what are you waiting for?"

It turned out I was waiting for her. Bonnie, I can never thank you enough for your love and partnership.